THE GOODMAN
OF PARIS

THE
GOODMAN
OF PARIS

(*Le Ménagier de Paris*)

A Treatise on
Moral and Domestic
Economy by
A CITIZEN
OF PARIS
c. 1393

*Translated and with
an Introduction and Notes by*
EILEEN POWER

THE BOYDELL PRESS

First published 1928
George Routledge and Sons Ltd

This edition first published 1992
The Folio Society

Paperback edition 2006
The Boydell Press, Woodbridge

Transferred to digital printing

ISBN 978–1–84383–222–5

The Boydell Press is an imprint of Boydell & Brewer Ltd
PO Box 9, Woodbridge, Suffolk IP12 3DF, UK
and of Boydell & Brewer Inc.
668 Mount Hope Ave, Rochester, NY 14604, USA
website: www.boydellandbrewer.com

A CIP catalogue record for this book is available
from the British Library

This publication is printed on acid-free paper

Le Ménagier de Paris is believed to have been written c. 1393 by
a citizen of Paris. The text used for this translation is that of
the first published edition of *Le Ménagier de Paris*, based on the
three existing fifteenth-century manuscripts of the *Ménagier*,
edited by Jérome Pichon for the Société des Bibliophiles
François, Paris, 1846

Contents

NOTES   205

INDEX   225

THIS TRANSLATION OF
LE MÉNAGIER DE PARIS
IS DEDICATED TO
M. CHARLES-V. LANGLOIS
BY THE TRANSLATOR,
WHO WILL
ALWAYS BE GRATEFUL
FOR HAVING BEEN
HIS PUPIL

Preface

The *Ménagier de Paris* was published in Paris in 1846 for the
Société des Bibliophiles françois and edited by Jérôme Pichon, president of the Society. The exact title of the edition is as follows:
'*Le Ménagier de Paris*, traité de morale et d'économie domestique,
composé vers 1393, par un bourgeois parisien; contenant Des
préceptes moraux, quelques faits historiques, des instructions sur
l'art de diriger une maison, des renseignemens sur la consommation
du Roi, des Princes et de la ville de Paris, à la fin du quatorzième
siècle, des conseils sur le jardinage et sur le choix des chevaux; un
traité de cuisine fort étendu, et un autre non moins complet sur la
chasse à l'épervier. Ensemble: L'histoire de Grisélidis, Mellibée et
Prudence par Albertan de Brescia (1246), traduit par père Renault
de Louens; et le chemin de Povreté et de Richesse, poème composé,
en 1342, par Jean Bruyant, notaire au Châtelet de Paris; publié pour
la première fois par la Société des Bibliophiles François (a Paris, de
l'Imprimerie de Crapelet, Rue de Vaugirard, 9, MDCCCXLVI)'; the
edition is in two volumes. Only 324 copies were published and the
book was never reprinted; it is consequently exceedingly rare.

The *Ménagier de Paris* was used by Thomas Wright, F. J.
Furnivall and other students of the social history of the Middle
Ages in England, and Furnivall added a long note upon it to his
edition of *A Book of Precedence* (Early English Text Society, 1869)
pp. 149–154. In the course of this note he remarked 'The book
well deserves translation into English . . . [it] is full of interest of
all kinds to the Englishman as well as the Frenchman'. It is now
nearly sixty years since those words were written, and here at last is
a long overdue translation, of one of the most delightful books of
its kind that has survived from the Middle Ages. The original is
very long and it has seemed best slightly to shorten it in translation,
more particularly as it has been possible to do so without leaving
out anything of first rate importance. The omissions made are as
follows: The section on the seven deadly sins and their corresponding virtues has been very slightly abbreviated and some well known
exempla drawn from the Bible have been omitted, as also have the
tale of *Melibeus and Prudence* and the long poem entitled *Le Chemin
de povreté et de richesse*, neither of which is the Ménagier's own

work. In the section on household management a short excursus on
the points and diseases of horses has been omitted and the cookery
book has been shortened by leaving out some recipes and general
instructions. Finally the whole of the treatise on falconry, which was
all that the Ménagier wrote of his third section, has been omitted,
as being somewhat technical and of less interest to the general reader
than the rest of the book.

My thanks are due to Messrs Methuen and Co. for allowing me
to repeat in my Introduction some paragraphs from the chapter on
'The Ménagier's Wife' in my book *Medieval People* (1924), and to
Mr W. P. Barrett, late of St John's College, Cambridge, who was
good enough to translate the greater part of the first three articles of
the first section; most of pages 31 to 50 of this book, including the
very felicitous versions of the Ménagier's beautiful prayers, is his
work. I have also to thank Miss Doris Leech for kindly making the
index.

EILEEN POWER

Introduction

1. LE MÉNAGIER DE PARIS

The Ménagier de Paris (the Householder or Goodman of Paris, as we might say) wrote this book for the instruction of his young wife between 1392 and 1394.[1] He was a wealthy man, not without learning[2] and of great experience in affairs, obviously a member of that solid and enlightened *haute bourgeoisie* upon which the French monarchy was coming to lean with ever-increasing confidence. He had travelled widely in France and Flanders[3] and he speaks of certain of the great men of the day in the terms of one who knew them personally, Jean Sire d'Andresel, with whom he was at Niort, Bureau de la Rivière and above all the famous Duke of Berry.[4] It seems probable that he himself was in some way connected with the affairs of government, and his French editor considers that he had at one time been employed in military finance (which would account for his presence at Melun in 1358 and Niort in 1374)[5] and that at the time he wrote he was a member of some judiciary body resident at Paris and concerned with the government of the town, such, for instance, as the *parlement* or the Châtelet. His detailed account of the dinner given by the Abbot of Lagny to the *président, procureur général* and *avocats du roi*, and of the wedding feast of Jean Duchesne, *procureur* at the Châtelet, seem to bear out the suggestion (p. 159); and in general his literary knowledge and his high connections make it more likely that he was an official than that he was a merchant. He retained, however, all the modesty and sturdy common sense of the bourgeois, who knew and was proud of his position and had no wish to move out of it; and from time to time he lets fall warnings against attending the entertainments of lords of too high a rank, or serving entremets which are beyond a simple citizen's cook.

When he wrote the book which is here translated he was approaching old age and he was certainly at least sixty, but he had recently married a young wife of higher birth than himself, an orphan from a different province. He speaks several times of her 'very great youth' and kept a sort of duenna-housekeeper with her, to help and direct her in the management of his house, and indeed she was only fifteen years old when he married her. Modern opinion is shocked by a discrepancy in age between husband and wife, with which the Middle Ages, a time of *mariages de convenance*, was more familiar. 'Seldom', the Ménagier says, 'will you see ever so old a man who will not marry a young woman.' Yet his attitude towards his young wife shows that there may have been compensations even in a marriage between May and January, and that Chaucer's incomparable *Marchantes Tale* is not the only possible version of such a situation. Time after time in the Ménagier's book there sounds the note of a tenderness which is paternal rather than marital, a sympathetic understanding of the feelings of a wedded child, which a younger man might not have compassed. Over all the matter of fact counsels there seems to hang something of the mellow sadness of an autumn evening, when 'beauty and death go ever hand in hand'. It was his wife's function to make comfortable his declining years; but it was his to make the task easy for her. He constantly repeats the assurance that he does not ask of her an overweening respect, or a service too humble or too hard, for such is not due to him; he desires only such care as his neighbours and kinswomen take of their husbands, 'for to me belongeth none save the common service, or less'.

In his Prologue, addressed to her, he gives a charming picture of the scene which led him to write his book, reminding her how in the week of their wedding she had prayed him one night in bed not to correct her before strangers, but to tell her what she had done wrong when they were alone and she would amend it. He assures her that all she had done hitherto had pleased him and all that she did thereafter with good intent would please him still, since her youth excused her from being very wise. Nevertheless he has taken heed of her words and has made a little book to show her how to comport herself; for he is sorry for this child, who has for long had neither father nor mother, and who is far from kinswomen, who might counsel her, having 'me only', he says, 'for whom you have been taken from your kinsfolk and from the land of your birth'. One characteristic reason, apart from his desire to help her and to be comfortable himself, he gives for his trouble and reverts to from time to time, surely the oddest ever given by a husband for instructing his wife. He is old, he says, and must die before her and she will marry again; and it will reflect the greatest discredit on *him* in the eyes of her second husband if she is not perfect in manners and morals and fully competent to run a house. It is characteristic of the Ménagier's reasonableness and solid sense that he regards his young wife's second marriage with equanimity. One of his sections is headed 'that you should love your husband (whether myself or another) after the ensample of Sarah, Rebecca and Rachel', and he constantly speaks of 'your husband that shall be'.

The plan of the book – 'in three sections containing nineteen principal articles' – is most exhaustive. The first section deals with religious and moral duties. In the words of the Ménagier the first section 'is necessary to gain the love of God and the salvation of your soul and also to win the love of your husband and to give you in this world that peace which should be in marriage. And because these two things, namely the salvation of your soul and the comfort of your husband, be the two things most chiefly necessary, therefore are they here placed first'. Then follows a series of articles telling the lady how to say her morning prayer when she rises, how to bear herself at mass and in what form to make her confession to the priest, together with a long excursus on the seven deadly sins and their corresponding virtues. These articles are to a certain extent what may be called common form; the excursus on the seven deadly sins should, for example, be compared with Chaucer's *Persones Tale*. But the Ménagier brings to these general moral and religious injunctions a charm that is all his own; the beautiful series of prayers, which he sets down for his wife's use, is particularly noteworthy, while here and there he illuminates his discussion of the deadly sins by little vignettes drawn from daily life, which are as vivid as the illustrations in an illuminated manuscript. Such is his picture of the false executors of wills, who heedless of the wishes of the dead 'devour their flesh like tyrants and grow fat upon their blood and substance'; or of the female glutton:

God commands us to go to church and rise early and the glutton saith, 'I must sleep. I was drunk yesterday. The church is not a hare, it will very well wait for me.' When she has with some difficulty risen, know you what be her hours? Her matins are: 'Ha! what shall we drink? Is there nought left over from last night?' Then says she her lauds, thus: 'Ha! we drank good wine yestreen.' Afterwards she says her orisons, thus: 'My head aches; I shall not be at ease until I have had a drink.'

But the greater part of the first section deals with the all-important subject of the wife's duty to her husband, and apart from the general picture which it gives of the medieval ideal of wifely behaviour, it is notable because it contains a series of stories (*exempla*, as they were commonly called), designed to illustrate the Ménagier's injunctions and to fix them in his wife's mind. These 'examples' are of two kinds, those which he drew from his somewhat extensive reading (he tells his wife that he possesses many books in French) and those which he drew from personal experience. Of the former the two longest were simply copied by him from books in his possession. One of these is the famous story of patient Griselda, originally told by Boccaccio and paraphrased in Latin by Petrarch, whose version was several times translated into French and once into English verse by Chaucer, who made it his *Clerkes Tale*. The second is the tale of Melibeus and Prudence, by Albertano of Brescia, which was translated into French by Renault de Louens, whose version the Ménagier copied, and adapted by Jean de Meung in the *Roman de la Rose*, from which in turn Chaucer took it to tell to the Canterbury pilgrims. It is a matter of some interest that the Ménagier's book, written at almost the same time as the *Canterbury Tales* (which were composed between 1386 and 1389), should have contained two stories which were also used by Chaucer, to say nothing of the parallel section on the Seven Deadly Sins and the tale of Lucretia, which Chaucer had previously included in his *Legend of Good Women*. Among the other stories which the Ménagier retells in his own manner are several taken from the Bible and the Apocrypha, the famous romance of *The Seven Sages of Rome*, Jacques de Cessoles' *Game of Chess Moralised*, and other sources into which all medieval story-tellers dipped. But all the tales are full of a vigour and colour imported into them by the Ménagier himself; whatever their origin and the period in which they are ostensibly set, the detail of medieval *exempla* is as invariably contemporary as is the detail of medieval painting. Even more interesting than these tales are the examples drawn from the Ménagier's own experience – the faithful dog, which he saw upon its master's grave at Niort, the wife whose obedience lost the Sire d'Andresel a wager at Melun, the story, told with such deep feeling, of the bourgeoise who gave her honour to save her husband's life after the rising of the Maillotins and the story of the *avocat*'s wife who cared for her husband's bastard daughter. Even where he is telling a variant of a well-known tale, he is sometimes at pains to give his informant. It was the bailly of Tournai who told him the story of the wager of the newly married husbands and his father who told him of the meek wife of Thomas Quentin.

Interesting as is the first section of the Ménagier's book, it is surpassed in interest by the second. Many treatises on the ideal of womanly behaviour were written in the Middle Ages and have come down to us, and the Ménagier's first section has much in common with the book which the Knight of La Tour-Landry, his contemporary, wrote for the edification of his three daughters.[6] But the second section of the Ménagier's book, in which he turns from theory to practice and from the soul to the body, is in its way unique, for it is by far the most exhaustive treatise on household management which has come down to us from the Middle Ages. It begins, it is true, with a very general dissertation on diligence and prudence in the shape of a long poem, written in 1342 by Jean Bruyant, a notary of the Châtelet, and called *The Way of Poverty and Wealth*, which the Ménagier copied out in full, but after that he cuts the cackle and gets to the 'osses, and the result might well earn for him the title of the Mrs Beeton of the Middle Ages. The section comprises a short treatise on gardening (of which more hereafter), careful instructions for the hire and treatment of servants, an excursus on the points and diseases of horses, and two long articles on the purchase of food, the arrangement of feasts and the choice of menus, ending with a very elaborate and detailed cookery book. If this section be taken together with some parts of the Ménagier's advice on making a husband comfortable in the preceding section, it provides us with an incomparable picture of home life among the wealthy bourgeoisie at the end of the fourteenth century.

The third section of the Ménagier's book was intended to contain three parts: first, a number of parlour games for indoor amusement; secondly, a treatise on hawking, the favourite outdoor sport of ladies; and thirdly, a list of amusing riddles and games of an arithmetical kind, presumably of the nature of our old friend, 'If a herring and a half cost three ha'pence'. Unfortunately the Ménagier seems never to have finished the book; the three MSS known to Pichon contain only the treatise on hawking and that is placed after the treatise on horses in the second section and not in its proper position, as indicated in the Ménagier's plan. It is possible that he tired of his labours, or more probably, that he died while still writing the book;

but, whatever the explanation, it is most regrettable that he should
have written the treatise on hawking instead of the two articles on
indoor amusements; for we have many similar books on hawking
and an account from the Ménagier's pen of the parlour games and
riddles with which medieval ladies amused themselves would have
been unique. What we have missed we may guess from his tantalis-
ing thumb-nail sketch of the occupations of the Roman ladies, in
the story of Lucretia:

Vindrent à Romme et trouvèrent les unes devisans, les autres jouans
au *bric*, les autres à *qui féry?* les autres à *pince-merille*, les autres jouans
aux *cartes* et aux autres jeux d'esbatemens avecques leurs voisines;
les autres qui avoient souppé ensemble, disoient des chançons, des
fables, des contes, des jeux-partis; les autres estoient en la rue
avecques leurs voisines jouans au *tiers* et au *bric*, et ainsi semblable-
ment de plusieurs jeux (see below, p. 69).

In those days, before the invention of printing had made books
plentiful, medieval ladies were largely dependent for amusement
upon telling and listening to stories, asking riddles and playing
games, which we have long ago banished to the nursery, and a
plentiful repertoire of such amusements was very desirable in a well
bred lady. The Ménagier was clearly anxious that his wife should
shine in the amenities as well as in the duties of social life; his many
examples provided her with a fund of anecdotes, and the missing
articles were to have contained her games and riddles. Personally I
can much more easily spare the lost books of Livy.

2. *THE PERFECT WIFE AND HOUSEWIFE*

Such was the monumental work which the Ménagier de Paris was
able to present as 'an easy introduction' to his wife. Though it has
been sadly neglected by historians, it deserves to be well known, for
it gives us a picture of a medieval housewife which it would be hard
indeed to surpass. There is hardly a side of her daily life upon which
it does not touch and it depicts in turn the perfect lady, whose deportment and manners do credit to her breeding, the perfect wife,
whose submission to her husband is only equalled by her skill in
ministering to his ease, and the perfect housewife, who runs her
house like clockwork.

The Ménagier's views on deportment are incongruously sand-wiched into his section on spiritual duties, under the general head-ings of getting up in the morning and going to church. His ideas on the subject of clothes are very clearly defined. A sweet disorder in the dress was in no way to his taste. 'See', he says, 'that you be honestly clad, without new devices and too much frippery, or too little. And before you leave your chamber or house, see you first that the collar of your shift, and your *blanchet*, your robe or your surcoat, straggle not forth one upon the other, as befalleth with certain drunken, foolish, or ignorant women, who have no regard for their honour, nor for the honesty of their estate or of their husbands, and go with roving eyes and head horribly reared up like unto a lion (*la teste espoventablement levée comme un lyon*), their hair straying out of their wimples and the collars of their shifts and robes one upon the other, and walk mannishly and bear themselves uncouthly before folk without shame'; and he recurs again later to 'those bold and foolish women, who go their ways in ribald wise, with their necks stretched forth like a stag in flight, looking this way and that, like unto a runaway horse'. In walking, his wife is to keep her head straight and her eyelids low, and to look upon the ground about four rods ahead, without glancing to right or left. Such instructions are common in all medieval books of deportment. So the English Good Wife teaches her daughter:

> *And whan thou goist in the way, go thou not to faste*
> *Braundische not with thin heed, thi schuldres thou ne caste,*[7]

and the Knight of La Tour-Landry, teaching by examples, bids his girls be like bloodhounds, which keep their noses straight in front of them, and not like tortoises and cranes, ever looking over their shoulders (p. 208, III[2]).

On the attitude of wife to husband the Ménagier's ideas are much the same as those of the other men of his age. They may be summed up as submission, obedience and constant attention. She must be buxom in bed and at board, even though her buxomness hide a heavy heart. Obedience and patience are the essential qualities for a wife; however unreasonable her husband's demands, they must be obeyed and however sorely he try her, she must never complain. Some of the best of the Ménagier's examples are set down to illus-trate this virtue of obedience, and one might assume from them that

the favourite wager of medieval gentlemen, who had drunk not
wisely but too well, was the superiority of their ladies in this quality.
They betted upon their wives as assiduously as their successors
betted upon their horses; and it is with considerable relief that one
gathers from the *exempla* that they usually lost. The Ménagier relates
no fewer than five of such wagers (including the one which occurs in
the course of the story of Lucrece); and two of them he purports to
have witnessed himself, the wager of the Sire d'Andresel and that of
the young husbands encountered at Bar-sur-Aube. How far patience
was expected to go in dealing with an unfaithful husband is well
illustrated in his tale of the wife of one of his friends, a famous
avocat in the *parlement* of Paris, who saw to the nurture and marriage of her husband's bastard daughter, 'and never did he know it
by one sign of ill-will, or one angry or reproachful word', and still
more by the charmingly told story of Jehanne la Quentine. The
stock example of wifely patience was, of course, Griselda, but no-
where does the essential moderation and good sense of the Ménagier
appear more clearly than in his comments on this tale; they are
Chaucerian, without the sub-acid flavour of Chaucer's Envoy. In
general, while subscribing to all the usual standards of his age, the
Ménagier contrives to keep hold upon the realities of life; in return
for obedience he was prepared to give trust and consideration, and
the wife that he wanted was a helpmeet and not a slave. In spite of
the insistence upon obedience which was characteristic of his period,
his ideal of marriage is by no means a low or an unequal one, and
the tone of his remarks contrasts very favourably with that of some
of the ecclesiastical or aristocratic writers, who also produced didactic
treatises for the guidance of women.

In the Ménagier's eyes no woman could be a perfect wife who
was not also a perfect housewife and his instructions to the housewife are (as has been pointed out) the most characteristic and valuable part of his book. He evidently had a large household and owned
a country as well as a town house, for he speaks several times of
overseeing the farm lands 'when you are in the village', and the
farm animals which are in the charge of Robin the shepherd, Josson
the oxherd, Arnoul the cowherd, Jehanneton the milkmaid and
Eudeline the farmer's wife, who looks after the poultry yard. To
assist his wife in superintending this large staff he has a *maître
d'hôtel*, called Master Jehan le Dispensier and a duenna, half house-

keeper and half chaperon for her young mistress, called Dame Agnes la Béguine. The Ménagier divides his servants and workmen into three classes, first, those engaged by the day or by the season for special work, such as porters and carriers, reapers and winnowers and coopers; secondly, those engaged on piecework, such as tailors, furriers, bakers and shoemakers; and thirdly, the ordinary domestic servants, who were hired by the year and lived in their master's house. He gives an amusing account, evidently based upon bitter experience, of the wiles of the French workman and his observations upon the engagement and management of maidservants are replete with the wisdom of the serpent, and incidentally show that the registry office and the 'character' are by no means modern phenomena. His instructions on how to look after servants when engaged are equally practical and marked both by benevolence and by good sense.

But it is perhaps in his capacity as Mrs Beeton that the Ménagier is most amusing. His infinite variety of household knowledge is shown in the incidental recipes, which he gives when he is describing the measures which a wife must take for her lord's comfort and the work of the servants. There are elaborate instructions concerning the costly medieval garments, worn year after year for a lifetime and handed down to another generation in their owner's will, instructions for cleaning dresses and furs and for preserving them from moths and instructions for removing stains and grease spots. The Ménagier gives seven recipes for taking out the latter, but he is somewhat sceptical about one or two of them, which he evidently copied from a book without trying them for himself. On the subject of moths his remarks recall those of John Russell,

> *In the warderobe ye must muche entende besily*
> *the robes to kepe well and also to brusche them clenly;*
> *with the ende of a soft brusche ye brusche them clenly,*
> *and yet ouer moche bruschynge werethe cloth lyghtly.*
> *lett neuer wollyn cloth ne furre passe a seuenyght*
> *to be vnbrosshen and shakyn, tend therto aright,*
> *for moughtes be redy euer in them to gendur and alight;*
> *therfore to drapery and skynnery euer haue ye a sight,*[8]

or of Laurens Andrewe, who writes,

The Motte bredethe amonge clothes tyll that they have byten it a
sonder and yt is a maniable worm, and yet it hydeth him in ye clothe
that it can scantly be sene and it bredethe gladly in clothes that haue
ben in an euyll ayre, or in a rayn or myst, and so layde vp without
hanging in the sonne or other swete ayre after . . . The erbes that be
bitter and well smellinge is good to be layde amonge such clothes, as
the bay leuis, cypres wode.[9]

The Ménagier, however, gives a recipe for drying rose-leaves to be
laid among clothes.

The chief impression left from a perusal of these domestic hints
is that the medieval housewife was engaged in a constant warfare
against fleas. One of the Ménagier's infallible rules for keeping a
husband happy is to give him a good fire in winter and keep his bed
free from fleas in the summer; and he gives six recipes for getting
rid of these 'familiar beasts to men'. A similar war had also to be
waged against flies and mosquitoes, which rendered summer miser-
able, and here too he has six infallible remedies to tell his wife.
Apart from this he is full of miscellaneous household hints; how to
look after wine and preserve fruit and vegetables; how to make
hippocras, that sovereign drink; how to prepare water scented with
sage, or camomile, rosemary, marjoram, bay-leaves or orange peel,
in which to wash the hands at table; how to make wine red and salt
white; how to preserve roses in winter; how to keep birds in aviaries
and make them breed; how to make ink, or sand for hourglasses, or
poison to kill wild beasts or rats; how to cure a toothache and the
bite of a mad dog (the latter a charm, to show that he was not
exempt from the superstitions of his age; he has another to cure a
horse).

The best commentary on the Ménagier in this aspect is to be
found in contemporary wills and household accounts, though of the
latter only the accounts of larger and more aristocratic households
than his have survived. But in literature a picture of domestic life
almost if not quite as vivid as that which he gives is to be found,
occasionally and rather unexpectedly, in certain medieval vocabularies. In the Middle Ages as in our own day a number of vocabularies and phrase books were compiled in order to teach foreign
languages, and then as now they consisted largely of words and
phrases which would be useful to the learner in daily life. Thus they

commonly give details as to food and household implements, shops and the market place, journeys and inns. Among these little books one in particular, a Franco-Flemish vocabulary of the fourteenth century, gives an amusing picture of a bourgeois ménage, somewhat smaller than that of our Parisian.[10] The apposite section is headed 'Concerning things in the house' and opens, after the manner of modern conversation books, with a dialogue between mistress and maid. 'Janet, listen to me.' 'What am I to listen to? Haven't I anything else to do?' 'And what hast thou to do that takes so long?' 'I am making the beds, setting straight the cushions on the forms, chairs, benches, tuffets and stools, and I am cleaning the solar [parlour], the chamber, the house and the kitchen.' 'Thou'rt a good girl and I praise thee.' 'Well, ma'am, I do your will not my own.' 'Tell Jehan that he is slow.' 'Where is he, ma'am?' 'How do I know? I expect he is by thy side.' 'Why do you say that, ma'am?' 'Because he is ready enough to follow thee round about the beds, when thou'rt alone.' 'Saint Mary, ma'am, what are you talking about? Upon my oath, he hates nothing so much as me.' Here follows a somewhat *inconvenant* anecdote of the rout of Jehan, whose intentions are not at all honourable, by Janet, which causes her mistress to exclaim 'O Dieu! Janet, art thou as innocent as thou makest out? Come down and bring towels and linen and coal, and take the bellows and blow up the fire, take the tongs and mend it so that it burns, boil the pots, fry some fat, lay the table and bring the long cloth, put water in the hand-basin.' 'Ma'am, where are the copper, the cauldron and our pans?' 'Art thou blind? dost thou not see them all beside the cupboard?' 'You're right, ma'am.' 'Thou hast still to wash and scour the pewter bottles, the quart and pint pots, platters, bowls and saucers, and put all this iron gear in its proper place, the roasting-iron, the flesh-hook, the trivet, the covers of the pots, and the spits, and then go for wine.' 'Where shall I go?' 'Go where you see most people and I will tell you what wine to get.' The exigencies of learning a language have somewhat crowded the poor maid-of-all-work's morning, but the picture is as clear as a little interior by Jan Steen or Van Dou.

Two articles of the Ménagier's section on household management demand rather more detailed notice than the rest. It will be observed that his book contains four little technical treatises, which are complete in themselves, the treatises on horses and on hawking (which are omitted in this translation) and those on gardening and on cookery. The two latter are among the most important parts of his work.

3. ON GARDENING

The treatise on gardening,[11] which occupies the second article of the second section, is exceedingly valuable in view of the comparative rarity of medieval writings on this subject. It is true that both the art and the literature of the Middle Ages are full of descriptions of gardens; the garden of the *Roman de la Rose*, the gardens scattered throughout Chaucer's poems and the innumerable gardens depicted with such loving detail in medieval illuminated MSS[12] would suffice to tell us a great deal about the subject. Occasionally, too, some didactic writer will give a list of the plants which ought to have a place in a princely garden, such a list as is found in Charlemagne's capitulary *De Villis* in the ninth century or in Alexander Neckam's treatise *De Naturis Rerum* in the twelfth, or again a maker of vocabularies will furnish similar names of plants, trees and agricultural implements. But vocabulary makers are somewhat to be mistrusted; their object is to teach the language — whatsoever it be — not to purvey exact and realistic information upon any subject, and just as their fish commonly range from minnows to mermaidens, just as their lord out hunting will shoot the phoenix among his wild duck and wood pigeons, so their gardens are apt to contain not only plants proper to all climates blooming happily in the same bed, but even such horticultural rarities as the mandrake. Nevertheless lists of garden plants such as those given by John de Garlande and Walter de Biblesworth in the thirteenth century are very valuable,[13] and even more valuable (so far as culinary herbs, vegetables and fruit are concerned) are the lists which may be compiled from medieval cookery books. Much, too, may be gleaned from the accounts of receipts and expenditure kept by the custodians of certain gardens; the account of the bailiff of Henry de Laci, Earl of Lincoln, of expenditure on and profits from his garden in Holborn in 1296 gives a valuable picture of a wealthy nobleman's garden at that date;[14] and similar accounts have survived from certain monastic houses; there is a good series concerning the garden of the monks of Norwich.[15]

But on the actual technique of medieval gardening little exact information is to be had. For the most part medieval gardeners relied either upon adaptations of ancient works, notably the treatises of Palladius and Columella, or upon empirical knowledge, handed on from gardener to gardener, which they failed to write down. Hence the Ménagier's little treatise is particularly valuable, especially as it bears some traces of originality. It may be compared usefully with three English treatises of the same date. Two of these are adaptations of Palladius, one entitled 'Godfrey upon Palladie de Agricultura', the other (in which the original element is stronger) by Nicholas Bollarde, a monk of Westminster.[16] But the third is much more original and attractive; it is a little treatise on 'The Feate of Gardeninge', written in verse in the first half of the fifteenth century by one 'Mayster Jon Gardener' and preserved in a manuscript in Trinity College, Cambridge.[17] Its particular and careful instructions for 'graffyng of treys', 'cuttyng and settyng of vyneys', 'settyng and sowyng of sedys', 'sowyng and settyng of wurtys', with dissertations on the habits of parsley and saffron and a long list of herbs and flowers growing in Master Jon's garden would persuade almost anyone to be a gardener, and ought to be compared with the Ménagier's instructions at every turn.

Our knowledge of the plan and appearance of a garden in the Ménagier's day is largely derived from pictures in illuminated MSS. His garden (whether in Paris or on his country farm) was probably not very large, surrounded by brick walls or wattles and very stiffly arranged. In the centre would stand a fountain or springhead, such as meets our eyes so often in illustrations of Susanna or Bathsheba bathing, or of the earthly paradise. The beds would be square or rectangular, raised from the ground, sometimes to a height of a foot or two, and faced with brick to keep them in place, and vegetables as well as flowers would be grown in them. There would be apple and cherry trees, to make a pleasant shade and provide fruit, and also vine arbours, for shelter and privacy as well as for their grapes. The grassy sward would be starred with low growing flowers and in the warm summer evenings the Ménagier and his wife would sit upon turfed mounds of earth, planted with sweet scented flowers and herbs, camomile, marjoram, pennyroyal, violets and perhaps periwinkles, 'the joy-of-the-ground', although (oddly enough) he does not mention this favourite flower. Perhaps there was also a *hortus*

conclusus, so beloved of medieval artists, because it was an emblem
of the Virgin ('a garden enclosed is my sister, my spouse, a spring
shut up, a fountain sealed'), a little closed garden within a garden,
with vines on the trellis round it and roses and lilies growing inside.

The contents of the garden fall into four classes, flowers, vegetables, herbs for culinary and medicinal purposes, or merely for
their sweet smell underfoot (which Bacon was to prize so greatly
some two centuries later), and fruit trees. The following plants are
mentioned in the Ménagier's treatise: (1) flowers: violet, gillyflower, peony, lily, rose; (2) vegetables: porray (p. 214²) and beet,
leek, cabbage, parsley, bean, pea, spinach, lettuce, pumpkin, turnip,
radish, parsnip; (3) herbs: lavender, marjoram, sage, mint, dittany,
basil, clary, dragonwort, savory, sorrel, borage, orage and hyssop;
(4) fruits: vine, raspberry, currant, cherry and plum. It should be
observed that the last three sections can be considerably increased
by adding vegetables, herbs and fruits mentioned in the cookery
book, though some of these were doubtless purchased and not
grown by him. Thus we have in addition carrots (which he specif-
ically says are bought in the market), shallots, cress, garlic, smallage,
tansey, rue, camomile, pennyroyal, herb bennet, chervil, fennel,
saffron and coriander among vegetables and herbs, and apples, pears,
peaches, medlars, quinces, figs, mulberries and various sorts of nuts
among fruits (besides oranges, pomegranates, dates and raisins).
The flowers mentioned are few, but prime favourites. Roses, white
and red, were the best loved flowers of the Middle Ages and are
found everywhere in art and literature; they have their apotheosis in
perhaps the most famous poem of the whole period, the *Roman de la
Rose*. Gillyflowers or clove pinks were also very popular, and the
nominal rent of a piece of land not infrequently took the form of a
red rose or a clove gillyflower tendered once a year; for they would
be found in every garden. Violets were prized not only for their
beauty and sweet scent, but as salad herbs, the flowers being either
eaten raw with onions and lettuce or sugared and served as sweet-
meats. Lilies and peonies also are often mentioned or depicted in
medieval gardens. These flowers were used for garlands, for both
men and women in the Middle Ages had the pleasant habit of gar-
landing themselves on festive occasions, and ladies are often represented in illuminated MSS plucking flowers for this purpose. The
Ménagier mentions the chaplet-maker as one of the personages re-

quired at a wedding feast and tells his young wife: 'I am pleased
rather than displeased that you tend rose trees and care for violets
and make chaplets and dance and sing.' One sees her in her garden,
like Chaucer's Emelye on May Day:

> *Y-clothed was she fresh, for to devyse;*
> *Hir yelow heer was broyded in a tresse,*
> *Behinde hir bak, a yerde long, I gesse.*
> *And in the gardin, at the sonne up-riste*
> *She walketh up and doun, and as hir liste*
> *She gadereth floures, party whyte and rede,*
> *To make a sotil gerland for hir hede,*
> *And as an aungel hevenly she song.*[18]

The Ménagier's collection of vegetables and herbs is much more
extensive than his collection of flowers and one suspects him of
regarding his garden with a somewhat utilitarian eye, and a mind
fixed on the black and white and green porrays, the herbolaces and
cold sages subsequently to appear upon his table. It will perhaps be
of interest to compare his list with others which are more or less
contemporary. John de Garlande was an Englishman living in Paris,
who drew up a *Dictionarius* just about a century before the Ménagier
wrote; and the garden described in it may, in Thomas Wright's
opinion, be considered as the garden of a respectable burgher of the
day.

In Master John's garden are these plants: sage, parsley, dittany,
hyssop, celandine, fennel, pellitory, the rose, the lily and the violet;
and at the side [i.e., in the hedge] the nettle, the thistle and fox-
gloves. There are also medicinal herbs here, to wit mercury and
mallow, agrimony with nightshade and marigold. Master John's
herb-gardener culls in his herb garden pot herbs [or perhaps specif-
ically *cole*]; there groweth borage, leek and garlic, mustard, porray
and cibols [a small onion] and scallions; in his grove grow pimpernel, mouseare, self-heal, buglos, adder's tongue and other herbs
good for men's bodies.

Master John's orchard contained cherry, pear, apple and plum
trees, quinces, medlars, peaches, chestnuts, nuts, walnuts, figs and

grapes.[19] Almost contemporary with the Ménagier's book there is an extremely amusing manual of French conversation, called *La Manière de langage,* which was also drawn up by an Englishman at Bury St Edmunds in 1396, in the course of which there occurs a model conversation with a gardener, which throws some further light upon the subject. 'Now tell me, fair sir, how much have you earned?' 'Willingly, my gentle comrade. I have grafted all the trees in my garden with the fairest grafts that I have seen for a long while, and they are beginning to put forth green; also I have dug another garden and I have very carefully planted cabbages, porray, parsley and sage and other goodly herbs; and furthermore I have pulled up and cleared away from it all the nettles, brambles and wicked weeds, and I have sown it full well with many good seeds; and in it I have likewise many fair trees bearing divers fruits, such as apples, pears, plums, cherries and nuts, and everywhere have I very well looked after them, and yet all I have earned this week is 3d. and my expenses; but last week I earned as much again, and I was very quick about it.' 'Hé, my friend, never mind, for one must earn what one can today.'[20]

A manuscript in the British Museum (MS Sloane 1201), which contains a cookery book and was written in the first half of the fifteenth century, that is to say shortly after *Le Ménagier de Paris,* contains a list of plants considered necessary for a garden, which has several times been printed.[21] After an alphabetical list, it classifies the plants as follows:

Of the same herbes for potage

Borage, langdebefe [buglos], vyolettes, malowes, marcury, daundelyoun, avence [herb bennet], myntes, sauge, parcely, goldes [corn marigold], margeroum [marjoram], ffenelle, carawey, red nettylle, oculus Christi [clary], daysys, chervelle, lekez, colewortes, rapez, tyme, cyves, betes, alysaundre, letyse, betayne, columbyne, allia [garlic], astralogya rotunda, astralogya longa, basillicam [basil], dylle, deteyne, hertestong, radiche, white pyper, cabagez, sedewale, spynache, coliaundre, ffoothistylle [probably sowthistle although under F in the list], orage, cartabus, lympens, nepte, clarey, pacience.

Of the same herbes for sauce

Hertestonge, sorelle, pelytory, pelytory of spayne, deteyne, vyolettes, parcely, myntes.

Also of the same herbez for the coppe [cup]

Cost, costmary, sauge, isope, rose mary, gyllofre [gillyflower], goldez, clarey, mageroum, rue.

Also of the same herbes for a salade

Buddus of stanmarche [the plant Alexander], vyolette flourez, parcely, red myntes, syves, cresse of Boleyne, purselane, ramsons, calamyntes, primerose buddus, dayses, rapounses, daundelyoun, rokette, red nettelle, borage flourez, croppus of red ffenelle, selbestryve, chykynwede.

Also herbez to stylle [distil]

Endyve, red rose, rose mary, dragans [herb serpentine], skabiose, ewfrace [eyebright], wermode, mogwede, beteyne, wylde tansey, sauge, isope, ersesmart.

Also herbes for savour and beaute

Gyllofre gentyle, margeroum gentyle, brasyle, palma Christi, stycadose, meloncez, arcachaffe, scalacely [Solomon's Seal], philyppendula [dropwort], popy royalle, germaundre, cowsloppus of Jerusalem, verveyne, dylle, seynt Mare, garlek.

Also rotys [roots] for a gardyne

Parsenepez, turnepez, radyche, karettes, galyngale, eryngez [eringoes], saffrone.

Also for an herbere [arbour]

Vynes, rosers, lyles, thewberies [? gooseberries], almondez, baytrese, gourdes, date-trese, pyneappulle, pyany romain, rose campy, cartabus, seliane, columbyne gentyle, elabre.

Finally, here is Jon Gardener's list of herbs, belonging to about the same date as the last:

Pelyter [pellitory], dytawnder [dittany], rewe and sage,
Clarey, tyme, ysope and orage,
Myntys, sauerey, tuncarse [town cress] and spynage,
Letows, calamynte, auans and borage,
Fynel, sowthrynwode [southernwood], warmot [wormwood] and rybwart,

Herb Ion [St John's wort], herb Robert, herb Water and walwort,
Hertystonge, polypody, parrow [? yarrow] and comfery,
Gromel, woderofe, hyndesall and betony,
Gladyn [iris], valeryan, scabyas and sperewort,
Verueyn, wodesour, waterlyly and lyuerworte,
Mouseer, egrimoyne, honysoke and bugull [buglos],
Centory, horsel, adderstong and bygull [bigold],
Henbane, camemyl, wyldtesyl and stychewort,
Weybrede, growdyswyly [groundsel], elysauwder [herb Alexander] and
    brysewort
Merege, lauyndull [lavender], radysche, sanycle and seueny [mustard],
Peruynke, violet, cowslyppe and lyly,
Carsyndyllys, strowberys and moder wort,
Langebefe, totesayne, tansay and feldewort,
Orpy, nepte, horehound and flos campi,
Affodyll, redeuay, primerole and oculus christi,
Rose ryde, rose whyghte, foxgloue and pympernold,
Holyhocke, coryawnder, pyony and the wold,
All this herby by seynt Mychaell
Wold be sette yn the moneth of Auerell.[22]

We are thus by no means ill-informed as to the contents of medieval gardens; but the Ménagier's treatise is particularly valuable for its practical instructions as to growing the different plants and trees. 'The processes of gardening', as Thomas Wright says, 'were simple and easy and the gardener's skill consisted chiefly in the knowledge of the seasons for sowing and planting different herbs and trees and of the astrological circumstances under which these processes could be performed most advantageously. The great ambition of the medieval horticulturist was to excel in the various mysteries of grafting and he entertained theories on this subject of the most visionary character, many of which were founded on the writings of the ancients; for the medieval theorists were accustomed to select from the doctrines of antiquity that which was most visionary and it usually became still more visionary in their hands.'[23] The Ménagier is as insistent upon the waxing or waning of the moon as he is upon dry or rainy weather as suitable for various operations; but although concerned, like all his fellows, to have grapes without pips and to graft cherry trees and vines upon each

other, he is guiltless of some of their worst absurdities, such as the
experiments in the colour and flavouring of fruits in which they delight. 'For to have frute of dyvers colourys,' says a little fifteenth-
century English treatise based on Palladius, 'thou schalt make an
hole in a tre nyghe the rote, evene to the pythe of the tre, and than
do therein good asure of Almayne, so hyt be nyghe fulle, and stope
the hole welle with a schort pyne and wrap hit welle with temperat
erthe, and wynd hit welle, as thou doste a graffe, and that frute
schalbe of blewe colour, and so hit may be do of a vyne, and this
may be do with alle manere colourys. Iff thou wylt that thy appyllys
be rede, take a graff of an appyltre and ympe hit opone a stoke of an
elme or an eldre, and hit schalbe rede appylles. Also Master Richard
saythe, to do the same thyngge, make an hole with a wymbulle, and
what colour that thou wylt dystemper with water, and put hit in the
hole, the frute schalbe the same colour.'[24] One cannot help feeling
that the Ménagier, confronted with such instructions, would sturdily
have added 'This do I not believe', as was his wont when copying
recipes which seemed to him unreliable.

Whatever may be said of his remarks on grafting, his instructions
dealing with the question of when and where and how to sow or set
vegetables and potherbs are obviously the work of a practical gardener, who knew what he was talking about. His careful description
of the different varieties of cabbage (which recurs in his cookery
book), his injunctions on the subject of parsley and his warnings
upon the method of transplanting are all based upon experience.
They may be compared with those set down in the little treatise of
Jon Gardener, who also clearly believed that an ounce of medieval
practice was worth a ton of ancient theory. Here are his instructions
for setting and sowing seeds:

Yn the day of Seynt Valentyne
Thu schalt sowe this sedys yn tyme
For they beth herbys un-meke [strong]
Thu schalt ham [them] set and sow eke.
They that beth stronge and nought meke
The names of hem is garlek and leke.
Oynet thu schalt sow then
Other [or] therafter sone Apon,
To set oynyns to make the sede

Y wul the tel for my mede.
In auerell [April] other yn mars, as y haue y-fownde,
To set other to sowe hem yn the grownde.
When they begynnyth to grow hye
Lete none of ham towche other nye.
Under hem than put thu schall,
That none of hem downe nought fall,
If thu wyl that hy the
Forkys y-made of asche-tre.
To haue hem saue [safe] and kepe hare prow [good]
They wolde aske askys [ashes] abowt ham y-strow.
When they rype they wyl schow
And by the bollus thu schalt hem know —
The sede w^t-yn wul schewe blake.
Then thu schalt hem vp take.
They wul be rype at the full
At lammasse of Peter Apostull [June 29th].
On thys maner thu schalt the sedys drye:
Uppon a clothe thu the sedys lye,
Agen the sonne his kynd ys
For to ly to dry, y-wys.

Here, again, are his instructions for the setting and sowing of herbs:

Wurtys we most haue
Both to mayster and to knaue.
Ye schul haue mynde here
To have wurtys yong al tyme of the yere.
Euery moneth hath his name
To set and sow, w^t-ought eny blame.
May for somer ys al the best,
July for eruyst [harvest, autumn] ys the nexst,
Novembr' for wynter mote the thyrde be,
Mars for lent, so mote y the.
The lond mote wel y dygned [dunged] be,
Y-dolue [delved], y-sturyd [stirred], syre parde [sir, parde!]
Whan thu hast y-sow thi sede on long,
Foore wykys theraftur thu let hem stonde.

Whan the iiij wykes beth al ouer gone
Take thy plontys euery-chone
And set ham yn kynd, fat lond,
And thay wul fayre wurtys [worts, herbs] be and long.
*W*t *yn too wykes that thay beth y-sett,*
Thu may pul hem to thy mete.
And so fro moneth to monethe
Thu schalt bryng thy wurtys forthe.
They that schal bere sede lasse and more
Let ham grow to make the store.

Finally, here are his remarks on parsley, to compare with the Ménagier's instructions on the cultivation of that indispensable herb:

Percell kynde [the nature of parsley] ys for to be
To be sow yn the monthe of mars, so mote I the,
He will grow long and thykke
And euer as he growyth thu schalt hym kytte [cut].
Thu may hym kytte by reson
Thryes yn one seson,
Wurtys to make and sewes also.
Let hym neuer to hye go.
To lete hym grow to hye hyt is grete foly,
For he wul then blest and wanchy [wither and become sickly].
Hys kynde ys nought to be sette;
To be sow ys al-ther best [best of all].
Thay that the sede schal bere the,
Kytte hym nought, but lete hym be
Fro mydwynter to the natyuyte
And he schal fayre sede be.
Of percell ys lyght to know —
Take hede he wul nought be set but sow,
For yf he be set he wul wax thynne,
And than he wul nought be gode to repyne.

4. ON FEASTS AND COOKERY

But if the Ménagier's treatise on gardening is strictly practical, even
more practical is his cookery book and it is very much longer and
more elaborate; for dear as were all the Ménagier's creature comforts to him, it is not difficult to guess that the inner man (with due
regard to the fact that gluttony was one of the seven deadly sins) was
dearest of all; and one of his most sapient hints as to the preservation
by his wife of his successor's affections, may certainly be summed up
as 'Feed the brute'. Not that anyone could possibly suspect the
Ménagier of gluttony. He was rather a genial epicure, like Chaucer's
Franklin:

> Of his complexioun he was sangwyn.
> Wel loved he by the morwe a sop in wyn.
> To liven in delyt was ever his wone,
> For he was Epicurus owne sone,
> That heeld opinioun, that pleyn delyt
> Was verraily felicitee parfyt.
> An housholdere and that a greet, was he;
> Seint Julian he was in his contree.
> His breed, his ale, was alwey after oon;
> A bettre envyned man was no-wher noon.
> Withoute bake mete was never his hous,
> Of fish and flesh, and that so plentevous,
> It snewed in his hous of mete and drinke,
> Of alle deyntees that men coude thinke.
> After the sondry sesons of the yeer,
> So chaunged he his mete and his soper.
> Ful many a fat partrich hadde he in mewe,
> And many a breem and many a luce in stewe.
> Wo was his cook, but if his sauce were
> Poynaunt and sharp, and redy al his gere.
> His table dormant in his halle alway
> Stood redy covered al the longe day.[25]

Everything that the Ménagier has to say about cooking shows a
discriminating taste and expert knowledge. The majority of his
recipes are doubtless neither his own nor set down in his own words,

though some may well be and to others he adds comments. He lived
in an age when the noble art of cookery was not merely prized, but
was beginning to be written down and to acquire a literature of its
own; the famous cookery books begin with the last half of the fourteenth century. In England about 1390 one was compiled by the
master cooks of Richard II, 'the best and ryallest viander of all
Christian kynges', under the name of *The Forme of Cury* and a little
later come other English cookery books which have been published, the *Liber Cure Cocorum*, the *Noble Boke off Cookry* and the two
fifteenth-century treatises published by the Early English Text
Society.[26] In these will be found variants of the majority of the
recipes given by the Ménagier. His own book is largely derived
from two French cookery books, which he evidently had in his possession and from which he copied. These books are the treatise
drawn up by the famous master cook Taillevent, who was cook to
Charles V in 1361 and *écuyer de cuisine* to Charles VI in 1386; and
another book entitled *Le Livre fort excellent de cuisine* or *Grand
Cuisinier de toutes cuisines*, which was afterwards several times printed
in the sixteenth century, and from which it is evident that the
Ménagier borrowed largely. But his own treatise is longer and far
more detailed than either and is certainly the fullest of its kind which
has survived from the fourteenth century. Here in profusion are the
recipes for cooking black puddings and sausages, meat and venison,
flesh and fowl, eels and herrings, freshwater fish, round sea-fish and
flat sea-fish, common pottages unspiced, spiced pottages, meat pottages and meatless pottages, pasties and entremets, sauces of all
sorts, and an excursus on invalid cookery.

In reading medieval cookery books a modern reader is inevitably
struck with the richness of the seasoning employed and the wide use
of spices in every sort of dish. It is no wonder that the Genoese and
Venetian merchants made their fortunes out of the spice trade. It is
sometimes said that this heavy spicing of meat was required by the
fact that since there were then no winter root crops or artificial
grasses (the turnip, as we see from the Ménagier's treatise on gardening, was still a garden vegetable), medieval farmers had to kill
and salt down at Martinmas all the sheep and cattle which their
supply of hay and pasture would not suffice to feed during the winter; consequently our forefathers ate a great deal of salt meat during
the winter months and needed spices to make it palatable. Doubtless

this is partially true; but all the cookery books show that they spiced fresh meat and poultry too, and most of the Ménagier's meat dishes appear to be made of fresh meat, so that the use of condiments would seem to have been a matter of taste rather than of necessity. The men of the Middle Ages inherited it from the ancient world and it does not seem to have died away until the seventeenth century, which saw the appearance of something much more like modern cookery. Occasionally they experienced some misgivings themselves over the increasing elaboration of the dishes set before them by their cooks. In the fifteenth century John Russell, usher and marshal to Humphrey, Duke of Gloucester, expressed himself with point on the subject in his *Boke of Nurture*:

> *Cookes with theire newe conceytes, choppynge, stampynge and*
> *gryndynge,*
> *Many new curies alle day they ar contryvynge and Fyndynge*
> *That provokethe the peple to perelles of passage through peyne soore*
> *pyndynge,*
> *and through nice excesse of suche receytes of the life to make a*
> *endynge.*
> *Some with Sireppis, Sawces, Sewes and soppes,*
> *Comedies, Cawdelles cast in Cawdrons, ponnes or pottes,*
> *leesses, Ielies, Fruturs, fried mete that stoppes*
> *and distemperethe alle the body, bothe bak, bely and roppes:*
> *some maner cury of Cookes crafft Sotelly y haue espied,*
> *how theire dischmetes ar dressid with hony not claryfied.*
> *Cow heelis and Calves fete ar dere y- bought some tide*
> *To medille amonge leeches and Ielies whan suger shalle syt aside.*[27]

But although we should probably dislike the spice powder scattered over broths and the seasoning of ginger, grain of paradise [cardamom], cloves, cinnamon and pepper, some of the Ménagier's dishes sound very good, especially the brewets (thick broths, with the solid chunks of meat etc., out of which they were made, in the bottom of the bowl and a powder of some sort scattered over them), the flawns and wafers and the herb and egg dishes. Some of his recipes are for dishes famous in their time, such as blankmanger and the delectable brewet of Almaign (Germany), without which no feast was complete. True to his race, he tells his wife how to prepare frogs and snails, but he also impresses upon her a 'delicate English broth', Lombard tarts and Norwegian pasties. Particularly interesting is his chapter on sauces, for he liked them 'poynaunt and sharp'; it may be compared with John Russell's injunctions (and indeed the *Boke of Nurture*, with its elaborate instructions for carving and serving every variety of food, is a sort of poetical commentary on this section of the Ménagier's book):

Also to know youre sawces for flesche conveniently,
hit provokithe a fyne apetide if sawce youre mete be bie;
to the lust of youre lord looke that ye have ther redy
suche sawce as hym likethe to make hym glad and mery.
Mustard is meete for brawne, beef or powdred motoun,
verdius to boyled capoun, veel, chiken or bakon;
And to signet and swan, convenyent is the chawdon;
Rooste beeff and goos with garlek, vinegre or pepur, in conclusioun.
Gynger sawce to lambe, to kyd, pigge, or fawn in fere;
To feysaund, partriche, or cony, Mustard with the sugure;
Sawce gamelyn to heyron-sewe, egret, crane and plovere;
Also brewe, Curlew sugre and salt, with watere of the ryvere;
Also for bustard, betowre and shovelere, gamelyn is in sesoun
Wodcok, lapewynk, Mertenet, larke and venysoun,
Sparows, thrusches, alle these – vij – with salt and synamome:
Quayles, sparowes and snytes, whan theire sesoun com,
Thus to provoke an appetide the Sawce hathe is operacioun.[28]

The Ménagier mentions the elaborate entremets (farced or stuffed pigs, swans or herons, or peacocks cooked and clad again in their skins and the like), which were borne aloft at great feasts; but he is careful to note, with his usual good sense, that such things are not for his bourgeois kitchen. 'But there is too much to do,' he says, describing how chickens may be farced and then coloured or glazed, 'it is not a work for a citizen's cook, nor even for a simple knight's; and therefore I leave it'; and the same for glazed shoulders of mutton, 'it is nought but pain and trouble,' says he, and for mock-hedgehogs made of tripe, 'it is a great expense and a great labour and little honour and profit, wherefore *nichil hic*'; he does not copy the recipes. Similarly his menus include no reference to the ingenious 'subtleties' or allegorical devices, which were brought in after each course in medieval feasts and since they were supposed to be appropriate to the occasion of the rejoicing, were sometimes surprising enough; at all events a modern bride might be somewhat taken aback to be faced at the fourth course of her wedding breakfast with 'a wif lying in childe-bed'.[29]

But the Ménagier does not content himself with providing his wife with a collection of recipes. He also gives her the menus of twenty-four dinners and suppers, for fish days and meat days alike, though from their elaboration it is clear that they were intended as models for great occasions and not for the simple bourgeois meals of everyday. From these and other menus of the sort which have survived elsewhere, it is clear that the meals followed a regular order. First came several courses of brewets and meat or fish dishes, which formed the more solid portion of the meal. Then on great occasions came the entremets, glazed and sugared dishes, and swans or pheasants with gilded beaks and claws and their feathered skins sewn round them again. Then came the dessert of compotes and fruit; then the issue, or 'departure from the table', usually composed of the sweet spiced drink called hippocras and a particular kind of wafer called *mestier*, or in summer, when hippocras was out of season, of apples, cheese and other light sugared wafers; and finally the *boutehors* or 'sally-forth' of wine and spices, followed by the washing of the guests' hands in rose-water, grace and adjournment to another room:

Afftur this, delicatis mo
Blaunderelle, or pepyns with carawey in confite,
Waffurs to ete, ypocras to drynk with delite,
now this fest is fynysched, voyd the table quyte.[30]

A particularly valuable introduction to the menus and recipes in the Ménagier's book is contained in his account of all the meat markets of Paris, together with the number of butchers to be found in each and the number of sheep, oxen, pigs and calves sold there every week, to which he adds the amount of meat and poultry consumed weekly in the households of the king, the queen and the royal children, the dukes of Orleans, Berry, Burgundy and Bourbon. Elsewhere also he speaks of other markets, the Pierre-au-Lait or milk market, the Place de Grève, where coal and firewood was sold, and the Porte-de-Paris, which was not only a meat market, but the best place in which to buy fish and salt and green herbs and branches to adorn rooms. Moreover, for his wife's further guidance, the Ménagier sets out a careful specification of the catering arrangements for several great feasts, which had taken place or were about to take place at the moment of his writing. Thus we have a dinner given by the Abbot of Lagny to the Bishop of Paris and the members of the King's Council, the wedding dinner and supper of Jean Duchesne upon a Tuesday in May and the arrangements for 'the Hautecourt wedding' in September. The description of the wedding feast of Jean Duchesne (arranged by one 'Master Helye', doubtless some such worthy steward as the Ménagier's own Master Jehan the Dispenser) is particularly full and valuable. The careful Ménagier has set down not only the menu of dinner and supper, but all the ingredients needed, their quantity and price and the shops or markets where they are to be bought, so that the reader may follow the *maître d'hôtel* and the cooks as they go from stall to stall, bargaining with butcher and baker, poulterer, sauce-maker, vintner, wafer-maker, spicer and chandler. He sets down likewise all the esquires and varlets who will be needed to serve such a feast as this. First the master cook, even such a one as Chaucer saw upon the road to Canterbury:

> *A Cook they hadde with hem for the nones,*
> *To boille the chiknes with the mary-bones,*
> *And poudre-marchant tart and galingale . . .*
> *He coude roste and sethe and boil and frye,*
> *Maken mortreux and wel bake a pye . . .*
> *For blankmanger, that made he with best.*[31]

(the Ménagier has recipes for all these dishes). The master cook brought his varlets with him and in Paris he took two francs for his hire, 'and perquisites'. There were ushers 'stout and strong' to keep the doors and a clerk to add up the accounts; bread-cutters and water-carriers, two squires to serve at the dresser in the kitchen where the plates and dishes were handed out, two others at the hall dresser to give out spoons and drinking cups and pour wine for the guests, and two in the pantry to give out the wine, which their varlet kept on drawing for them. There were two *maîtres d'hôtel* to set out the silver salt-cellars for the high table, the four great gilded goblets, the four dozen hanaps, the four dozen silver spoons, the ewers and alms mugs and sweetmeat dishes and to usher the guests to their places, a sewer and two servitors for each table, a flower girl to make garlands for the guests and women to see to the linen and dight the bridal bed. The floors were strewn with violets and green herbs and the walls and tables decorated with branches of greenery (all bought in the market outside the Paris gate in the early morning); there was a good stock of torches and candles, small candles to stand on the supper table and great torches to be set in sconces on the walls, or to be carried in procession by the guests, for the supper ended with 'dancing, singing, wine and spices and lighted torches'; and there were also musicians to play during the meal and acrobats to amuse the company.

5. CONCLUSION

Such is the general outline of the book which this unknown citizen of Paris wrote for the instruction of his wife. Out of it there emerges clearly a picture of the Ménagier de Paris, sensible, yet full of sensibility, deeply religious, yet a man of the world, gravely dignified, yet modest at heart, a worthy representative of that great bourgeoisie, which at the end of the fourteenth century was rapidly becoming more influential than the aristocracy, which had once despised it. As a full-length portrait of a bourgeois and his wife it has indeed only one equal, the portrait of Jean Arnolfini and his wife, which Van Eyck painted in 1434 and which now hangs in the National Gallery. They were born in one bourgeois civilisation – that of Lucca – and had settled in another – that of Bruges. They stand, facing the spectator, hand in hand, dignified, with serious and rather sad faces, 'married friends', to use the phrase of a sixteenth-century Flemish weaver. She is richly dressed, with enormous flowing skirts like a lady, but there is no frivolity in her air. At her feet stands her little dog, and all round them are their household goods, the great scarlet bed, the glass-paned windows, the brass chandelier and the concave mirror in which the scene is seen small as in a miniature. And above it is written '*Johannes de Eyck fuit hic*' – Jan Van Eyck was here. If Jan Van Eyck had been there when the Ménagier and his wife stood in their chamber, he might have painted just such a picture of them. The Ménagier was an old man, but if we set upon Arnolfini's shoulders the head of the man with the carnations in the Kaiser Friedrich Museum, or of the Canon Van der Paele in the great picture at Bruges, we may perhaps imagine to ourselves something of how these two looked. But indeed it is not necessary; for the Ménagier himself has drawn them as clearly with his pen as even Jan Van Eyck could have done with his brush.

EILEEN POWER

Prologue

Dear Sister,[1]
You being the age of fifteen years and in the week that you and I were wed, did pray me to be indulgent to your youth and to your small and ignorant service, until you had seen and learned more; to this end you promised me to give all heed and to set all care and diligence to keep my peace and my love, as you spoke full wisely, and as I well believe, with other wisdom than your own, beseeching me humbly in our bed, as I remember, for the love of God not to correct you harshly before strangers nor before our own folk, but rather each night, or from day to day, in our chamber, to remind you of the unseemly or foolish things done in the day or days past, and chastise you, if it pleased me, and then you would strive to amend yourself according to my teaching and correction, and to serve my will in all things, as you said. And your words were pleasing to me, and won my praise and thanks, and I have often remembered them since. And know, dear sister, that all that I know you have done since we were wed until now and all that you shall do hereafter with good intent, was and is to my liking, pleaseth me, and has well pleased me, and will please me. For your youth excuses your unwisdom and will still excuse you in all things as long as all you do is with good intent and not displeasing to me. And know that I am pleased rather than displeased that you tend rose trees, and care for violets, and make chaplets, and dance, and sing: nor would I have you cease to do so among our friends and equals, and it is but good and seemly so to pass the time of your youth, so long as you neither seek nor try to go to the feasts and dances of lords of too high rank, for that does not become you, nor does it sort with your estate, nor mine. And as for the greater service that you say you would willingly do for me, if you were able and I taught it you, know dear sister, that I am well content that you should do me such service as your good neighbours of like estate do for their husbands, and as your kinswomen do unto their husbands. Take counsel privily of them, and then follow it either more or less as you please. For I am not so overweening in my attitude to you and your good intent that I am not satisfied with what you do for me therein, nor with all other services, provided there be no disorder or scorn or disdain, and

that you are careful. For although I know well that you are of gentler birth than I, nathless that would not protect you, for by God, the women of your lineage be good enough to correct you harshly themselves, if I did not, if they learnt of your error from me or from another source; but in you I have no fear, I have confidence in your good intent. Yet although, as I have said, to me belongs only the lesser service, I would that you know how to give good will and honour and service in great measure and abundance more than is fit for me, either to serve another husband, if you have one, after me, or to teach greater wisdom to your daughters, friends or others, if you list and have such need. For the more you know the greater honour will be yours and the greater praise will therefore be unto your parents and to me and to others about you, by whom you have been nurtured. And for your honour and love, and not for my service (for to me belongs but the common service, or less), since I had pity and loving compassion on you who for long have had neither father nor mother, nor any of your kinswomen near you to whom you might turn for counsel in your private needs, save me alone, for whom you were brought from your kin and the country of your birth, I have often wondered how I might find a simple general introduction to teach you the which, without the aforesaid difficulties, you might of yourself introduce into your work and care. And lastly, me-seems that if your love is as it has appeared in your good words, it can be accomplished in this way, namely in a general instruction that I will write for you and present to you, in three sections containing nineteen[2] principal articles.

THE FIRST SECTION

The first section of the three is necessary to gain the love of God and the salvation of your soul, and also to win the love of your husband and to give you in this world that peace which should be in marriage. And because these two things, namely the salvation of your soul and the comfort of your husband, be the two things most chiefly necessary, therefore are they here placed first. And this first section contains nine articles.

The first article speaketh of worshipping and thanking our Saviour and his Blessed Mother at your waking and your rising, and of apparelling yourself seemingly.

The second article is of fit companions, and of going to church, and of choosing your place, of wise behaviour, of hearing mass and of making confession.

The third article is that you should love God and his Blessed Mother and serve them continually and set and keep yourself in their grace.

The fourth article is that you should dwell in continence and chastity, after the ensample of Susanna, of Lucrece, and others.

The fifth article is that you should love your husband (whether myself or another) after the ensample of Sarah, Rebecca and Rachel.

The sixth article is that you should be humble and obedient to him after the ensample of Griselda, of the woman who would not rescue her husband from drowning, and of the Mother of God who answered '*fiat*' etc., of Lucifer, of the *puys*,[3] of the bailly of Tournai, of the monks and the husbands, of Madame d'Andresel, of Chaumont and of the Roman woman.

The seventh that you be careful and heedful of his person.

The eighth that you be silent in hiding his secrets, after the ensample of Papirius, of the woman who laid eight eggs, of the Venetian woman, of the woman who returned from St James (of Compostella), and of the advocate.

The ninth and last article showeth that if your husband try to act foolishly or so acteth, you must wisely and humbly withdraw him therefrom, like unto Melibeus and Dame Jehanne la Quentine.[4]

THE SECOND SECTION

The second section is necessary to increase the profit of the household, gain friends and save one's possessions; to succour and aid oneself against the ill fortunes of age to come, and it contains six [*sic*] articles.

The first article is that you have care of your household, with diligence and perseverance and regard for work; take pains to find pleasure therein and I will do likewise on my part, and so shall we reach the castle whereof it is spoken.[5]

The second article is that at the least you take pleasure and have some little skill in the care and cultivation of a garden, grafting in due season and keeping roses in winter.

The third article is that you know how to choose varlets, door-keepers, handymen or other strong folk to perform the heavy work that from hour to hour must be done, and likewise labourers etc. And also tailors, shoemakers, bakers, pastry-makers, etc. And in particular how to set the household varlets and chambermaids to work, to sift and winnow grain, clean dresses, air and dry, and how to order your folk to take thought for the sheep and horses and to keep and amend wines.

The fourth article is that you, as sovereign mistress of your house, know how to order dinners, suppers, dishes and courses, and be wise in that which concerns the butcher and the poulterer, and have knowledge of spices.

The fifth article is that you know how to order, ordain, devise and have made all manner of pottages, civeys (p. 216)²¹, sauces and all other meats, and the same for sick folk.

THE THIRD SECTION

The third section tells of games and amusements that be pleasant enough to keep you in countenance and give you something to talk about in company, and contains three articles.

The first article is all concerned with amusing questions, which be shown forth and answered in strange fashion by the hazard of dice and by rooks and kings.

The second article is to know how to feed and fly the falcon.

The third article tells of certain other riddles concerning counting and numbering, which be subtle to find out and guess.⁶

First Section

The beginning and first article of the first section speaks of worship and of rising; by which rising you must understand the morning. And morning, according to the interpretation of the matter whereof we have to speak, is called matins. For as among us country folk we call it day from dawn to dusk, or from the rising to the setting sun, clerks in subtler wise say that this is but artificial day and that natural day, which is always twenty-four hours long, begins at midnight and ends the following midnight. I have said that morning is called matins, and this I have said because the matins ring at that hour to waken the monks to sing matins and praise to God, and not because I mean that you, dear sister, nor married women, should rise at this hour. But I intend by this to have said that at the hour when you hear the matins ring then you should pray and praise Our Lord with some intercession, prayer or orison before going to sleep again; and for this purpose you will find hereafter fit prayers and orisons. So for waking at this hour of matins or for rising at dawn I have here written two prayers to say to Our Lord and two others for Our Lady. And first there follows one for midnight, in which you thank Our Saviour for his mercy in bringing you to this hour. And you will say: *Gracias ago tibi, Domine*, etc. That is, in the French tongue: Dear Father God Almighty Three in One Who wert, art, and shall be blessed world without end, I thank Thee that Thou hast kept me from nightfall to the hour of morning, I pray Thee to grant in Thy holy pity that this day I fall into no sin, so that at eventide I may again give thanks, praise and blessing unto Thee, my Lord and Saviour.

Next follows the other prayer to Our Saviour, saying: *Domine sancte, Pater* etc. That is, in the French tongue: Dear Lord God Almighty and Father Everlasting Who hast safely brought me to the beginning of this day by Thy holy power, grant that this day I fall into no sin, neither run into any kind of danger, but that by Thy restraining care my thoughts be set to keep Thy holy laws and to do Thy holy will.

Then follow the two prayers to Our Lady, and first: *Sancta Maria*, *mater Domini*, etc. That is, in the French tongue: Mary, holy Mother of our Lord Jesus Christ, into thy hands and those of thy blessed Son now and forever I commit myself, body, soul and spirit. Lord, deliver me from all evil, from all sins and from all the temptations of the Devil and keep me in all perils. Sweet Lord Jesus defend me, giving my body strength and my soul health, enduing me with the will to do what is right, and to live justly in this world, and not to fail. Grant me remission of all my sins. Lord, save me waking, save me sleeping, that I may sleep in peace and awake in Thee in the glory of paradise.

Then follows the other prayer to Our Lady that is all in French: Most certain hope, O Lady the defence of all who seek thy aid. Glorious Virgin Mary, I pray thee now, that in the hour when my eyes shall be so heavy with the darkness of death that I cannot see the brightness of this world, nor move my tongue to pray or call to thee, when my frail heart that is so faint shall tremble from fear of the enemies of hell and shall be so stricken that all my limbs shall melt away in sweat from the pain of the agony of death, then, sweet and piteous Lady, deign to look upon me with compassion and aid me that I may see with thee the company of angels and the knighthood of paradise, and that the troublous and frighted enemies by thy help shall have no sight, presumption or suspicion of evil against me, nor any hope or power of banishing me from thy company. Instead, most gentle Lady, may it please thee to remember my prayer to thee now, to receive my soul in thy blessed faith, in thy keeping and defence, to present it to thy glorious Son to be apparelled in robes of glory and made one of the company of the blisful feast of the angels and of all the saints. O gate of paradise! O Lady of the patriarchs, of the prophets, apostles, martyrs, confessors, virgins, and of all the saints. O day star brighter than the sun and whiter than snow, I clasp my hands and lift up mine eyes and bend my knee before thee. O most gentle Lady, by thy joy when thy holy soul departed thy body unspotted and fearless, to be borne in the midst of angels and archangels, and was presented singing to thy glorious Son and was received there to dwell in eternal joy, I pray thee that thou wilt succour and prevent me in this dread hour. When death shall be so near, Lady, be to my soul comfort and refuge and defence, so that the cruel enemies of hell, so fearful to behold, may not confront me with the sins I have committed, but that these shall be pardoned at thy prayer and blotted out by thy blessed Son. And wilt thou, O sweetest Lady, present my soul to thy blessed Son, to attain by thy prayer the possession of eternal peace and joy that shall never fail. Amen.

These orisons may you say at matins, or at your awakening at morn, or at one and the other, whilst you rise and dress, and afterwards; they are good for all these occasions, and let it be with fasting and before all other tasks. And since I have said whilst dressing, I will here speak a little of dress. Wherefore, dear sister, know that if you would follow my advice, you will have great care and regard for what you and I are able and can afford to do, according to the estate of your kinsfolk and mine, with whom you will have to resort and repair daily. See that you be honestly clad, without new devices and too much frippery, or too little. And before you leave your chamber or house, see you first that the collar of your shift, and your *blanchet*, your robe or your surcoat,[1] straggle not forth one upon the other, as befalleth with certain drunken, foolish, or ignorant women, who have no regard for their honour, nor for the honesty of their estate or of their husbands, and go with roving eyes and head horribly reared up like unto a lion, their hair straying out of their wimples and the collars of their shifts and robes one upon the other, and walk mannishly and bear themselves uncouthly before folk without shame. And if one speaks to them about it, they excuse themselves on the ground of diligence and humility, saying that they be so diligent, hard working and human that they have no care of themselves; but they lie, for they have such great care of themselves that if they were in an honourable company, they would fain be in no wise less waited upon than the wise ladies, that be their equals in rank, nor have fewer salutations, bows, reverences and be less spoken to in public than the others, but rather more, and they are not worthy of it, since they know not how to maintain the honourable estate either of themselves alone, or even of their husbands and their lineage, on whom they bring shame. Beware then, fair sister, that your hair, your wimple, your kerchief and your hood and the rest of your attire be full neatly and simply ordered, so that none who see you can laugh nor mock at you, but you should be made an ensample of good and simple and decent array before all the others. And this must suffice you as to this first article.

THE SECOND ARTICLE

The second article saith that when you go to town or to church you should be suitably accompanied, according to your estate, and especially by worthy women, and flee suspicious company and never go near any suspected woman, or suffer one to be in your company. And as you go, bear your head straight, keep your eyelids lowered and still and look straight before you about four rods ahead and upon the ground, without looking nor turning your gaze upon any man or woman to right or to left, nor looking up, nor glancing from place to place, nor laughing, nor stopping to speak to anyone in the road.[2] And when you have come to church, choose a secret and solitary place before a fair altar or image, and there remain and stay without moving hither and thither, nor going to and fro, and hold your head upright and keep your lips ever moving saying orisons and prayers. Moreover keep your glance continually on your book or on the face of the image, without looking at man or woman, picture or else, and without hypocrisy or feint, keep your thoughts always on heaven and pray with your whole heart; and so doing go to mass each day and often to confession; and if you do this and fail not therein, honour will befall you and all good will come unto you. And what is said above should be sufficient for a beginning, for the good wise dames whom you frequent, and the good examples you take from their ways and teaching, the good wise honest old priests to whom you confess and the sound mother-wit God has given you will increase this and provide the rest of the second article.

THE THIRD ARTICLE

The third article says that you should love God and keep yourself in His grace. Wherefore I counsel you, that straightway, and putting aside all tasks, you give up eating and drinking even a little, at night or vespers, and that you take your mind from all earthly and worldly thoughts, and stay in a secret place, far from other folk; that you think of nothing but hearing mass at an early hour on the morrow, and after this of accounting to your confessor for your sins, in a good, thoughtful and modest confession. And as these two things, hearing mass and confession, are separate, we will speak first of mass and then of confession.

And as for mass, dear sister, you must learn that mass hath several dignities, in three estates or degrees, the which it is meet to describe and explain to you. And first, when the priest is robed and has said his *Confiteor* and is ready, he begins his mass: and this is called the *Introit* of the mass; it is the beginning or entry of the mass, at which point should every man and every woman restrain their thoughts and think of no worldly thing they may erewhile have seen or heard, for when men and women be at church to hear divine service, their hearts should not be at home or in their fields, nor in any other things of this world, and they should not think of temporal things, but of God, in purity, singleness and sincerity, and should pray devoutly to Him. After the Introit, sung or said, is said nine times *Kyrie eleison, Christe eleison*, to signify that there are nine hosts of angels called hierarchies, and of each host or hierarchy some come to the mass, not all the order, but of each order a few. Then should every man pray to these blessed angels to intercede with our Lord for him, saying: O ye blessed angels who descend from glory to our Lord to minister for Him and serve Him on earth, pray Him to pardon our transgressions and send us His grace.

After this is said *Gloria in excelsis Deo*; then should we praise our Saviour in these pleasant words: 'Most Gentle Lord, glory and honour be unto Thee, and unto Thee praise, and blessing, and prayer, etc., etc.' Then come the orisons to the saints and to Our Lady; we ought to beseech the most gentle Mother of God and the saints to pray for us, saying: 'Most glorious Mother of God who art a way between thy gentle Son and penitent sinners, pray to thy Child for us, and you, blessed saints, whom we commemorate, help us and pray with the Queen of the angels that God in His mercy shall pardon our sins and light our hearts with His Grace.' After this is said the Epistle, which is as if to remind us that a messenger is come bringing letters that report that the Saviour of the world is soon to come. After this is sung the Gradual or the Alleluia or Tract in Lent, and the Sequence is said: this shows that there are heralds who come before and declare that the Saviour is already on His way, and who sound their trumpets to gladden the hearts of those who wait and believe in the coming of the Lord and Saviour. After that is read the Gospel, which is the truest and nearest message: for here are the banners, the pennants and the standard to show beyond doubt that now the Lord is near, and now should everyone be silent and

stand upright, and set his heart to hear and mark what the Gospel
saith, for these are the very words that our Lord spake with His lips,
these are the words to teach us how to live, if we wish to be of the
family of the Lord. Therefore ought all men to observe and give ear
to the words of the Gospel, and be mindful of them. After this the
Offertory is made, when we ought to offer into the priest's hand
something to signify that we offer our hearts to God, saying: 'Holy
Trinity, receive my heart that I bring as an offering: enrich it with
thy grace.' And whilst saying this we should make our offering.
After this, when the priest is come again to the altar, he asks us to
pray for him; and we ought diligently to pray, for he enters into our
needs and makes orisons for us.

Then the priest says – *Per omnia saecula saeculorum*, and then
Sursum Corda. That is to say: 'Lift up your hearts to God'; and the
clerks and others reply: *Habemus ad Dominium*: 'We lift them up
unto the Lord'. Then ought we to prepare ourselves and look upon
the priest. After this are sung the praises of the angels, namely:
Sanctus, Sanctus, Sanctus. At which the angels come down and make
ready and surround and defend the table whither God will descend
and by His look alone feed His friends, and then we hope to see His
coming and we ought to prepare ourselves as loving subjects when
the King enters His city, and we ought lovingly and with great joy
of heart to look upon Him and receive Him, and looking upon Him
to be grateful for His coming and give praise and blessing, and in
our hearts and with a low voice beseech Him to grant us remission
and pardon for past errors. For He cometh on earth for three things:
the first is the forgiveness of our sins, if we are worthy, the second is
the gift of His grace, if we know how to ask it, and the third our
salvation from the path of hell.

After this is the *Paternoster* which teaches us to call Him Father
and to pray Him to forgive us our trespasses as we forgive them that
trespass against us, and to lead us not into temptation, but deliver
us from evil, Amen. Then is said thrice the *Agnus Dei*, praying God
to have mercy upon us and give us peace; which may be taken as
peace between body and soul, that the body may be obedient to the
soul, or peace between us and our enemies, in whatsoever sense it is
understood.

Next is sung the Post-communion and then ought we to beseech
our Lord not to withdraw from us, nor to leave us orphans and

fatherless. Afterwards are said the last orisons and then ought we to withdraw and commend ourselves to the blessed Virgin Mary and beseech her to pray her blessed Son to dwell with us. And when all is said and finished, and the priest has taken off his robes, then should we thank our God that He has given us sense and understanding to hear His blessed mass and to behold His blessed sacrament, so keeping us in remembrance of His blessed birth and of His blessed passion and resurrection, and we should pray Him that, continuing not to fail, He may grant us true and perfect absolution. And then dear sister, be all alone, with your eyes inclined to the ground and your heart to heaven, and think earnestly and sincerely with your whole heart of all your transgressions so that you may rid and deliver yourself of them at this hour. But to advise you henceforth how this should be done I will here treat of it a little according to my knowledge and belief.

Dear sister, believe me in this that whoever, man or woman, desires faithfully to confess his sins for the salvation of his soul, he must know that three things be necessary: to wit, contrition, confession and penance. And he or she must know that contrition demands sorrow of heart in deep agony and repentance and that it is meet for the sinner with a most humble and contrite heart to ask pardon and mercy and to beseech most earnestly Our Creator and Sovereign Lord for forgiveness in that wherein he has angered and distressed Him. The sinner must know that without contrition his prayer is unavailing, since he has his mind and heart elsewhere. And, dear sister, remember the ensample of the man to whom a horse had been promised if he said a *Paternoster* and kept his thoughts on that alone, but who whilst praying, wondered whether the giver of the horse would leave him the saddle also, and so wretchedly lost both. So it is with him who makes intercession with Our Lord without thinking of his prayer nor of Him to Whom it is made: who, if he has, by chance, committed some sin by which he merits hanging on the gallows of hell, yet sleeps in this sin, and heeds it not. Yet how would the same man, condemned in this mean world by a petty provost to be hanged on a gallows of wood or stone, or even less, to pay a great fine, if he thought he might escape by contrition, by weeping and imploring the provost or judge, how he would implore him with his whole being in sincerity and tearfulness, with groans and promises of penance, though now he cannot weep, nor earnestly

pray the great Lord his Sovereign and Maker, Who from the lofty
windows of His providence, where He reigns above, sees all the
passions of the sinner's heart. And the transgressor knows that his
Lord is so piteous and merciful that for the smallest prayer, if it
comes from a humble and contrite heart, He would have forgiven
all – even if the sentence against the sinner had already been pro-
nounced, or the sinner but lately condemned to death, yet can this
Lord recall and cancel everything, though there is neither provost,
nor judge, save Him alone, Who for the weeping or prayers that a
guilty prisoner may make can cancel the judgement He has given
against him. See then dear sister, what comparison this is! Yet there
is worse to come, for when a man is sentenced to death by the
Sovereign Judge, if He cancel not his doom, it meaneth that the
agony of death is eternal and everlasting, but when he is condemned
by a provost the punishment of death is but for a moment. So, fair
sister, there is no comparison of the power of the judges, nor of the
penalties they are able to inflict. Therefore is it wiser, fair sister, to
weep and be contrite and address our prayers to Him Who has
sovereign and absolute power, rather than to him who has no power,
save what is lent and conditional and may not be exceeded. For the
Sovereign Judge is He Who will finally examine and judge us.
Therefore, fair sister, what account shall we render to Him of the
riches of fortune and nature He has lent to us, that we have with
folly expended for our own use and pleasure, having made no gift of
alms to Him or to the wretched and patient sufferers, who for love's
sake and in His name have asked it of us? If He accuse us of robbing
Him, as in this theft, what shall we reply? Likewise touching our
soul, His daughter that He gave unto us clean and healthy, without
stain or blemish, which we have poisoned with the draughts of mortal
sin, if He accuse us of murder, saying that we have slain His daughter
that He gave into our keeping, what defence shall we have? Likewise
touching our heart, our body that is the castle which He gave us to
defend and we have delivered it unto His enemy, to wit the Devil of
hell, what excuse shall we have? Certes, fair sister, if the blessed
Virgin Mary His mother plead not for us as advocate, I can in no
wise see how we may escape being, by the good judgement of that
Sovereign Judge, punished and chained to the gibbet of hell forever
as thieves and murderers and traitors, unless the hot tears of our
heart's contrition drive the enemy from within us in this our life;

but that may be done even as easily as hot water driveth the dog out of the kitchen.

After contrition cometh confession, which has six conditions, or it is nothing worth. The first condition of confession is that the confession be wisely made; wisely to wit in two ways, that is to say that the sinner choose a wise and worthy confessor. And the sinner ought thus to mark how every sick creature desireth health, and to have and recover health, desireth rather to find the better than the worse physician. And ought the sinner also to mark how, since every creature must desire bodily health, which is a fleeting pleasure that time devours, by greater reason should he care for his noble soul, which it is ordained shall be visited either with eternal good or evil without end. And therefore ought he to choose a most skilful, wise and excellent physician, that he may soon regain the health of his sick and wounded soul, for if by chance he take for his physician one who knows not the remedy to his sickness, he will die. This you see for example when the blind lead the blind, for it is no marvel that they both fall into the ditch. Therefore should a sinner seek out a most wise and far-seeing counsellor, who shall be able to cure him of all his sins and advise him, who can discriminate one sin from another and so cure them; and the confessor should set his whole thought and mind to hear and receive what the sinner shall say unto him, and should have power to absolve him. And then ought the sinner to be aware of and have thought beforehand long and earnestly of all his sins, as I have said before, so that he may be able to tell of them and recount them in order and describe their circumstances to his confessor and counsellor, and should have sorrow in his heart that he has committed the sins, and great fear of the vengeance of Our Lord, great shame and great repentance for the sins, from hope and sure intent of amending his ways and of never falling back into his errors, but rather of hating them like poison, and of desiring gladly to receive and joyfully to perform, to the end that he may be cured and recover his health, whatsoever penance his confessor shall prescribe for him.

The second condition is that as soon as we are fallen into sin we ought with haste and speed to make confession. For thou knowest not when God will take from thee speech and health; therefore is it good to make frequent confession. Beggars prove it abundantly, who from day to day and hour to hour display their wounds to kind folk for alms; wounded men from day to day show their sores to the doctor to gain speedy and fresh healing; so ought the sinner immediately to reveal his sin to gain a new healing and a fuller mercy.

The third condition of confession is that we ought to confess everything and reveal everything at one and the same time, to display and open to the surgeon the whole wound. It is meet to tell everything in great humility and repentance and to forget naught, and leave naught unsaid, and however great the morsel be it must needs come forth from thy lips. And if the proud heart of the sinner cannot endure this, let him make the sign of the cross before his lips that the enemy who is stopping up the passage of his words shall depart from him; then should the sinner constrain himself to tell the heavy sin that is killing his soul, for if he delay longer, he will forget it in his delay, and so will never confess it, and will thus dwell in such peril that by reason of this sin wherein he has remained, that he has not remembered, there shall be no good deed of his that shall not be blotted out, save by the grace of God. Then what pardon shall he ever gain by fasting, or by alms, or by toil of pilgrimage that he undertakes, if he have not fully confessed? Behold him also who has not truly confessed, how shall he dare to receive his Creator? and if he receive Him not, how he deceives himself and in what peril he runs. Perchance he hides on this occasion his sin, thinking to confess it another and very near occasion, and remembering not that he is in God's power, Who may at will snatch from him his speech, or cause him suddenly to die at His desire. If this happen he will be damned for his omission, and on the Day of Judgement he will not know what to reply.

The fourth condition of confession is that we must make an orderly confession, and tell our sins in order and according to how theology places them, and they should be put one after another without interference or dissimulation, nor should the first be put last, nor anything diminished, and we should not excuse ourselves nor accuse others. The sinner must tell the circumstances of the sin: how he thought of it, the cause and motive of his thought; how he has since pursued and committed it, spoken thereof and caused it to be committed; he should tell the time, the place; why and how he performed it; if the sin is natural or against nature; if he did it wittingly or in ignorance, and he should tell everything concerning it, its circumstances and conditions, that may burden his soul.

The fifth condition is that we should confess all our sins at the same time, and to one confessor, and not to several confessors. We ought not to divide our sins into two parts and tell half to one confessor and half to another, for confession made in this vicious manner would be unavailing, and would make us even greater sinners inasmuch as we were attempting to deceive our confessor, who represents the person of Our Lord Jesus Christ.

The sixth condition is that we ought to confess devoutly and with great meekness, with our eyes turned earthward to signify our shame and abasement for our sin, and our thoughts and mind in heaven, for we ought to remember that we are speaking with God and should address our heart and words to Him, and pray Him for forgiveness and mercy. For He sees the whole depth of your heart's wile, another understands only that which he hears.

Now have you heard, dear sister, how we ought to confess; but know there are five things that prevent confession, namely: shame of confessing the sin, an evil fear of having great penance to do, hope of long life, and despair that we take so great delight in our sin that we cannot eschew it nor repent of it, and think therefore that confession would be worthless, since we should presently fall again — and for this there is death.

After confession comes penance. This must we do according to the decision and counsel of the wise confessor, and it is performed in three manners: to wit by fasting, by alms, or by prayer, according as you will hereinafter learn.

I have said earlier that for confession three things be necessary, to wit contrition, confession and penance, then I showed and taught you, as far as I could, the meaning of contrition, and then of confession, and how confession should be made, and I passed lightly over the five things that hinder it greatly, which you will please to mark and be mindful of, at fit time and place, and finally I showed you what penance is. Now will I show you how to know wherein you have erred; and we will take first the names and conditions of the seven deadly sins that be so evil that all sins derive from them, and they are named deadly by reason of the death that cometh to the soul when the adversary can command the heart to commit them. And also, to keep you henceforth from these sins, I will show and teach you the names and the power of the seven virtues that are contraries of the seven aforesaid sins, and are fit medicine and remedy against them when they are committed, and are so hostile to the sins that immediately the virtue is come the sin flies away.

And first follow the names of the failings you may confess when you have erred therein, and after them the virtues, in which henceforth you ought to continue.

Pride is the sin, the opposite virtue is Humility.
Envy is the sin, the opposite virtue is Loving Kindness.
Wrath is the sin, the opposite virtue is Gentleness.
Sloth is the sin, the opposite virtue is Diligence.
Avarice is the sin, the opposite virtue is Generosity.
Gluttony is the sin, the opposite virtue is Temperance.
Lechery is the sin, the opposite virtue is Chastity.

Now you have heard the names of the seven deadly sins, and also of the seven healing virtues, now shall you hear their conditions, first of the seven deadly sins, and afterwards shall you learn of the virtues which are contraries to them.

Pride is the root and beginning of all other sins. The sin of pride has five branches: to wit, disobedience, vainglory, hypocrisy, discord and aloofness. Disobedience is the first branch and through this a man loses God, forgets His commandments and in disobedience to Him does the will of the flesh and performs his heart's desire against God and against reason and all this cometh from pride.

The second branch of pride is vainglory, that is when a man exalts himself and is puffed up with pride either at the good or at the evil he has done, is doing, or shall do. But these two things, good and evil, come not from ourselves. For the good a creature does comes from God Who is good and from His mercy, and the evil comes from the evil state of the creature and from his evil nature, because he betrays himself to the power of his adversary, which is evil. And truly when a person does good, since it cometh from the wise providence of God Who is good, it is He Who should have the honour and glory, and the person doing good should have the profit; and for evil we ought to hate the enemy who entices and leads us thereto through pride.

The third branch springing from pride is hypocrisy, when a person pretends to be full of virtue within, and to do and say more good deeds and words than he does. And when he sees he is believed to be a good man, he is filled with great joy and vainglory. Vainglory is the Devil's coin with which he buys all the fair commodities in this world's market, and the commodities are the gifts of nature and of fortune and of mercy that God has given to man and woman. The gifts of nature come from the body, and are beauty, valour, fair speech, intelligence, understanding. The gifts of fortune are wealth, eminence, honour, prosperity; and the gifts of grace are virtue and good works. All these gifts will a proud man barter to the Devil for the false coin of vainglory. All these things are blasted by the tempest of vainglory. And you must know that in these gifts of grace, which are virtue and good works, as I have said, is man or woman tempted in three ways. The first, when a creature rejoices in the good deeds he performs; the second when he delights to be praised for his actions, and the third when he performs these good deeds to the end that he may receive praise and be esteemed righteous. And such hypocrites are like a foul and stinking dunghill covered with cloth of gold and silk, to have greater honour and glory. In like fashion these hypocrites cover themselves, who wear a fair garment without, with intent to acquiring friends and through them greater office than they hold, in spite of their unworthiness, and to gain the riches that other folk possess more worthily than they. Hence it often happens that they desire and seek the death of him who holds the office that they covet, and so become evil murderers. When it happens that they live long in this hope without success, and die with this wicked longing which burns them up, in this envious hope wherein they are all consumed, they fall straight into the pan where the Devil is frying over his hell-fire. And their good works are lost and affect them only as having been done with evil intent. Alas! false coin, whence all this loss of souls. And this third branch of hypocrisy springs from pride.

The fourth branch of pride is discord or strife, that is when a man will agree neither with the acts nor the words of other folk, and desires that his own words and deeds shall be esteemed strong and true, whether so or not, even though all others and wiser than he deem them of no account; and all this springs from pride.

The fifth branch of pride is aloofness, that is when a person does and says what no other could do, and would conquer and be aloof in word and in deed excellently in all things, wherefore he becomes hateful and for this it is said that there is no proud man who is not continually engaged in law suits, nor is there. And all these, namely, disobedience, vainglory, hypocrisy, strife and aloofness, spring from pride.

A sinful man or woman in confession should begin in this manner: Lord Who art vicar and viceroy of God, I make confession to God Almighty and to the blessed Virgin Mary and all the saints of paradise, and to you, dear Father, of all the sins I have in many ways committed. First of pride: I have been proud of and have vaunted of my beauty, my strength, my praise, my excellent apparel, the skill of my limbs, and have given matter and example of sin to many men and women who looked upon me with pride, and when I saw this I thought of the power my children should have in their day, and of my power, my wealth, my estate, my friends and my birth, and how none could compare with me in all these things I have spoken of, and through this sin of pride I fell into its many branches.

The first branch of pride is disobedience, and through such pride I have disobeyed God and have not rendered Him honour or reverence as to my Creator, Who made me and gave me the riches of nature, of grace and of fortune with which I have strayed, which I have abused and expended in evil uses, in worldly vanities and honours, and have not rendered Him thanks, nor for His sake given aught to the poor, but have held them in shame and despite, and since they appeared to me disfigured and foul, I would not suffer them to approach me, but turned from them so that I might not see them. I have not honoured and reverenced my friends who are of my flesh and blood, especially my father and mother and the ancestors from whom I am sprung, my natural brothers and sisters, my husband and other benefactors and lords, nor my other brothers and sisters, children of Adam and Eve, for I have esteemed none other but myself. And when folk wished to help me or correct the evil I had done I would not suffer it, but turned in anger and despite towards those who helped me, being worse towards them and more cruel than before, blaming them and speaking scandal of them in their absence; and I have often spoken evilly of them and this sprang from pride and its branch of disobedience.

Through vainglory, which is the second branch of pride, I have zealously listened to calumny of others, and have believed and willingly repeated it, or have added to it. And sometimes from vengeance or evil nature, I have said things touching others that I did not know. I puffed myself up and vaunted of the evil things I had done and said, and took great delight therein. And if anything was said of me touching understanding, or good repute, or beauty, in my presence and bearing, but not to me, I did not correct it and say it was not in me, but held my peace in agreement and was well pleased. I puffed myself up and had pride in the great expenditure I sometimes incurred, in my great extravagances and superfluities, as in giving abundant and excessive dishes, having great halls and fair chambers, gathering together great companies, presenting jewels to ladies and lords and their officers and retinue, in order to hear them praise me and say that I was noble and brave and generous; indeed of poor folk I cared very little. In truth, Lord, I have affirmed many things to be true of which I was not certain, doing this to please such folk as were present and about me, and speaking thereof; and all this I did through vainglory.

Through hypocrisy I pretended to be holy and took great pains to appear so and acquire such a reputation before men, nevertheless I kept not from sin, nor from great sin, when I saw that I might commit it privily and in secret, and truly I have done penance and given alms to the poor before men's eyes to the sole end that my name might be in their mouths with honour and praise and not for the grace of God. And oft have I shown myself outwardly to desire good that in my heart I desired not, and this I did that I might be glorified by men, even though I knew it to be against the will of my Creator. And at times I have offered to many folk to do things for them for which I had no desire or heart, moreover I thought much good of myself in which there was little truth, and if there was a little therein, I did not remember that the good came from God (as I said earlier) nor was I thankful to God for it; and all this I did from hypocrisy and great pride.

I have been obstinate in discord and strife, which is the fourth branch of pride. For if I began to uphold something or the deed of someone, to uphold his good or to overcome another, in upholding or confounding the which I set great store, I sometimes in abuse of another told lying tales and affirmed them to be true, that I might do the will and pleasure of certain people; and in despite I moved certain persons to wrath and anger and discord, whereof great evils came sometimes thereafter; and others I made to swear and perjure themselves and to lie, and by the discord I moved and the lying words that I said and affirmed were true and had them so sworn to and affirmed, I have full sore shocked and angered several persons by my ill behaviour. Once when I confessed I excused myself in my confession and set my excuse first, and afterwards coloured in favour of myself that which caused my sin, or I laid my fault upon another and said that hers was the fault whereof I was the rather guilty, and excused myself, saying: such an one made me do it, and I was not keeping watch, and thus spake I to excuse my sins, which seemed to me too heavy, and moreover I left out and was silent concerning great and horrible sins; and likewise concerning small and light ones, whereof I spoke, I spoke not of the circumstances belonging to those sins, as of the persons, time and place, etc. Long have I dwelt in my sin and by long dwelling have I fallen into other mortal sins. To one of my confessors [I told my least faults] and to another, who peradventure was more pleasing to me, I told the other and greater sins, with intent to be less severely corrected by him and to have a smaller penance, by reason of the familiarity between him and me. I desired vainglory, seeking for honours and to be like to the greatest in clothes and other things likewise, and took pride in being honoured by great persons, and to have their grace and to be saluted with great reverence, and to be honoured and admired for my beauty, my wealth, my nobility, my lineage, to be fairly adorned, to sing and dance full well and sweetly to laugh and play and talk. I desired and laboured to be the most honoured everywhere; I was ready to listen to divers instruments and melodies, to charms, to wagers and divers other games that be disreputable and disorderly and which were neither according to God nor to reason, for I laughed and bore myself right proudly and in great disport. I desired to have and use revenge and to have the punishment of those, concerning whom I did but think that they had wished or done me ill, and I was fain to have my desire accomplished fully and completely, albeit right or wrong, without sparing them nor having mercy upon them, and that, dear Father, I did in my pride, and I repent me of it; and I beg of you pardon and penance.

Afterwards followeth the sin of envy, which groweth out of pride. Envy hath five branches: to wit, hatred, malice, murmuring, detraction and being glad of another's ill and wrath at his good hap. Envy is born of the sin of pride, for when a person is proud, he is fain that none be like unto him and envieth another that is as high or higher in any thing, or in any possessions, graces or knowledge, or of more worth than he, and therefore he holdeth that other in great hatred and hateth him and seeketh ever by speech and blame to prevent the praise or good fortune of another; and this is the first branch of envy.

The second branch of envy is malice: to wit when a person repeats ill words concerning certain persons out of envy and beareth evil from one person to another by ill sayings, that detract from the good and increase the evil concerning another.

The third branch is murmuring: to wit when the heart murmurs, because a greater than he commandeth him, or because all is not done and said unto him as to the others, and he dares not speak thereof.

The fourth branch of envy is detraction: to wit when a person saith ill, and speaketh behind the back, and saith that which he knows and that which he knows not of someone, and contriveth and thinketh how he can say somewhat that may harm or wound him of whom he speaks, and when he heareth ill spoken of that person, he helpeth with all his might to increase and exalt it, and speaketh of it full weightily when he has the chance, for that he knows that he can in no wise harm him more and knows that he cannot restore his good name that he taketh from him, and so is he slain.

The fifth branch is to rejoice over another's ill or hindrance, and to labour to destroy his good when it cometh to him, and to be sad and mournful over that good. And for all these things thou shouldst say in thy confession: Sire, in all these things that I have before named, I have sinned full sore; for in my heart I have thought it and of my wicked will I have done it and by my false mouth I have said it and sown it wheresoever I could, and if I have spoken well concerning him or another, I have done it faintly and as a feint and nathless I was mocking; and in treuthe concerning those whose honour and good I ought to have kept and could have had I willed, I have turned it to ill; and when I saw that ill was being spoken, I betook myself and went there and consented to ill speech with all the power of my heart and mouth and body. And all, dear father, have I done out of envy, and I repent thereof, and I seek pardon of you.

After envy comes the sin of wrath, which groweth from envy. The sin of wrath has five branches: to wit, hatred, contention, presumption, indignation and swearing. Hatred is when a person cannot bring another into subjection, or cannot command or subject another as he is fain to do, and is fain to have the lordship and domination over that other, then is he sorrowful and wrathful and his heart swelleth within him; that is the first branch of wrath.

The second branch of wrath is when the heart swelleth and maketh a person to do and say ill in speech, and when he speaks in foul and disorderly wise in wrath against another.

The third branch of wrath is when out of speech come mêlées and battles and dissentions, and then the person should bethink him whether any upon his side or the other were wounded in substance or in limb by reason of his words; for then would that person be the cause of all the ill that had befallen.

The fourth branch of wrath is when in thy wrath thou hast offended God by swearing.

The fifth branch of wrath is when by thy wrath thou hast moved and caused others to be moved to anger, and concerning this you should confess in these words: Sire, I have taken the name of God in vain in my wrath and I have spoken foully of God and of the blessed Virgin Mary, His sweet Mother and of all the saints of paradise; I have been roused against others and in my wrath have refused speech with them; I have angered my lord father and my lady mother by my wrath and I have spoken despitefully to them and in wrath I have looked evilly upon them and desired the end of their days; I have spoken right despitefully to the poor and called them caitiffs in my wrath. Sire, I have by my wrath moved many to swear foully and by right foul oaths; my servants and many others have I moved to anger and I have moved them to do ill. And I have full oft time thought how I might revenge me upon those that I hated and gladly did I do them ill, if I could, when my heart was turned against them. Much and for long have I dwelt in hatred, whereof I repent, wherefore dear father, I require of you pardon and penance.

After this comes the sin of sloth, which is the fourth of the mortal sins, from which is born and groweth idleness, which is a foul blame and a foul stain on one that would fain be good. For it is said in the Gospel that on the Day of Judgement every idle person shall have to account for the time that he hath lost by his idleness. Now it will be a marvel if the idle have any defence, when they be charged before God. In another part of the Gospel it is said that an idle body is the mortal enemy of the soul and my lord Saint Jerome saith thus: be thou ever doing something lest the enemy find thee in idleness, for he is wont to find his own work and employment for those that be idle. And my lord Saint Augustine says in the book of the labour of the monks,[3] that no man that is able to labour ought to be idle. Too long would it take to recite the sayings of all the wise men who blame idleness.

The sin of sloth has six branches. The first branch is negligence, the second grudging, the third carnality, the fourth vanity of heart, the fifth branch despair, the sixth presumption.

Negligence is when a man loves and fears and remembers God so little and holds Him in so small account, that he does no good deed for Him or for love of Him, and so to act is slothful and negligent, for one is not slothful and negligent in seeking pleasure and ease. Certes, it is a great sin to be slothful in well doing. For it is written in the Scriptures that if a man had never once sinned and yet had never done any good and so let the time pass by, he might go to hell; and this first branch of negligence is bred of sloth.

The second branch is when a person grudgeth in his heart against another, and for the ill will that he has against him, setteth himself to seek vengeance, and noddeth and sleepeth therein and leaveth to do his penances, and alms and other good deeds. For ever doth this grudging person think how he may harm whom he hateth, and day and night setteth all his thought thereto; thus ceases he to do the good which he ought to do; and that is the second branch of sloth.

The third branch of sloth is carnality. Carnality is when one seeks the desire of the flesh, as to sleep in good beds and to rest long, and to lie late abed, and in the morn when one is in great ease in one's bed and hears the bell ringing for mass, one pays no attention and turns over upon the other side to sleep again, and such vain and craven folk had rather lose four masses than warmth and a nap; and that is the third branch of sloth.

The fourth branch of sloth is vanity: to wit when a person knows well that he is in sin and is so vain of heart that he cannot, or will not, or deigns not to return to God by confession and devotion, thus ever thinks he and promises himself to mend his life from one day to the next, and doth not correct himself and so is slothful and negligent in recovering himself and cares not to do any good and to follow God's commandments, as a good person ought to do, and keep them; and that is the fourth branch of sloth.

The fifth branch is despair; it is a manner of sin that God hateth full sore, and he that is taken in this sin is damned like unto Judas, that hanged himself in despair, for he thought that he had so sinned before God that never could he ask for mercy, and whosoever dieth in this sin and hath no hope in the mercy of God he sinneth against the Holy Ghost and against God's goodness; wherefore ought one in no wise to fall into this sin of despair nor linger therein. For if thou fall and do a full great sin, as to burn the houses and goods of Holy Church by force, the which is sacrilege, thou dost worse than all the seven deadly sins, yet again say I that the mercy of God is the greater to pardon. Nathless if thou wouldst confess and return to God, in troth if thou hadst done more evil than tongue might tell or believe, or heart conceive, yet shouldst thou find mercy in Him; and that is the fifth branch of sloth.

The sixth branch is presumption: that is when a person is so overweening and proud that he thinks that he cannot be damned for any sin that he doth or may do; and such folk be of such mind that they say God hath not made them for damnation. And they ought to know that God would not be just if He gave paradise as well to those that have not deserved it as to those that have. It would not be a just judgement if each took away as much as the other, for if it were thus, no one would ever do good, since he that served not Our Lord should have as fair a reward as he that served Him. Certes, they that think thus sin against the good justice of God and against His loving kindness and gentleness. For though He be merciful, as I have said before, yet is He a just Judge, and every man is made to serve Him and do His will, and thus may one have and deserve the Kingdom of Heaven, and not otherwise, for he that is negligent and slothful to do His service, sinneth. Wherefore, thou that art slothful shouldst confess the branches of sloth, saying thus: Sire, I have also sinned in all the branches of sloth; by my negligence I have been slow in God's service, slothful and negligent in the faith, and I have taken great care and thought for the ease of my vile body, and I have not remembered the words of the Scriptures, nor followed after them, by reason of my sloth. Again have I not given thanks to God, as I should, for the spiritual and temporal blessings that He has given and sent me, and furthermore I have not served God as I ought, according to the blessings and virtues that He has given me. I have neither said nor done those good things which I might have said or done, and I have been slow and slothful in the service of Our Lord, and done and busied myself in the service of worldly things, and also I have better served myself and mine own flesh and have set more store thereby, than in the service of my sweet Creator. I have long been full idle, whence many evils and ill thoughts and meditations be come to me.

Then shouldst thou say in confession that when mass was being sung or some other time, or when thou wast in devotion or saying thine hours, thou wast in vain meditation and evil and unprofitable thoughts, and harmful to thy salvation. Wherefore behoves thee to say thus: Sire, when I perceived these things, I returned not to God, nor made my peace with Him as I should. And furthermore, sire, when God's service was being said and done, I chattered and spake idle words such as were unseemly to be said in church. Sire, I slept in church while others were praying God. Sire, once I did not confess when my conscience smote me and so made my ill doing worse, and even when there was place and time fitting, turned I not myself thereto, but I said in my heart through my sloth, 'thou canst well do it another time, or another week, or another day,' and by such delays and negligences I forgot many of my sins; afterwards by negligence and sloth did I forget to do my penances enjoined upon me. I set not a good example to my people. For by my full unseemly talk, the which they noted because I was their lord, I set them in the way of sin. Sire, when I heard my folk swearing foully, I neither reproved nor corrected them, but I heard them and let it pass by reason of my sloth. Then, sire, when I came to confess I did not bethink me beforehand concerning my sins that I must tell, nor ever thought I thereof; thus when I came forth from confession, I found myself more full of sin and of greater sin than before, and I was not diligent to return to my confessor, and so the time passed; and all this did I from sloth, wherein I have dwelt and kept myself and whereof I repent; wherefore, dear father, I seek pardon and penance from you.

After the sin of sloth cometh avarice. Avarice is straitly to restrain oneself and niggardly to spend, in an excessive will and desire to acquire this world's goods, whether rightly or wrongly, caring not how, and nathless reason telleth a man whether he doth ill or well. Certes full many scholars be avaricious, that be executors of wills and enrich themselves and keep back the possessions of the dead, who showed such love to them at their end that they chose them above all others to have care of their salvation; and after their death these executors devour their flesh like unto tyrants and grow fat upon their blood and substance; these be the scholars of avarice. Likewise there be wicked lords that by great fines seize the substance of their poor subjects; innkeepers and merchants that sell things for more than their just price and have false weights and measures; false lawyers, that by litigation and trickery steal their possessions from poor folk and persecute them in the courts of great lords so sore and so long that they have their desire of them, whatsoe'er it be. Avarice, as I said, is born of sloth; when a person is slothful and negligent to do or perform what is necessary to sustain his body and profitable to him, and by such sloth is careless and fails to gain a livelihood, then to restore his fortune there cometh to him the desire for rapine and the will to take what is another's, unjustly and without reason. If thou art rich and powerful and hast enough and to spare, and fearest lest thy possessions should fail thee and so givest not when need and occasion is to the poor, and returnest not that which thou hast ill gotten of another, be it by borrowing or otherwise, thou dost sin in avarice.

Avarice has seven branches: the first is theft, the second rapine, the third fraud, the fourth deceit, the fifth usury, the sixth gambling and the seventh simony.

Theft is when a person unjustly and by night takes a thing without the knowledge and against the will of him to whom it belongs; and that is the first branch of avarice.

The second branch of avarice is rapine, that is when a person seizes a thing from another and, when he has it, will not render it or send it to him to whom it rightfully belongs, but by avarice keeps and conceals it because it pleases him, and if peradventure he hears it asked for, he will not tell of it, but conceals and hides it so that none can find it.

The third branch of avarice is fraud, that is when a person, by deception, by trickery or by fraudulent purchase or sale telleth lies unto him, from whom he would fain purchase a thing or to whom he would sell it, causing him falsely to think that the thing is worth more than it is.

The fourth branch of avarice is deceit: to wit when a person shows the outside of a thing that seems good, and the fault does not show, and he leaves it and says nought concerning it and swears that the thing is good and true, and well he knows that it is not so. And thus do false merchants, who set the fairest and best on the top and the worst underneath and swear that all is good and true and this is deceit, because they deceive folk and swear false oaths.

The fifth branch of avarice is usury: to wit when a person lends his money to have a larger sum for a long term, or sells his corn and wine dearer because he gives long credit, and so with all other merchandise, which I pass over for the present, for usury is a full long thing to tell and full wicked.

The sixth branch of avarice is gambling, that is when one plays at dice to win another's money and therein is much trickery, covetousness, avarice and deceit, as in false counting and lending money for gain, as to lend twelve pence for thirteen; and in such games many and evil oaths be spoken, as swearing by God and Our Lady and all the saints of paradise and much evil is said and done; wherefore one should beware thereof.

The seventh branch of avarice is simony: to wit when the sacraments of holy church be bought or sold or the prebends of churches; and such sins come of clerks and monks, and they come likewise when tithes be ill paid and penances ill performed and the commandments of holy church ill kept, and alms ill distributed.

The Devil giveth six commandments to the avaricious man: the first, that he take good care of his own; the second, that he lend not without gain and do no good before his death; the third, that he eat all alone and do no courtesy nor almsgiving; the fourth that he restrain his household from eating and drinking; the fifth that he give away neither crumb nor remnant; the sixth that he seek diligently to pile up for his heirs.

All these things wherein thy conscience accuses thee and all concerning the sin of avarice wherein thou feelest thyself guilty, thou shouldst confess one after another, in the above order, and at the end thou shouldst say: Sire, dear father, I repent full sorely of all the sins that I have sinned through avarice and have told you, and I require of you pardon and penance.

After the sin of avarice comes the sin of gluttony, which is divided into two parts: the first is when one takes too abundantly of meat and the second is ribald and wanton speech. The sin of too much eating and drinking pleaseth the Devil. It is written in the Gospels that God gave the Devil power to enter into the belly of the swine, by reason of their gluttony, and the Devil entered into them and drove them into the sea and they were drowned; even so enters he into the body of gluttons, who lead a dishonest life, and pushes them into the sea of hell. God commands fasting, and the woman that is a glutton saith, 'I will eat.' God commands us to go to church and rise early and the glutton saith, 'I must sleep. I was drunk yesterday. The church is not a hare, it will very well wait for me.' When she has with some difficulty risen, know you what be her hours? Her matins are: 'Ha! what shall we drink? Is there nought left over from last night?' Then says she her lauds, thus: 'Ha! we drank good wine yestreen.' Afterwards she says her orisons, thus: 'My head aches; I shall not be at ease until I have had a drink.' Certes, such gluttony putteth a woman to shame, for from it she becomes a ribald, and a wanton and a thief. The tavern is the Devil's church, where his disciples go to serve him and where he doth his miracles; for when people go there, they go upright and well spoken, wise and sensible and well advised, and when they return they cannot hold themselves upright, nor speak; they are all fools and madmen and they return swearing, beating and giving the lie to each other.

The other part of the sin of the mouth is foolish speaking in many ways, idle words, boasting, flattering, swearing, gossiping, grumbling, rebelling and blaming. There is no word so small that thou hast spoken that thou shalt not account for before God. Alas! how much sayest thou in the morning which thou hast forgotten at midday. Idle babblers be like unto the clappers of the mill that cannot be still; boasters and pestles speak only of themselves.

This sin of gluttony, which, as I have said, is divided into two parts, has five branches. The first branch is when a person eateth before he ought: to wit too early in the morning, or before saying hours and going to church and hearing the word of God and His commandments; for every creature ought to have the good sense and discretion not to eat before the hour of tierce, save by reason of illness, or weakness or some necessity constraining thereto.

The second branch of gluttony is when a person eats more often than behoveth and without need. For, as the Scripture saith: once upon the day to eat and drink it is angelic, and to eat twice a day is human, and thrice or four times or more often is the life of a beast and not of a human being.

The third branch of gluttony is when a person eats and drinks so much in a day that ill befalls him, and he is drunk and sick and must take to his bed, and is sore burdened thereby.

The fourth branch of gluttony is when a person eats so greedily of a dish that he doth not chew it and swallows it whole and before he ought, as the Scripture telleth of Esau, that was the first-born of all his brothers, and made such haste to eat that he was nigh choked.

The fifth branch of gluttony is when a person seeks out delicious viands, howsoever costly they be, and can do good to fewer others and cannot withhold himself so that he may help a poor man, or two, or more. And it is this sin concerning which we read in the Gospels of the wicked rich man, that was clad in purple, and each day ate so plenteously of meat and would do no kindness to the poor lazar, and concerning him, we read that he was damned, for that he lived too delicately and gave not for God's sake as behoved him. And these things aforesaid you should confess . . .

Afterwards cometh the sin of lechery, which is born of gluttony, for when the wicked man has well drunken and eaten more than he ought, then is he moved and warmed to this sin and then come dis-ordered thoughts and evil meditations and from the thought he goeth to the deed. And this sin of lechery hath six branches . . . Wherefore all these things the sinner ought humbly to tell to his confessor and ask pardon saying: I have sinned these sins and on great feast days and vigils and perchance on the vigils of Our Lady, on feasts or in Lent, or in a holy place, as in church. And he should say whether it be once, or twice, or several times, and with whom he sinneth more than with others. And at the end he should say: Dear father, I have erred and sinned as I have said with the sin of lechery, and I repent me truly thereof, so I beg of you pardon and penance.

Hereafter follow the names and conditions of the seven virtues, whereby one may keep oneself from deadly sin, and first:

Humility is against pride; for even as pride cometh of a wicked and proud and despiteful heart, and causeth body and soul to be condemned and lost and done to death, so humility is born of a piti-ful heart and causeth the body to be honoured in this world and the soul to be set in everlasting bliss, wherefore is humility compared to the Virgin Mary . . .

Loving kindness is against the sin of envy; for even as that sin poisons and burns the heart of the envious man, as thou hast heard, so doth the holy virtue of loving kindness, which is the gift of the

Holy Ghost, make the heart humble and mistrustful of itself; and therefore it is called *the gift of fear*. The virtue of loving kindness is a sweetness, a dew, a medicine against envy; for even as the envious man is ever sad and wrath because of the possessions of others, so a good heart full of loving kindness is ever glad of the good of his neighbour and is sorrowful and hath compassion over his enemies. The virtue of loving kindness casteth envy altogether out of the heart and maketh a man content with that which he hath. Never shalt thou envy the possessions of thy good friend that thou lovest well . . . God and the Gospel giveth heaven to the poor and maketh the loving and debonnair to inherit the earth; look thou then, where shall the envious and unkind be save in the torment of hell?

Gentleness is against wrath. The holy virtue of gentleness and temperance seeketh ever peace, equity and justice, without harming, or angering, or hating anyone and hateth and despiseth none. Even as wrath is the fire that spoileth all the goods that be in the house of the felon heart, so gentleness is the precious medicine that spreadeth peace everywhere and seeketh equity and justice. Equity has eight steps that be full good to note, whereby the peaceable and worthy man marketh the snares and gins of the Devil, who sees us when we see him not and proves us sorely and in more than a thousand ways. The Devil is a philosopher, he knows the state and habits of man and his complexion and what vice he most inclineth to by nature or custom, and assails him most strongly upon that side; the choleric with wrath and discord, the sanguine with jollity and lechery, the phlegmatic with gluttony and sloth, the melancholy with envy and sorrow. Wherefore everyone should defend himself upon that side where he knoweth that his castle is weakest, and fight against that vice wherewith he findeth himself most sorely assailed. The gentle man spreadeth peace everywhere. Peace vanquishes all malice and wrath and without peace none may have the victory . . .

Prowess, that is the same as diligence, is a holy virtue against the sin of accidie[4] and sloth; for even as the citizen seeks to win wealth for himself and his children, so the knight and the noble seek to win prize and praise in the world, and each man according to his estate in this world seeks to win worldly things. Alas! how few there be that labour to win spiritual possessions! Good men and not vainglorious, that be weary of the world and seek to come before God, are wise to despise the world for the dangers and difficulties wherewith it is full; it is a forest full of lions, a mountain full of serpents and bears, a battle full of treacherous enemies, a shadowy valley full of tears, and nought is there stable therein; there is no peace of heart or of conscience for him that would trust in the world and love it. The good folk that be weary of the world turn their hearts towards God, whither they hope to come, and misprize all worldly possessions; but it is a thing so great that few who undertake it persevere therein. By this virtue, saith Jesus Christ, all the other virtues fight and this gaineth the victory; all labour but this beareth away the wage at eventide.

Mercy or charity is against avarice, for mercy is, as it were, to have sorrow and compassion over the ill fortune, or necessity, or poverty of another and to aid, counsel and comfort him with all one's might. Thus, even as the Devil giveth his commandments to the miser, as thou hast heard, so the Holy Ghost giveth His commandments to him that is merciful and charitable, bidding him to despise worldly goods, to give alms, to clothe the naked, to give drink to the thirsty, to feed the hungry and to visit the sick. Even as the miser is son to the Devil and like unto him, so the charitable is like unto God his father. Even as avarice taketh thought both night and day to gain and to heap up, whether by fair means or foul, so charity and mercy take thought to accomplish the seven works of mercy . . .

Mercy hath seven branches: the first is to give food and drink to the poor; the second is to clothe the hungry; the third is to lend to the poor and needy and forgive them the debt; the fourth is to visit the sick; the fifth, to house the poor; the sixth, to visit those that be in prison; and the seventh, to bury the dead. And all these things it behoveth you to do in charity and compassion, for the love of God only and without vainglory. You ought to give alms out of your own true possessions, buxomly, speedily, secretly, devoutly and humbly, without despising the poor in thought or deed. He does well who gives to them at once when they ask him, but he does better still who gives without being asked.

Temperance is against gluttony; for even as the holy virtue of temperance is right measure against the mortal sin of gluttony, so is it the virtue which the gift of wisdom giveth and planteth in the glutton's heart against excess. Temperance is a tree full precious, for it guardeth the life of body and soul; for from too much drinking and eating cometh death and from too ill speech the head hath sorrow and the body and soul be slain. By temperance the body lives long and in peace in this world and the soul has life everlasting. This virtue ought to be kept above all the others by reason of the great good that it doth. First, temperance is the guard of reason, understanding and sense and the man without sense is a beast. He that is drunken is so full of wine that he loses reason and understanding and so he thinks that he is drinking the wine, but the wine is drinking him. The second is that temperance delivers the glutton from the servitude of the belly, to which he is serf. Saint Paul saith that a man lowereth himself much that loseth his freedom to be serf to a lord, but he lowereth himself more that maketh himself serf to his belly, from which nought but filth cometh forth. Temperance keeps a man in his own lordship, for spirit and sense ought to be lords over the body and the body ought to serve the spirit. The glutton by his drunkenness and gluttony loses sense and spirit and knows not how to govern his body. The third is that it keeps well the gate of the castle that the Devil may not enter man's body by deadly sin; the mouth is the gate whereby the Devil enters into the castle to fight with the good virtues and he enters therein by reason of the false traitors, lords Glutton and Evil-Speech, who leave the gate of the mouth open to the Devil. This virtue hath lordship over the body, for by temperance is the body mastered, even as a horse by the bridle. Temperance fighteth the first battle of the host and guardeth the other virtues. The Devil tempts man through the mouth, even as he did Our Lord, when he bade Him to turn a stone into bread, and Adam, when he made him to eat the fruit. Among the other creatures, man's mouth is smallest in proportion to his body; man has the other members double: two ears, and two nostrils and two eyes, but he hath but one mouth, and this shows us that he ought to eat and drink and speak temperately. Temperance is none other than right measure, which is midway between too much and too little; man ought to have measure in all things in his heart, and in his sense, for he is even as a bird that guideth itself by the eye of temperance, and oftentimes flieth away and falleth into the net of the fowler, to wit of the Devil, who often hunteth to take that bird.

Chastity is against lechery and the holy virtue of chastity is to have a conscience pure from all evil thoughts and the members pure from touch . . . It behoveth the chaste, as thou hast heard, to have a clean conscience; to have a clean conscience three things be neces-

sary: the first is willingly to hear God spoken of; the second is well
and often to confess to Him; the third is to hold in remembrance the
passion of Jesus Christ and to remember why He died and that thou
shalt die and shalt not escape death; and that is the first degree of
chastity. The second degree of chastity is to beware of evil words,
for evil communications corrupt good manners. The third degree is
well to keep the five bodily senses: the eyes from foolishly looking,
the ears from foolishly hearing, the nostrils from too much smelling
and delighting in sweet odours, the hands from foolishly touching,
the feet from going into evil places; these be the five doors and the
five windows through which the Devil cometh to steal chastity from
the castle of the soul and of the caitiff body. The fourth degree is to
fast and ever to remember that death may suddenly seize thee and
bear thee away, if thou be not ware. The fifth degree is to shun evil
company, as did Joseph, who fled from the lady that would have
tempted him to sin. The sixth degree is to be busy with good works;
for when the Devil findeth a person idle, fain is he to occupy him
about his own business. The seventh degree is to pray; and for
prayer there be three things needful: to wit, true faith, the hope of
having that for which one asks and a devout heart, without wander-
ing thoughts. Prayer without devotion is a messenger without letters.
In prayer God looketh for a humble and devout heart and taketh no
heed of outward show nor of an ostentatious bearing, like to that of
those bold and foolish women, who go their ways in ribald wise,
with their necks stretched forth like unto a stag in flight, looking
this way and that like unto a runaway horse.

And this, dear sister, will suffice you concerning this matter. For
the mother wit that God has given you and your good will to be
devout and virtuous towards God and the Church, and the preach-
ings and sermon you shall hear in our parish and elsewhere, together
with the Bible, the *Golden Legend*,[5] the Apocalypse, the *Life of the
Fathers*,[6] and divers other good books in French which I have and
whereof you are mistress and free to take them at your pleasure,
these will teach you all the rest at God's good pleasure, and may He
guide you and incline your heart towards these things.

THE FOURTH ARTICLE

The fourth article of the first section saith that you must keep your-self in continence and live chastely.

I am sure that so you do, and I doubt not concerning it, but because I know that after you and me this book will fall into the hands of our children or other our friends, I readily set down all that I know, and I say that you ought also to lesson your friends and especially your daughters, and tell them, fair sister, that in sooth all good is departed from maid or woman who faileth in virginity, continence and chastity; not riches, nor beauty, nor good sense, nor high lineage, nor any other merit can ever wipe out the ill fame of the opposite vice, above all if in a woman it be but once committed, in sooth if it be but suspected, wherefore many wise women have kept themselves not only from the deed but from the suspicion thereof, in purpose to win the name of virginity; concerning the which name the holy writings of my lord Saint Augustine and my lord Saint Gregory and many others say and bear witness that all worthy women who have been, are and shall be, of whatsoever estate they be or have been, may be named and called virgins. And my lord Saint Paul confirmeth it in the eleventh chapter of the second epistle that he made unto the Corinthians, where he said thus: *Despondienim vos*, etc. I would have you know, saith he, that a woman who is wedded unto a man and liveth chastely without thought of another man, she may be called a virgin and presented unto Our Lord Jesus Christ. Concerning every good and worthy woman Jesus Christ in the thirteenth chapter of the Gospel of Saint Matthew speaketh thus in a parable: *Simile est regnum coelorum thesauro abscondito in agro*, etc. The Kingdom of Heaven, he saith, is like unto a treasure hid in a field, the which when a man digging therein hath found, he hideth and goeth and selleth all that he hath and buyeth that field. In the same chapter Our Lord saith this parable: The Kingdom of Heaven is like unto a merchant man, seeking goodly pearls, who, when he had found one pearl of great price, went and sold all that he had and bought it. By the treasure found in a field and by the precious stone we may understand every good and worthy woman; for in whatsoever estate she be, maid, wife, or widow, she may be compared unto the treasure and the precious stone; for she is so good, so pure, so stainless that she is pleasing unto God Who loveth her as a holy virgin, whatsoever be her estate, maid, wife or widow. And certes, a man in whatsoever estate he be, noble or not, can have no better treasure than a worthy and wise woman. And that may he know well and have proof who will study the acts and good bearing and good deeds of the glorious ladies that were in the time of the old law, as Sarah, Rebecca, Leah and Rachel; who were wives to the holy patriarchs Abraham, Isaac and Jacob who is called Israel, and who were all chaste and lived chastely and as virgins.

Item, upon this matter we find written in the thirteenth chapter of the book of Daniel, how that after the Babylonish migration, to wit after that Jechonias King of Jerusalem and the people of Israel were led into prison and captivity in Babylon and the city of Jerusalem was destroyed by King Nebuchadnezzar, there was in Jerusalem a rich and worthy Jew hight Joachim, and Joachim took to wife the daughter of another Jew that was called Belchias; and the maid was called Susanna, and she was very fair and feared God, for her father and mother that were just and good people had right well taught and lessoned her in chastity according to the law of Moses. This Joachim, husband of Susanna, was rich and had a right fair garden full of fruit trees. There the Jews were wont to come to take their pleasure, for the place was more seemly than all others, and Susanna herself went often to take her ease in this garden. Now it befel that two old priests of this same law were set up by the people to be their judges for a year, the which judges saw that Susanna was very fair and were taken and inflamed with fleshly love. So they took counsel together and sought how they might deceive her, and they were of accord that they would spy upon her in the aforesaid garden and speak to her if they found her alone.

One day it befel that after the midday hour they were musing in a corner of the garden, and Susanna came to the garden to bathe herself, as their law ordained, and with her brought two of her maidens, whom she sent back to her house, that they might bring oil and ointments to anoint her. And when the two elders saw her alone, they ran to her and said: 'Suffer peacefully that which we would do with thee, and if thou dost not so, we will bear witness against thee and will say that we found thee in adultery.' And when Susanna beheld and knew the wickedness of the judges, she avised her in her heart and said thus: '*Angustie michi sunt undique*, etc. God! Pitfalls lie all about me, for if I do this thing I am dead before God and if I do it not, I may not escape from their hands save I be tormented and stoned; but better behoveth me to fall into their power without sinning than to sin before God.' Then she cried out in a loud voice and the two elders cried out likewise, until the servants of the house ran to them, and the judges said that they had found her in sin with a young man that was strong and lusty, and escaped them, so that they knew not who he might be. Then were the servants marvellously abashed and astonied, for never before had they heard tell such a thing of their lady nor seen any evil in her; nathless she was cast into prison.

And the next day the judges were seated in judgment and all the people assembled before them to see the marvel, and Susanna was brought to judgment; her parents and friends looked upon her, weeping right tenderly. Susanna had her head covered, for the shame and abashment that she had, but the judges caused her visage to be uncovered for great disgrace and despite. Then weeping, she lifted her eyes to heaven, for she trusted in Our Lord and in her innocence. Then the two priests told before the people how that they were walking and taking their ease in the garden and saw Susanna come therein and with her two of her maidens, the which she sent away and barred the door behind them; and they said that then came there a young man, the which they saw lie with her, wherefore they ran thither and the young man fled away through the door, and they could not stop him nor take him, but only the aforesaid Susanna, who would not name his name; 'and of this crime we two be witness, and for this crime we do condemn her to death'. Then Susanna cried aloud and spake thus: 'O Everlasting God, thou knowest all hidden things and all things that be done and thou knowest well that they bear false witness against me; remember and have mercy upon me!'

After this they led her to her torment, and as they passed along a road, Our Lord moved the spirit of a young and little child hight Daniel, the which began to cry with a loud voice: 'O people of Israel, this woman is falsely judged, return to judgment, return, for the judgments are false!' Then the people cried out and brought Susanna back to the place where she had been judged, and led there the judges and the child Daniel, who spake these words: 'Separate these judges and lead one here and the other there.' When this was done he came to the one and asked him under what tree he had seen the man and Susanna doing their sin, and that judge answered that

it was beneath an oak. Afterwards the aforesaid Daniel went to the
other judge and asked beneath which tree he had seen Susanna with
the young man, and he answered, 'Beneath a tree called *Lentsicus.*'
Lentsicus is a tree that giveth forth oil and the root thereof is a spice
called mace. Thus was their lie discovered and Susanna set free and
proved pure and clean, without stain of evil embraces. And it is well
proven that she was full of the virtue of chastity when she spake
these words to the false judges: 'Rather would I fall into your hands
that be mine enemies and die without sin, than sin before God our
Lord.' O woman full of faith and great loyalty, who feared so God
and the sin of breaking her marriage vow, that she preferred rather
to die than to deliver her body to evil embraces! And certes, true it
is that the Jews, men and women, that be now in this realm, hold
this sin in such horror and their law is such, that if a woman be taken
in adultery she shall be stoned and wounded with stones unto her
death, according to their law. Even the wicked keep this law and we
ought to keep it well, for it is a good one.[7]

Another example there is, as Cerxes[8] the philosopher telleth in his
book of *Chess*, in the chapter concerning the queen, and he saith that
the queen ought in all things to keep her chaste and to lesson her
daughters, for, saith he, we read of many maids that have been
queens because that they guarded their virginity or maidenhead.
Paul, the historian of the Lombards, telleth how that in Italy there
was a duchess that was named Raymonde[9] and she had a son and
two daughters. It befel that the king of Hungary hight Cantamus
quarrelled with the aforesaid Raymonde and came before one of her
towns and laid siege thereto. She and her children were within the
fortress and she looked forth and saw her enemies making a sally
against the folk of her town, that hotly defended themselves, and
among the enemy she saw a knight who was fair to look upon. She
was so afire with love of him that she sent word unto him that
secretly, through her fortress, she would deliver up the town to him,
if he would take her to wife. And the knight answered yea and thereafter she opened the gates of the fortress unto him and he and his
folk entered therein. When they were within the castle, his folk
entered thereby into the town, and took men and women and all that
they could; and the sons of that woman had so great shame and grief
for her treason that they left her and betook themselves away, and
afterwards they were so worthy that one of these children that was

hight Grimault, to wit the younger, was duke of Benevento and afterwards king of Lombardy. And the daughters, that knew not whither
they might flee, and feared lest they should be ravished by the Hungarians, killed pigeons and laid them beneath their breasts, so that
at the warmth of their breasts the flesh of the pigeons stank, and
when the Hungarians would have come near unto them, then smelt
they the stink thereof and their lust cooled and they turned and left
them, saying one to the other, 'Fie, how these Lombards stink!' And
at the last these maidens fled by sea to keep their virginity and nathless by reason of this good deed that they did and their other virtues,
one was afterwards queen of France and the other queen of Germany.
The aforesaid knight took that duchess and had his pleasure of her
for one night to save his oath, and the next day he made her common
unto all the Hungarians. The day after he caused a parchment to be
set upon her from waist to throat, on the which was writ: 'Even such
a husband should the whore have who by her bawdry hath betrayed
her city and delivered her people into the hands of her enemies.' And
these words he caused also to be writ upon several parts of her garment, and bade bind and tie her all dead to the outer walls and before
the gate of her city, that all might see her, and so left her.

Again he giveth another example how to cherish the marriage
[vow] and chastity and saith how Saint Augustine in the book of the
City of God telleth (and I have seen it likewise in Livy) that there
lived in Rome a very good lady, of great and virtuous heart, hight
Lucrece, that was wife to a Roman hight Collatine, who once bade
and invited the Emperor Tarquin the Proud and his son Sextus to
dine with him. And they dined and were feasted and after dinner
they took their pleasure, and Sextus looked upon the countenance of
all the ladies that were there, and among all and above all the others,
Lucrece and her beauty pleased him well. A short while afterwards,
the people of a castle which stood five leagues away, near unto Rome,
rebelled against the emperor, who went to lay siege thereto, and with
him went Sextus his son, in whose company were several of the
young men of Rome and among them Collatine, the husband of
Lucrece. Long time were the Romans in siege before that place, and
on a day that was fair and fine, there were in company and drinking
together, Sextus, the emperor's son and several of these same young
Romans, among whom was Collatine, and they plotted among themselves to sup betimes, and afterwards to go speedily to Rome to the

houses of each of these young men, that they might see the bearing and behaviour of each of their wives and their governance, agreeing that he whose wife should be found in best disposition of mind, should have the honour of lodging Sextus the emperor's son in his house. Thus they were accorded, and came to Rome; and some ladies they found talking, others playing at *bric*, others at hot cockles, others at 'pinch me[10],' others playing at cards and other games of play with their neighbours; others, who had supped together, were singing songs and telling fables and tales and asking riddles; others were in the road with their neighbours playing at blind-man's buff and at *bric* and so likewise at other games; save only Lucrece, who within and in the innermost part of her house, in a great chamber far from the road, had with her workers in wool, and there, all alone, seated in little space away from her workers and apart, she was holding her book devoutly and with bent head, and saying her hours full humbly. And it was found that neither then nor at other times when her husband Collatine was away, in whatever company or feast she was, could man or woman make her to dance or sing, save only on the day when she had letters from him or when he came back to see her; and then she sang and danced with the others, if there were a feast. Wherefore Collatine bore away the honour of their coming and Sextus the emperor's son was lodged in his house, and there was served and companioned by all the others and their wives; and the next day very early was awakened and dressed by the ladies and heard mass and they saw him mount and take the road. And on this journey was Sextus smitten with love for Lucrece, so deeply that he bethought him to return to her in company with other folk that were not friends of her nor of her husband. Thus did he and came at eve to Lucrece's house, who received him full honourably, and when the time came to sleep, they prepared a bed for Sextus as for the emperor's son, and this evil emperor's son spied where Lucrece lay, and after all that were there were abed and sleeping, came Sextus unto her and set one hand on her breast and the other on his sword and said unto her, 'Lucrece, be silent! I am Sextus, son to the emperor, Tarquin, if thou speakest thou art dead.' And she cried out in fear, and Sextus began to beseech her. It availed not. Then offered he and promised her gifts and services. It availed not. And then he threatened her that she should yield to him or he would destroy her and all her line. It availed not. When he saw that nought of all this availed him, he spake thus to her: 'Lucrece, if thou dost not my will, I shall slay thee and I shall slay likewise one of thy varlets, and then shall I say that I found you both abed together, and for your bawdry slew you.' And she, who feared rather to be shamed before the world than to die, consented to do his will.

And as soon as Sextus was gone away, the lady sent letters bidding her husband, who was with the army, that he should come to her, and she sent also to seek her father, her brothers and all her friends and a man that was hight Brutus and was nephew to Collatine her husband. And when they were come, she said unto them full dreadfully, 'Sextus, the emperor's son, came yesterday as a guest unto this house, but he went not forth as a guest, but as a foe to thee, Collatine, for know that he hath dishonoured thy bed. Nathless, if my body be dishonoured, so is not my heart, wherefore do I absolve me of the sin but not of the punishment.' Then Collatine her husband saw that she was all pale and wan and her face all white and tearful, for the mark of tears was upon her visage from her eyes even to her lips and her eyes were large and swollen, the lids thereof dead and blue, and within red from the running of her tears, and she looked and spake piteously. Then began he to comfort her full gently and to pardon her, and showed unto her many fair reasons why her body had done no sin, sith that the heart had not consented thereto nor taken delight therein, and he fell to quoting ensamples and authorities. But it pleased her not; she brake into his words, saying full sharply, 'Oh, oh, nay, nay! 'Tis too late, all is of no avail, for I am not worthy now to live; and he that hath done this to me hath done it to his own great mishap, if ye be worth aught, and for that no bawdry may prevail by example of Lucrece, let him who would take example of the sin and the loss, take likewise example of the amends.' And straightway with a sword that she had beneath her robe, she struck herself through the body and died before them all.

Then Brutus the counsellor, and Collatine the husband of this same Lucrece, and all her friends, weeping and mourning, took the sword all stained with blood, and swore upon the blood of Lucrece that never would they hold their hand until they had destroyed Tarquin and his son, and pursued him with fire and bloodshed, and cast forth all his race, so that none henceforth might rise to any honour. And even so was it shortly done, for they bore her through the town of Rome and so moved the people thereby that each man swore to destroy the Emperor Tarquin and his son by fire and by bloodshed. Then shut they the gates that none might go forth to warn the emperor of their intent, and they armed and sallied forth, hurrying like mad folk to the place where lay the emperor's army. And when they drew near to the emperor and he heard the noise and the tumult and saw the people all dusty and the smoke of the horses, and heard what was told him, then he and his son fled away, fearful and all undone. Whereupon the *Romance of the Rose* saith thus:

> *N'onc puis Rommains, pour ce desroy,*
> *Ne vouldrent faire à Romme roy.*
>
> *Ne never was ther king in Rome toun*
> *Sin thilke day.*[11]

So have you two ensamples, the one to keep honourably widowhood or virginity or maidenhood, the other to keep marriage or chastity. And wot you that riches, beauty of form and face, lineage and all other virtues be all perished and wiped out in a woman that hath any stain or suspicion against one of these virtues aforesaid. Certes, then all is lost and blotted, all is fallen never to rise again, after a woman hath once been suspected or bruited to the contrary; and even supposing that she be wrongly so suspected, never can that ill fame be wiped away. See then in what ceaseless danger a woman sets her honour and the honour of her husband's line and her children, when she shunneth not such blame, which she may easily do. And upon this it is noteworthy, as I have heard tell, that the queens of France, after that they be wed, read never sealed letters, save such as be by the hand of their husband, as is said, and those read they all alone, and for the others they call company and bid them to be read by others before them, and say often that they know not how to read letter or writing, save that of their husband; and this they do by wise teaching and full well, that they may be far even from whisper and suspicion, for there is no fear of the deed itself. And since ladies so great and so honourable act so, the lowly ones that have as great need of their husband's love and of good fame ought in troth to do so too.

And I counsel you that you receive with great joy and reverence the loving and private letters of your husband, and secretly and all alone read them unto yourself, and all alone write again unto him with your own hand, if you know how, or by the hand of another very privy person; and write unto him good and loving words and tell him your joys and diversions, and receive not nor read any other letters, nor write unto no other person, save by another's hand and in another's presence, and cause them to be read in public.

Item, they say likewise that after the queens be wed, they never kiss any man, nor father, nor brother nor kinsman, save only the king as long as he liveth. Why they forbear and whether it be true, I know not. These things, dear sister, be enough to give unto you for this article, and they be given you rather for the tale, than for the teaching. There is no need to teach you in this matter, for, thanks be unto God, from this danger and suspicion you are well kept and shall be.

THE FIFTH ARTICLE

The fifth article of the first section telleth that you ought to be very loving and privy towards your husband above all other living creatures, moderately loving and privy towards your good and near kinsfolk in the flesh and your husband's kinsfolk, and very distant with all other men and most of all with overweening and idle young men, who spend more than their means, and be dancers, albeit they have neither land nor lineage; and also with courtiers or too great lords, and with all those men and women that be renowned of gay and amorous and loose life[12] . . .

For to show what I have said, that you ought to be very privy and loving with your husband, I set here a rustic ensample, that even the birds and the shy wild beasts, nay the savage beasts, have the sense and practice of this, for the female birds do ever follow and keep close to their mates and to none other and follow them and fly after them, and not after others. If the male birds stop, so also do the females and settle near to their mates; when the males fly away they fly after them, side by side. And likewise wild birds, be they ravens, crows, jackdaws, nay, birds of prey such as hawks, falcons, tercels and goshawks and the like, that be nurtured by persons strange to them in the beginning, after that they have taken food from those strangers, they love them more than others. So likewise is it with domestic and field animals, as with wild beasts. Of domestic animals you shall see how that a greyhound or mastiff or little dog, whether it be on the road, or at table, or in bed, ever keepeth him close to the person from whom he taketh his food and leaveth all the others and is distant and shy with them; and if the dog is afar off, he always has his heart and his eye upon his master; even if his master whip him and throw stones at him, the dog followeth, wagging his tail and lying down before his master to appease him, and through rivers, through woods, through thieves and through battles followeth him.

Another ensample may be taken from the dog Macaire, that saw his master slain within a wood, and when he was dead left him not, but lay down in the wood near to the dead man, and by day went to find food afar off and brought it back in his mouth and there returned without eating it, but lay down and drank and ate beside the corpse of his master, all dead within the wood. Afterwards this dog several times fought and attacked the man that had slain his master, and whenever he found him did assail and attack him; and in the end he overbore the man in the fields on the island of Notre-Dame at Paris, and even to this day there be traces there of the lists that were made for the dog and for the field [of battle].

By God, at Niort I saw an old dog, that lay upon the pit wherein his master had been buried, that had been slain by the English, and Monseigneur de Berry and a great number of lords were led there to see the marvel of this dog's loyalty and love, that day and night left not the pit, wherein was his master that the English had slain. And Monseigneur de Berry caused ten francs to be given to him, the which were delivered to a neighbour to find food for him all his life.[13]

So likewise is it with the beasts of the field; you shall see it in a sheep and a lamb, that follow and be privy with their masters and mistresses and with none other; and so too wild beasts, as boar, or stag or hind, that be wild by nature, follow and keep near unto their masters and mistresses and leave all other. *Item*, it is likewise even with wild beasts that be devouring and ravening, as with wolves, lions, leopards and the like, that be fierce, and proud and cruel, devouring and ravening; they too follow and serve and are privy with those who feed them and whom they love and are strange with all others.

Now have you seen divers strange ensamples, which be true and visible to the eye, by the which ensamples you see that the birds of the sky and the shy wild beasts and even the ravening beasts have the sense perfectly to love and be privy with their owners and those that be kind to them, and to be strange with others; wherefore for a better and stronger reason women, to whom God has given natural sense and who are reasonable, ought to have a perfect and solemn love for their husbands; and so I pray you to be very loving and privy with your husband who shall be.

THE SIXTH ARTICLE

The sixth article of the first section saith that you shall be humble and obedient towards him that shall be your husband, the which article containeth in itself four particulars.

The first particular saith that you shall be obedient: to wit to him and to his commandments whatsoe'er they be, whether they be made in earnest or in jest, or whether they be orders to do strange things, or whether they be made concerning matters of small import or of great; for all things should be of great import to you, since he that shall be your husband hath bidden you to do them. The second part or particular is to understand that if you have some business to perform concerning which you have not spoken to him that shall be your husband, nor hath he bethought him concerning it, wherefore hath he nothing ordered nor forbidden, if the business be urgent and it behoves to perform it before he that shall be your husband knoweth it, and if you be moved to do after one fashion and you feel that he that shall be your husband would be pleased to do after another fashion, do you act according to the pleasure of your husband that shall be, rather than according to your own, for his pleasure should come before yours.

The third particular is to understand that if he that shall be your husband shall forbid you to do anything, whether he forbid you in jest or in earnest or whether it be concerning small matters or great, you must watch that you do not in any manner that which he has forbidden.

The fourth particular is that you be not arrogant and that you answer not back your husband that shall be, nor his words, nor contradict what he saith, above all before other people.

Taking the first of the four particulars, which biddeth you to be humble and obedient to your husband, the Scripture bids it, *ad Ephesios* v°, where it is said: *Mulieres viris suis subdite sint sicut domino, quoniam vir caput est mulieris, sicut Christus caput est Ecclesie.* That is to say, it is the command of God that wives be subject to their husbands as their lords, for the husband is the head of the wife, even as our Lord Jesus Christ is the head of the Church. Thus it followeth that even as the Church is subject and obedient to the commandments, great and small, of Jesus Christ, as to her head, even so wives ought to be subject to their husbands as to their head and obey them and all their commandments great and small. And so did Our Lord command, as Saint Jerome saith, and likewise the *Decretal,* xxxiii[a] *Questione, quinto capitulo: Cum caput.* Wherefore the apostle writing unto the Hebrews saith in the xiii[th] chapter: *Obedite prepositis vestris et subjacete eis* etc. That is to say, obey them that have rule over you and submit yourselves.

Again it is plainly shown unto you that it is our Lord's word, for that it is said in the beginning that woman ought to be in subjection to man. For it is said that when at the beginning of the world Adam was made, our Lord spake these words, and said, 'Let us make him an help meet for him.' And then from Adam's rib he made woman as help and subject, and so it useth to be, and it is reason. Wherefore a woman ought to consider well of what condition is he that she shall take, before that she taketh him. For it is as a poor Roman said, who without his knowledge or desire, was elected emperor by the Romans, and when they brought him unto the throne and the crown he was all astonied; and one of the first things that he said unto the people was this: 'Have a care what you do or have done, for so it is that when you have elected me and I be made emperor, wot you surely that thenceforth my words shall be sharp as razors newly ground.' That is to wit that whosoever obeyed not his commands when he was made emperor, should be under pain of losing his head.

Thus let a woman watch well how and to whom she shall be wedded, for however poor or lowly he may have been before, nathless for all time to come after the marriage, he ought to be and is sovereign and can increase or diminish all [that she hath]. Wherefore you should think rather of character than of fortune in your husband, for you cannot change him afterwards, and when you have taken him, hold him in love and love and obey him humbly. For many women have made great gain and come to great honour by their obedience, and others by their disobedience have been hindered and brought low.

Concerning this matter of obedience, and the good that cometh to the woman that is obedient unto her husband, I can draw an ensample that once was translated by master Francis Petrarch, who was crowned poet at Rome,[14] the which tale runneth thus:

On the borders of Piedmont in Lombardy, as 'twere at the foot of the mountain that divideth France and Italy and is called in those parts Monte Video, there is a long and lusty country, full of castles and towns and adorned with woods, meadows, rivers, vines, hayfields and ploughed fields; and this land is hight the land of Saluzzo, the which of old times ruled over the neighbouring country and of old times to this day hath been ruled by certain nobles and powerful princes hight marquises of Saluzzo, whereof one of the noblest and most powerful was named Walter, to whom all the other folk of this land, as barons, knights, squires, burgesses, merchants, and labourers were obeisant. This Walter, Marquis of Saluzzo, was fair in person, strong and nimble, of noble blood, rich possessions and great lordship, full of all honour and courtesy, and perfectly furnished with the precious gifts of nature. There was one vice in him, for he much loved solitude, and considered not the time to come, and by no means would he marry. All his joy and delight was in rivers and woods, in hounds and birds, and he took no thought for the government of his signory; wherefore his barons besought and admonished him to marry, and his people were in great sadness, and most of all because that he would not incline him to marriage. One day they came together in great number, and the worthiest among them came unto him, and by the mouth of one of them spake these words unto him: 'Oh thou, our lord marquis, the love that we bear to thee giveth us courage to speak these poor words. Since we like well and ever have liked thee and all the things that are in thee, and we hold ourselves happy to have such a lord, yet one thing lacketh in thee, the which if thou wilt grant it to us, we hold ourselves in better felicity than all our neighbours: it is to wit that you will please to incline your heart to the bonds of marriage and that your past liberty be a little restrained and brought within the marriage law. Thou knowest, Sire, how that the days pass and flee away and never return. And although thou art in thy green youth, nathless, from day to day death menaceth and approacheth thee, for it spareth no age and no man may escape it. All must die, but none knoweth how, nor when, nor what day, nor by what end. We, then, thy people, who never yet refused thy behest, we pray thee very humbly that we have liberty to choose thee a lady of fit lineage, of noble birth and fair person, adorned with goodness and good sense, whom it shall please thee to take in marriage and through whom we hope to have lineage and a lord of thy line to succeed thee. Sire, do this grace to thy loyal subjects; if ought were to befal thy high and noble person and thou wert to depart from this world it should not be without heir and successor and thy sad and mournful subjects should not be left without a lord.'

When they had made an end the marquis was moved to pity for his subjects and replied to them very gently, saying, 'My friends, you constrain me to that in which I can never find my heart; for I rejoiced me in liberty and in that free will which seldomtime is found in marriage, as they know well that have proved it. Nathless for your love do I submit me to your will. True it is that marriage is a doubtful thing and oftentimes children be not like their father. Nathless if the father have any good of them, he ought not therefore to say that it is his by right, but that it cometh from God above; to Him do I commend the fate of my marriage, in hope that of his bounty he will grant me a wife with whom I can live in the peace and quiet that be necessary to my salvation. I grant you, my friends, and promise you that I will take a wife; but I am in mind to choose her myself, and I charge you that you promise me one thing: assuredly it is this, that whomsoever I shall take to wife, be she daughter to the Prince of the Romans, or a serf, or another, you shall love her and honour her entirely, and that none of you be ill content with her after my choice, nor grudge nor murmur against her.'

Then all the barons and subjects of the marquis were rejoiced that they had their will, of the which thing they had oftentimes despaired. With one voice they thanked the marquis their lord, and promised with hearty will the reverence and obedience which he had asked of them. Great joy was there in the palace of Saluzzo, and the marquis granted a day for his bridal whereon he should take a wife, and he bade make great preparations, greater than ever before was made by any other marquis, and likewise bade summon kinsmen and friends, neighbours and ladies of the land for the aforesaid day; the which thing was solemnly performed and while the preparations were a-making, the Marquis of Saluzzo, as was his custom, went forth to take his delight in hunting and hawking.

Not far from the castle of Saluzzo there stood a little village wherein dwelt a few labourers, by the which village the marquis was often wont to pass, and among the aforesaid labourers was an old man and poor, who could not help himself, and was called Janicula. This poor man had a daughter hight Griselda, fair enough to sight, but fairer still in life and virtuous ways; she had been poorly fostered up by the labour of her father; never had she known delicious meats nor delicate things. A ripe and virtuous heart dwelt sweetly in her virgin breast; gently and in great humility she supported and sustained her father's age and fostered him; and she diligently kept a few sheep that he had, going with them and spinning continually with her distaff in the fields. And when Griselda homeward came at eve and brought back her beasts to her father's house, she gave them forage, and prepared for herself and her father the food that God gave them. And in brief all the courtesy and service that she might do unto her father, she gently performed it.

The marquis was aware by common renown of the virtue and great goodness of this same Griselda, and when he rode to take his pleasure he oftentimes looked upon her, and her fair ways and great goodness laid hold upon his heart. And in the end he determined in his heart that Griselda and none other should by him be raised to be his wife and lady of Saluzzo, and he bade his lords to the wedding on the day determined. That day drew near, and the lords, nothing knowing of the maid that the marquis was minded to take, were sore astonied. Nathless they knew well that the marquis had caused to be made rich robes, girdles, brooches and rings measured upon a maiden like in stature to Griselda. So it befel that the wedding day was come and all the palace of Saluzzo was filled with barons and knights, with ladies and damsels, burgesses and other folk, but no news was there of their lord's bride, whereat they marvelled much; nay, more, the hour of the dinner drew near, and all the officers were ready each to do his office. Then the Marquis of Saluzzo, as one that would go forth to meet his bride, set out from his palace, and a great troop of lords and ladies, minstrels and heralds followed after him.

But the maid Griselda knew nought of all this, for that same morning she arrayed and cleaned and ordered her father's house, that she might go with the other maidens, her neighbours, to see their lord's bride. And even as the marquis drew nigh Griselda was bearing a water-pot upon her head to her father's house, and then came the marquis with all his company, and called the maid by name and asked her where her father was. Griselda set her pot upon the ground and on her knees, humbly and with great reverence, answered, 'Lord, he is in the house.' 'Go to him', said the marquis, 'and bid him come speak with me.' And she went. Then the poor man Janicula came out of the house. The marquis took him by the hand and led him aside, and said thus to him secretly: 'Janicula, I wot well that thou hast ever loved and dost love me, and what pleaseth me should please thee likewise. One thing I would have of thee, to wit that thou wilt give me thy daughter to wife.' The poor man dared not speak, and after a short space he answered very humbly on his knees, 'Lord, I ought neither to like nor to mislike aught save what pleaseth thee, for thou art my lord.' Then said the marquis, 'Go into thine house alone, thou and thy daughter, for I would ask her something.' The marquis went into the house of the poor man Janicula, as is aforesaid, and all the people remained outside and much they marvelled; and the maiden kept her close to her father, fearful, shamefast and abashed at the sudden coming of her lord and his great and noble company, for she had never learned to see so great a guest in their house. The marquis spoke to her and these were his words: 'Griselda, it pleaseth thy father and me that thou shalt be my wife, and I suppose well that thou wilt not refuse me, but I have a thing to ask thee before thy father; to wit, that if I take thee to wife, the which thing shall be even now, I would know if thou wilt incline thy heart entirely to do my will, in such manner that I may do with thee and all that concerneth thee, as best meseemeth, without argument or contradiction by thee, either in word or deed, in sign or thought?' Then Griselda, abashed and marvelling much at this great thing, answered, 'Lord, I know well that I am not worthy to be called thy wife, nor even to be called thy servant wench, but if it please thee and fortune offer it to me, never will I wittingly do or think anything against thy will, and never will I deny anything that thou mayst do against me.' 'It is enough,' said the marquis, and took the maiden by the hand and led her forth from the house into the midst of his lords and his people and spoke thus, 'My friends, this is my wife, your lady; love and fear and honour her, and if you love me, love her very dearly.' And for that she should bring with her no relic of the ill hap of poverty, the marquis ordered the ladies and matrons to undress her all naked from foot to head, and clothe her anew in rich robes and bridal array.

Then set the ladies to work: some dressed her, others shod her, others set on her girdle, others pinned brooches upon her, and sewed her with pearls and precious stones, others combed their lady's hair and dressed her head and set a rich crown thereupon, that she had never seen the like and it was small wonder that she marvelled. Who then saw a poor girl, brown with the sun and thin from poverty, so nobly adorned and richly crowned and suddenly transformed so that the people scarce knew her, well might he marvel thereat.

Then the lords took their lady and joyfully led her to church and there the marquis set a ring upon her finger and wedded her after the ordinance of Holy Church and the custom of the country. And when the divine office was over, the Lady Griselda was seated on a white palfrey and by all the throng was accompanied and brought to the palace, where all manner of instruments sounded forth. And the wedding was celebrated and the day was passed in great joy and consolation by the marquis and all his friends and subjects. And the lady was so filled with sense and bore her so worshipfully with her lord and husband, this poor Lady Griselda shone so with divine grace, that each man said she seemed not to be brought up and nurtured in a shepherd's or labourer's cot, but rather in a royal or imperial palace. And she was so loved and cherished and honoured by all that had known her from her childhood, that they could scarce believe that she was the poor man Janicula's daughter.

The fair maid was of such discreet life and sweet eloquence that she drew the hearts of all to love her, not only the marquis's subjects and neighbours, but the folk of all the provinces round about; and the lords and ladies came to visit her by reason of her good fame, and all went from her rejoiced and comforted. And thus the marquis and Griselda lived happily in the palace in peace and quiet, in the grace of God and men; and this lady not only busied herself wisely and diligently with all the homely arts that belong unto women, but at the behest of her lord and in his presence she wisely and diligently busied herself likewise with public affairs. For when there arose debate and discord among nobles, she so appeased them by her fair words, ripe judgement and good equity, that all with one voice said that this lady had been sent them by heaven for the salvation of the people.

Not long time after, the Lady Griselda grew big with child and then bore a fair daughter, and the marquis and all the people of the land had thereof great joy and consolation, albeit they had liever that she had had a boy. Time passed and the days came when the marquis's daughter was weaned. Then the marquis, who loved his wife much for the great virtue that he saw increase in her daily, bethought him to assay her and tempt her sorely. He came into her chamber, showing her a troubled countenance and as one wrathful said thus, 'Oh thou, Griselda, although that thou art at present raised to this pleasant dignity, yet I trow thou hast not forgotten thine estate in time past, and how and in what manner thou didst enter this palace; thou hast been honoured and to me thou art still lief and dear; but it is not as thou thinkest in the minds of my vassals, and especially since thou hadst a child. For they have great scorn to be subject to a lady born of such small parents and low estate, and I desire, as their lord, to have peace with them; so must I bow and consent to their will and not to my own, and do with thy daughter a thing that could not be more sorrowful to my heart, the which thing I would not do without thy witting. So will I that thou shouldst assent and lend thy free will thereunto, and bear patiently what shall be done, showing me the patience that thou didst promise at the beginning of our marriage.'

When the marquis ended these words, which in good sooth pierced her to the heart, the lady neither changed hue nor showed any sign of sadness, but humbly to her lord she answered, 'Thou art my lord, and I and this little maid be thine; do what thou wilt with thine own. Nothing can be pleasing to thee that ought not likewise to please me, and this have I so rooted in the midst of my heart that no length of time, nor death itself can efface it, and all other things may happen before I change my mind in this.' Then the marquis, hearing his wife's reply, and seeing her steadfast and humble mien, had great joy in his heart, but he hid it and departed from her with sad and dreary looks.

Soon after this the marquis called to him a loyal and secret man of his, in whom he had all trust, and committed to this sergeant all his intent in the matter of his daughter, and sent him to his lady. The sergeant came before the lady and soberly spake these words to her: 'Madam, I pray thee to forgive me and impute not to me that which I am constrained to do. Thou art a wise lady and knowest what it is to be beneath lords whose behests never by force nor by guile may be resisted. Madam, I am enforced to take this child and perform what I am bidden.' Then the lady, remembering her lord's words in her heart, understood well and misdoubted that her daughter must die. She took heart virtuously and comforted herself, vanquishing nature for to fulfil her promise and acquit herself and do her lord's bidding. And sighing not nor showing other mark of sorrow, she took her child and looked long upon it and gently kissed it and made the sign of the cross upon it; then gave she it to the sergeant, thus saying, 'Go now and do and accomplish fully all that my lord hath commanded thee; yet would I pray thee that the tender body of this maid be not eaten by birds or wild beasts, save it be so ordered thee.'

The sergeant left the lady, carrying the child, and privily came to the marquis and showed him his daughter, and told him how that he had found the lady of great courage, and without contradiction obedient to him. The marquis considered his wife's great virtue and looked upon his daughter and had fatherly compassion upon her, and he would not change the hardness of his purpose, but he bade the sergeant, in whom he had trust, to wrap up the child as gently as might be for her ease, and to set her in a pannier upon a mule with gentle paces, and without delay carry her secretly to Bologna the Rich, to his sister that was wife to the Count of Perugia; and to show to his sister upon the love she bore him, that she should have the child fostered and taught in all gentleness, and do it so privily that neither her husband the count nor any living wight should ever know thereof.

The which sergeant forthwith departed by night and carried the maid to Bologna the Rich and delivered his message full diligently as he was bidden. And the countess received her niece with great joy and did very wisely all that the marquis her brother had asked of her.

Thus patiently did Griselda pass this stormy time, the which pierced her entrails, and firmly in her heart she believed that her child was dead and slain; and the marquis bore himself as aforetime to his wife, nor spoke word to her of her daughter, and often looked upon her face, her bearing and her cheer, to see and subtly to assay whether he could see in her any sign of grief, but no change of heart could he understand or see in her, but ever the same glad service, the same love, the same courage; for the lady was ever as she had been unto her lord, nor showed she any sadness nor spake of her daughter in the presence of the marquis or in his absence.

Thus the marquis and his wife passed four years together in great love, leading a loving and peaceful life. And at the end of four years the Lady Griselda bore a son of marvellous beauty, wherefore the marquis and his friends and subjects and all the country were full of joy. When the child was weaned from his nurse and two years old, growing in great beauty, the marquis was moved again to try his marvellous and perilous assay and came to his wife and said: 'Thou knowest and hast heard how that my people were ill content with our marriage and especially since they have seen that thou art not barren and bearest children. Nathless never were my barons and my people so ill content as they be now, especially for that thou hast borne a male child, and they say often and mine ears have heard them murmur and say mockingly, "When Walter is agone, then shall the goodman Janicula be our lord; lo, to what a lord shall this noble land be subject!" Every day there rise such murmurs; and by reason of these words and fears, I, that would live in peace with my subjects, and am in great fear for my life, am constrained and moved to do with this child as I did with his sister, the which thing I tell unto thee, that a sudden sorrow may not shake thy heart.'

O what sorrowful thoughts must this lady have hid in her heart, remembering the foul death of her daughter and that the like was ordained for her only son of two years old! Who is there, not only say I among women, that be tender of nature and loving to their children, but among the strongest men of courage that could be found, who could support such a sentence on his only son? Listen, ye queens, princesses and countesses and all other women, and hear what answer the lady made unto her lord and take example: 'My lord,' quoth she, 'I said before and again I say it, that naught will I or will I not save that which pleaseth thee. Thou art lord of me and of my children. Do therefore as thou wilt with thine own and ask not my consent. When first I entered thy palace, I put off my poor clothes and my own will and affection and put on thine, wherefore all that thou desirest, I desire. Certes, if I had prescience to know thy thoughts and desires before thou toldest them to me, whatsoever they were I would accomplish them after my power, for naught is there in the world, neither parents, nor friends, nor mine own life that can compare with thy love.'

The Marquis of Saluzzo, hearing his wife's words and marvelling in his heart at her great virtue and steadfastness without compare and at the true love that she bore him, answered her not, but went forth with eyes cast down, as though heavy at that which he must do unto his son, and soon afterwards, as he had done aforetime, sent a loyal sergeant secretly to the lady. The which sergeant after many excuses, showing her gently that he must needs obey his lord, very humbly and piteously prayed his lady's pardon if before he had done aught to displease her and so must do again, and besought her to forgive his great cruelty and asked for the child. The lady, without delay or sign of grief, took her fair son in her arms, and without tear or sighing, looked long upon him, and as she had done to his sister, she signed him with the sign of the cross, and blessed him, tenderly kissing him, and delivered him to the sergeant, saying, 'Take him, my friend, and do as is bidden thee; one thing I pray thee as I did before, if it may be, that thou wilt save the tender limbs of this child that they be not disturbed or devoured by birds and wild beasts.'

The sergeant took the child and bore him secretly to his lord and told him all that he had heard from his lady, and more than ever did the marquis marvel at the great and steadfast courage of his wife, and had he not known well the great love she bore her children he might have thought that such courage came not of humanity but of beastial cruelty, and he saw full clearly that his wife loved nothing beneath heaven more than her husband.

The marquis sent his son secretly to Bologna to his sister, even as he had sent his daughter, and his sister, the Countess of Perugia, after the will of her brother the marquis fostered his daughter and son so wisely that none might know whose children they were, until the marquis ordained as shall appear hereafter.

Now certes, the assay which the Marquis of Saluzzo, as a cruel and exacting husband, had made of his wife might well have sufficed him, without trying nor tormenting her more. But some there be who, when that they have set forth upon the path of suspicion, know not how to end nor slake their purpose.

When it had befallen thus, the marquis conversing with his wife looked often upon her, to see whether she showed him any change by reason of the things that were past, but never saw he in her any variance or altered cheer. Day after day he found her joyous and loving and more obedient, so that all could see that in these two persons there was but one mind, the which mind and will was chiefly the husband's, for as is aforesaid, she had no desire of her own, but laid all to her husband's will. While the marquis lived thus lovingly with his wife, in great repose and in great joy, he learned that ill fame was abroad concerning him, to wit that the marquis was shamed that, taking no heed of his great lineage, he had taken in marriage the daughter to the poor man Janicula, and had had of her two children, and therefore he had had them done to death and cast away none knew where. And although they loved him well aforetime as their natural lord, nathless for this reason they held him in hatred, the which he well knew. Nathless, by no means would he stint nor soften his cruel purpose, but took thought again and again to prove and tempt his wife by a yet stronger argument and harder test, by wedding another woman.

Twelve years were then passed since his daughter's birth; the marquis sent privily to Rome to the Holy Father the Pope and sought of him sacred bulls, by the which the rumour should go forth to his people that the marquis had leave of the Pope of Rome, for the peace and repose of himself and his subjects, to lay aside his first marriage, and take in lawful wedlock another woman. The rude people thought full well that it had been so, and were roused against their lord. The cold tidings of this bull, by which the marquis should take another wife, came to the ears of Griselda, daughter of Janicula, and her heart was full of woe, as is no marvel. But she that once had submitted herself and all that was hers to her lord's will, freely considered and took counsel with herself, and steeled her heart and took comfort, disposing her to await all that he to whom she was in submission should ordain.

Then did the marquis send a note to the Count of Perugia and his sister, bidding them bring home his children, without saying whose they might be, and his sister wrote that she would do his will. Their coming was speedily spread abroad and the rumour went forth throughout all the land that a fair virgin sprung of a great lineage was coming to wed the Marquis of Saluzzo.

The Count of Perugia accompanied by great lords and ladies set forth from Bologna and brought with him the son and daughter of the marquis. And the boy was of the age of eight years and the maiden of twelve, and she was full fair of form and face and ripe for marriage, and she was arrayed in rich stuffs and garments and gems, and was to reach Saluzzo upon a certain day ordained.

While that the Count of Perugia and his children were on the road, the Marquis of Saluzzo called Griselda his wife and in the presence of some of his barons spake to her thus, 'In time past I had pleasure enow in thy company in marriage, for thy fair ways and not for thy lineage, but now, as I see well, great fortune beareth heavily upon me and I am in great servitude, and I may not consent that a poor labouring man such as thou art sprung from should have so great lordship over my vassals. My people constrain me and the Pope alloweth me to take another wife than thee, and she is upon the road and soon shall be here. Be thou then strong of heart, Griselda, and void thy place to this other who cometh. Take thy dower and be appeased. Go forth to thy father's house; for nothing that befalleth man or woman in this world can last for ever.'

Then answered Griselda and said thus, 'My lord I wot well or at least I wist it, that betwixt thy magnificence and my poverty there might be neither proportion nor likelihood, neither did I ever deem myself worthy to be thy wife, nor so much as thy chamberer; and in this palace where thou broughtest me and didst make me lady, I take God to witness that I ever deemed and demeaned myself thy servant, and for all the time that I have dwelt with thee I give thee thanks, and now I am ready to return to my father's house, wherein to pass my age and die a happy and honourable widow, that to such a lord was wed. I leave my place to God, and may it please Him to send a full good virgin to that place where I have very joyfully dwelt, and since thus it pleaseth thee, I go without ill or hard thought. And as to my dower that thou hast bidden me to take with me, I see what it is. Thou knowest well that when thou didst take me at the door of my father Janicula's house, thou didst cause me to be stripped naked and clad in thy robes, wherein I came to thee, nor ever brought I with me other riches or dowry, save only faith, loyalty, reverence and poverty. See here this robe which I strip from me, and the ring with which thou didst wed me, which I restore to thee; the other rings, jewels, garments and adornments wherewith I was adorned and enriched are in thy chamber. Naked came I from my father's house, and naked must I return there, save that I think it would be an unworthy thing that this womb, in which thy children lay, should appear all bare before the people; wherefore, if it please thee and not otherwise, I pray thee in guerdon of my maidenhead, which I brought to thy palace and bear not thence again, that ye vouchsafe to order that a smock be left me, wherewith I may cover the womb of her

that was thy wife and lady, and that for thine honour I go forth at
eventide.'

Then the marquis could scarce restrain his tears for the ruth that
he had for his very loyal wife. He turned away his face and weeping
bade them to give her a single smock at eventide. Thus it was done;
and at eventide she stripped her of all her clothes, and put off her
shoes and the ornaments that were on her head, and humbly she clad
herself in the one smock that her lord had given her, and was content therewith, and with head and feet all bare she departed from the
palace, and with her went barons and knights, ladies and maidens,
weeping and considering her great virtues and loyalty, and marvellous goodness and patience. All wept, but she shed no tear, but
honestly and simply, with eyes upon the ground, fared towards the
house of her father Janicula, who heard the noise of this great company drawing nigh. And because that Janicula was old and wise and
had always held his daughter's marriage in suspicion, thinking that
when his lord was weary of so lowly a marriage, with so poor a
creature, he, that was a great lord, would lightly send her away, he
was adrad and came quickly to the door and saw that it was his
daughter all naked; then hastily took he the poor, torn dress which
she had left long ago, and weeping ran to meet his daughter and
kissed her and clad and covered her with this old dress. And when
Griselda was come to the threshold of her father's house, showing
no semblance of scorn or anger, she turned her to the lords, ladies
and maidens that had accompanied her, and very gently and humbly
thanked them for their escort and company, and said and showed to
them by fair, soft words how that for the love of God they should
not say, or think, or believe that her lord the marquis had done her
any wrong, and that it was not so, but that he had good cause to do
all that he pleased with her, that was bound to suffer and bear it.
And she bade them wot well that naught was displeasing to her, and
admonished them for the love of God to love their husbands truly
and full cordially and to serve and honour them with all their might,
and that they could have no greater good, nor higher renown, nor
better praise than this, and bade them farewell. And thus she entered
her father's house and the lords and ladies who had accompanied
her returned, weeping and sore sighing and moaning, so that they
might not look upon each other nor speak.

Griselda with all things was content; forgetting and caring naught for the great riches that she had had, and the great service, reverence and obedience that had been shown to her, she dwelt humbly with her father as aforetime, poor in spirit and in full great humility towards her poor friends and her father's old neighbours and lived a full lowly life. And well may the sorrow and small comfort of poor Janicula be imagined, that in his old age saw his daughter in such poor and small estate, after such great and high honour and wealth; but it was a marvellous good thing to see how benignantly, humbly and wisely she cared for him, and when she saw him heavy how wisely she comforted him, and afterwards led him to speak of another matter.

Many days passed as hath been said, and the Count of Perugia and his noble company drew nigh, and all the people of the country murmured against the nuptials of the marquis. The Count of Perugia, brother to the marquis, sent several knights ahead to show his brother the Marquis of Saluzzo the day of his coming and that he was bringing with him the virgin that the marquis was to wed; for in troth the Count of Perugia knew not that the children that the countess his wife had bred up were that same marquis's children, for the Countess of Perugia had hidden the matter from her husband, when she looked to the nurture of her niece and nephew, and from the countess's words the count thought them children of some strange land, as the children showed by their fair ways. And the count hoped that, when the maid should be wedded to the marquis and the fame thereof should go forth through the world, it should soon be known who the father might be.

Then the Marquis of Saluzzo bade seek Griselda, and bid her come forthwith to his palace; and she refused not and came. And the marquis said to her, 'Griselda, the maiden that I must wed shall be here tomorrow at dinner, and for that I desire that she and the count, my brother, and the other lords of their company be honourably received, so that each be honoured according to his estate, and especially for love of the virgin that cometh to me, and I have in my palace no woman or chambermaid that knoweth so well how to do it after my will as thou dost (for thou knowest my ways and how such folk should be received and thou knowest all the rooms and places and governance of my palace); therefore it is my will that thou take no thought for times past, nor be shamed of thy poor array, and notwithstanding thy small estate do thou take upon thee the ordering of all my affairs and all the officers of my house shall obey thee.'

Quoth Griselda gladly, 'My lord, not only willingly but with all my heart will I do all that I may to do thy pleasure, and never shall I be weary or burdened thereby, nor feign therein, as long as the relics of my poor spirit shall remain within my body.'

Then Griselda like unto a poor serving maid, took the lowly tools and delivered them to the household and bade some to clean the palace and others the stables, and prayed the officers and the chambermaids that each should do her own task in due place, and she began to dight the beds and the chambers, spreading the rich carpets and all the broideries and needlework that belonged to the garnishing of the palace, as befitted the reception of her lord's wife. And albeit Griselda was in poor estate and in the garment of a poor maid, yet seemed she to all who saw her a woman of great honour and marvellous prudence. Such virtue, such honour and such obedience were enow that all ladies should marvel thereat.

The next day at the hour of tierce, the count and with him the damsel and her brother and all the company entered Saluzzo. And all marvelled at the beauty of the maiden and her brother and at their goodly port, and some there were that said, 'The Marquis Walter doth well to change his marriage, for this wife is tenderer and of nobler birth than Janicula's daughter.' Thus in great joy they entered and dismounted before the palace. Griselda beheld all and seemed of good comfort in this great thing that so closely touched her, and naught was she abashed of her poor robe, but with glad cheer came from afar to meet the damsel, and from afar greeted her upon her knees, saying, 'Welcome, madam,' and so likewise to the son and then to the count and humbly saluted them saying, 'Be you welcome with my lady.' And she led each to his room that was richly arrayed. And when they had seen and considered the deeds and the bearing of Griselda, all marvelled how that such honour and reverence could be in so poor a garb.

Griselda after this went to the damsel and to the child, and could in no wise leave them. For an hour she gazed upon the maiden's beauty and the gracious bearing of the young boy, and she wearied not in praising them. The hour drew near when all should sit down to meat; and then the marquis called Griselda to him before them all and in a loud voice quoth he, 'How likest thou this my wife, Griselda? Is she not fair and honourable enow?' Griselda, wisely and aloud and upon her knees answered, 'Certes, my lord, I trow that never saw I a fairer and more honourable. My lord, with her you may lead a joyful and honourable life, the which thing in good faith do I desire; but, my lord, I do beseech and warn you that you prick not with strange torments this new wife, for, my lord, you shall bethink you that she is young and sprung of a great line and tenderly fostered, and she could not endure them as the other hath endured, to my thinking.'

Then the marquis, hearing Griselda's wise and gentle words and considering the good cheer and great constancy that she showed and ever had, felt a piteous ruth in his heart and could no more withhold to show his will, and in the presence of them all and in a loud voice he spake thus, 'O Griselda! Griselda! I see and know and am content with thy true faith and loyalty; and thy love for me, thy constant obedience and true humility I have assayed and well proved, and am constrained thereby to say that never, I wist, hath any man beneath heaven assayed his wife as sore as I have thee.' Then Griselda blushed, with bent head, in honest shame for the great praise wherewith she was praised by the marquis her lord before so many people. The marquis, weeping, took her in his arms and kissed her and said, 'Thou only art my wife and none other will I ever have. This is thy daughter, whom thou hast supposed to be my wife, and this child is thy son; the which children all our subjects wist were lost. Know then, all ye that thought the contrary, that I was in mind curiously and rigorously to prove this my loyal wife, and not to contemn nor to despise her, and I have had her children privily bred up by my sister at Bologna and have nor harmed nor slain them.'

And when the Lady Griselda heard her husband's words, she fell in a swoon before him to the ground, for the joy that she had to see her children. They raised her up and when she was recovered she took her two children and gently embraced and kissed them, so that they were covered with her tears, and none might take them from her arms, the which was a piteous thing to see. The ladies and the damsels, weeping for joy, took their Lady Griselda and led her to a chamber and stripped her of her poor dress and array, and clad her in others and honoured her as befitted a marquise. Then was there such great and solemn rejoicing for that the marquis's children were come back, to the inestimable comfort of their mother and of the marquis and his friends and subjects, that the great joy thereof was spread throughout the land, and many tears of pity were shed that

day in the palace of Saluzzo, and none wearied of faithfully recording the great and unmatched virtues of Griselda, who seemed rather
the daughter of an emperor for her bearing, or of Solomon for her
prudence, than the child of the poor Janicula. Greater and more
joyous was the feast than was the revel of their bridal, and the marquis and his lady lived together in great love and peace and concord
for the space of twenty years. And as to Janicula, father of Griselda,
of whom he had taken no heed in time past, to prove that old man's
daughter, the said marquis brought him to the palace of Saluzzo and
there held him in great honour all the days of his life. And the marquis married his daughter to a great and powerful lord, and when
his son was of age he married him likewise, and they had children
whom he lived to see; and after his gracious end, he left his son as
his heir and successor in Saluzzo, to the great consolation of all his
friends and subjects.

Dear sister, this story was translated by master Francis Petrarch,
crowned poet at Rome, in no wise only to move good ladies to be
patient in the tribulations that they suffer from their husbands for
the love of those same husbands alone, but 'twas translated to show
that since God and the Church and reason will that they be obedient
and since their husbands will that they have much to suffer, and
since to escape worse things it behoves them of need to submit them
in all things to the will of their husbands and to suffer patiently all
that those husbands will, and since again and nathless these good
ladies ought to hide and be silent concerning them and notwithstanding appease them and recall them and ever with good cheer bring
themselves nigh again to the grace and love of those husbands that
be mortal, by how much the greater reason behoveth it for men and
women to suffer patiently the tribulations which God, who is immortal, eternal and everlasting, sendeth unto them. And notwithstanding the death of friends, the loss of goods and children and
lineage, discomfiture by enemies, captures, slayings, losses, fire,
tempest, storms of weather, floods of water, or other sudden tribulations, ever ought we to suffer patiently and return, join and recall
ourselves lovingly and beseechingly to the love of the immortal ruler,
eternal and everlasting God, by the ensample of this poor woman,
born in poverty, of lowly folk without honour or learning, who so
much suffered for her mortal friend.

And I, that have set the tale here merely to lesson you, have not

set it here to apply it to you, nor because I would have such obedience from you, for I am not worthy thereof, and also I am no marquis nor have I taken in you a shepherdess, and I am not so foolish,
so overweening nor of so small sense that I know not well that 'tis
not for me to assault nor to assay you thus, nor in like manner. God
keep me from trying you in this way or in others, under colour of
false simulations! Nor otherwise in any manner would I assay you,
for sufficeth unto me the proof I have already made by the good
fame of your predecessors and yourself, together with what I feel
and see with mine eyes and know by true experience. And excuse
me if the story telleth of cruelty too great (to my mind) and above
reason. And wot you that it never befel so, but thus the tale runs,
and I may neither correct it nor make another, for a wiser than I compiled and told it. And I would that since others have seen it, you also
should see and know how to talk about all things, like to the others.[15]

Thus, dear sister, as I have said before that it behoves you to be
obedient to him that shall be your husband, and that by good obedience a wise woman gains her husband's love and at the end hath
what she would of him; even so may I say that by default of obedience, or by arrogance if you anger him, you destroy yourself and
your husband and your household. And for an ensample I set a tale
which saith thus: It befel that a wedded pair had a dispute with each
other, to wit the wife against the husband; for each of them said that
he or she was the wiser, the nobler in lineage and the worthier, and
like fools did they argue against each other, and the wife so bitterly
maintained her violence against her husband, who in the beginning,
perchance, had not lessoned her gently, that friends were driven to
intervene to save a harmful slander. Many meetings of friends were
held, many reproaches exchanged, and no remedy could be found,
but the wife must needs in her pride have her rights set down clearly,
point by point, and the obediences and services that the friends told
her she must pay to her husband set down and written in articles on
the one hand, and this and that from her husband to her on the other
hand, and thus might they dwell together, if not in love, at least in
peace. Thus it came about, and for some time they dwelt together,
and the wife narrowly guarded her rights by her charter against her
husband, who was fain, to avoid worse things, to have or to feign
patience in the despite that he had thereby, for he had begun to
amend her too late.

One day they were going on a pilgrimage and it behoved them to pass by a narrow plank over a ditch. The husband went first, then turned and saw that his wife was fearful and dared not come after him; and the husband was adrad lest if she should come, the fear itself should make her fall, and kindly he returned to her and took and held her by the hand; and leading her along the plank, held her and talked to her, assuring her that she should have no fear, and so went the good man backwards and talking the while. Then fell he into the water, that was deep, and he struggled hard in the water to save him from the danger of drowning, and caught and held on to an old plank that had fallen therein long time past, and was floating there, and he cried to his wife that with the help of her staff that she bore, she should draw the plank to the bank of the stream and save him. But she answered thus, 'Nay, nay,' quoth she, 'I will look first in my charter whether it be written therein that I must do so, and if it be therein, I will do it, and otherwise not.' She looked therein, and because that her charter made no mention thereof, she answered that she would do naught and left him and went her way. Long time was the husband in the water until he was at point of death. The lord of the land and his people passed by the place and saw him and rescued him when he was nigh dead. They caused him to be warmed and eased, and when that speech returned to him, they asked him what had befallen and he told them. Then the lord caused the wife to be followed and taken and had her burnt. Now see you to what an end pride brought her, that in her great disobedience was fain so straitly to keep her rights against her husband.

And, by God, it is not always the season to say to one's ruler: 'I will do naught, it is not reasonable'; greater good cometh by obeying, wherefore I take my ensample from the words of the Blessed Virgin Mary, when the Angel Gabriel brought her tidings that Our Lord should be conceived in her. She did not answer, 'It is not reasonable, I am maid and virgin, I will not suffer it, I shall be defamed'; but obediently she answered, '*Fiat mihi secundum verbum tuum*,' as who should say, Be it unto me according to thy word. Thus was she truly humble and obedient, and of her humility and obedience great good hath come to us, and by disobedience and pride cometh great ill and a foul end, as is aforesaid concerning her that was burnt and as ye may read in the Bible of Eve, by whose disobedience and pride she and all women that were and shall be after her, were and have been accursed by the word of God. For, as the Historian[16] saith, because Eve sinned doubly she had two curses. First, when she uprose in her pride and would have been like unto God: wherefore was she cast down and humbled in the first curse, wherein God spake thus, *Multiplicabo aerumnas tuas et sub potestate viri eris, et ipse dominabitur tibi.* To wit: I will greatly multiply thy sorrow and thou shalt be in the power of man and he shall rule over thee. The History saith that before she sinned, she was somewhat in subjection to man, for that she had been made of man his rib, but that subjection was full gentle and mild, and born of right obedience and true will, but after this curse she was subject in all things of necessity, whether she would or no, and all other women that sprang and shall spring from her, have had and shall have to suffer and obey all that their husbands would, and shall be forced to do their commandments. The second curse was this: *Multiplicabo conceptus tuos; in dolore paries filios tuos.* God said, 'I will multiply thy conception and in sorrow shalt thou bring forth children.' The History saith that the curse was not for the child, but concerning the pain that women have in bringing forth children.

See ye likewise the curse that our Lord set upon the disobedience of Lucifer. For once Lucifer was the most solemn angel and the most beloved and the nearest to God that was then in paradise, and therefore he was hight Lucifer, which is as 'twere *lucem ferens*, to wit bearing light, for in the eyes of the others all light and joy was there where he came, for that he represented and brought remembrance of that sovereign Lord, who so loved him and from whom he came and to whom he was so near. And as soon as this same Lucifer set aside humility, and puffed up his heart with pride, Our Lord set him further away from Him, for He caused him to fall lower than all others, to wit to the lowermost depths of hell, where he is the lowest, the worst and the most wicked of the evil ones. And likewise wot you that you shall be so close to your husband that wheresoever he goeth he will carry the memory and remembrance of you. And you may see it in all wedded folk, for no sooner do we see the husband than we ask him, 'How doth your wife?' and likewise when we see the wife, 'How doth your husband?' So close is wife to husband.

Thus see you, as well by the judgements of God Himself as by the ensamples above written, that if you be not obedient in all things great and small to your husband that shall be, you shall be more to be blamed and punished by your said husband than any other that shall disobey him, inasmuch as you be nearer to him. If you be less obedient, and your chambermaid, by good disposition or by service or otherwise, showeth him such obedience that he leaveth you and committeth unto her those duties which he should commit to you, and committeth naught to you, but leaveth you aside, what will your friends say? And what will your heart feel when it perceiveth this? And when he shall have transferred his pleasure there, how shall you withdraw it afterwards? Certes, it will be in no wise in your power.

And, for God's sake, have a care lest this ill hap come, that once only he take other service than yours. And so let his commandments, even the small ones that on the surface seem to you worthless or strange, be near to your heart, that you care naught for your own pleasures but only for his, and watch you that by your hand and by yourself and in your own person his pleasure be accomplished; and as for him and for those of his affairs that concern you, let none come near or set hand thereto but yourself, and let your own affairs be committed and laid by you upon your children and your privy servants that be under you, and if they do them not, do you punish them.

And for that I have told you to be obedient to your husband that shall be, to wit more than to any other and above all living creatures beside, this word obedience shall be explained and made clear to you; to wit in all matters, in all terms, in all places and in all seasons, you shall do and accomplish without argument all his commandments whatsoever. For know that since he is a reasonable man and of good natural sense, he will command nothing without due cause and will let you do naught that is unreasonable. Nathless some women there be that are fain to gloze and pick over the reasons and sense of their husbands, and again, to be thought wise and masterful, they do it more before folk than otherwise, which is worst of all. For although I am not minded to say that they ought not to know everything and that their husbands ought not to tell them everything, nathless it must be said and done apart, and ought to come of the will and courtesy of the husband and not of the authority, mastery and lordship of the wife, that questioneth him and domineereth before folk. For before folk, that she may show her obedience and keep her honour, she should say no word thereof, lest it should seem to the folk listening that the husband was wont to render account concerning his desires to his wife, and the wife ought not to wish this to be perceived, for in such case they show themselves mistresses and rulers and do great blame to themselves and great villainy to their husbands.

Again others there be whose husbands bid them to do things that seem to them small and of small value, and they regard not the thwarting of him from whom the order cometh, nor the obedience that they owe to him, but only the value of the thing, the which value they judge after their own ideas and in no wise sometimes after the truth, for they know it not, since it hath not been told them. An ensample that may serve: A man hight Robert, that oweth me two hundred francs, cometh to bid me farewell and saith that he wendeth over the sea and saith thus to me, 'Sire,' saith he, 'I owe you two hundred francs, the which I have delivered unto my wife who knoweth you not, but I have told her to deliver them to him that shall bring her name written in my hand and here it is.' So much from him, and when he is gone from me, without telling the circumstance, I bid my wife in whom I set my trust to keep it, and my aforesaid wife causeth another to read it, and when she perceiveth that it is a woman's name, she thinketh ill and casteth it on the fire, and cometh to me in wrath, saying that she scorns to be my bawd. There is fine obedience!

Item, I deliver her a straw, or an old nail or a pebble that have been delivered unto me for a witness in some great affairs, or a thread or a twig of wood for remembrance of some important business, whereof, by forgetfulness or other hazard, I say naught unto my wife, but give her the things to keep in safety; she regardeth only the value of the thread or the twig and taketh no other account of my orders, in despite because I did her not the honour and reverence of telling her the business at length. And such women be commonly rebellious, arrogant and sly, and when they have spoilt all in order to prove their mastery, they think in excusing themselves to make their husbands believe that they thought it a thing of naught, and therefore have not done as they were commanded, but if their husbands be wise they see well that it is done through disdain and despite, because they have not done their wives the honour of telling them the matter at once and without delay, and perchance they hold the commandment for naught in their pride, nor care they at all for their husbands' displeasure, provided only that they have occasion to excuse themselves and say, 'It was naught, but had it been important, I should have done it.' And for this, think they, they shall be excused, but they think wrong, for howbeit the husband saith nought at the time, nathless they lose ever the name of virtuous obedience, and the stain of the disobedience remaineth long time afterward so deep in the husband's heart, that he will remember it at another time, when the wife thinketh that there is peace and that the husband hath forgotten it. So let woman avoid this perilous danger and have a care of what the apostle saith *ad Hebreos* XIII: *Obedite*, etc.

Now this article saith again that the wife ought to obey her husband and do all his commandments whatsoever, great and small and even very small; nor behoveth it that your husband tell you the cause of his commandment, nor what moveth him, for that would seem a sign of your willing to do or not to do it according as the cause appeared good to you or otherwise, the which ought not to fall upon you nor upon your judgement, for it behoveth him alone to know it, and it behoveth not you to ask him, save it be afterwards, by your two selves alone and in private. For in doing his commandment you ought to show in no wise withdrawal, refusal, slowness or delay, and that which he forbiddeth ought you in no wise to do, or correct, or increase, or diminish, or loosen, or take away from, in any way; for in all things and everywhere, be it good or ill that you have done, you are quit and free when you say, 'My husband ordered me to do it.' Furthermore, if ill come of your deed, then it is said of a wedded woman, 'She did well, for her husband bade her, and in so doing she did her duty.' And thus if worse befal, you shall not merely be excused but praised.

And concerning this, I will tell you a very piteous and marvellous thing, whereof I have great ruth.[17] I know a woman of a very great family among citizens, who is married to a good person and they be two good creatures, peaceful young people, that have fair little children. The wife is blamed for that she received a great lord into her company, but, by God, when it is spoken of, other men and women who know the story, and even those who hate that sin, say that the wife ought no wise to be blamed, for her husband commanded her. The truth is that they dwell in one of the greatest cities of this realm. Her husband and several other burgesses were imprisoned by the king by reason of a rebellion that the commons had made. Each day the heads of three or four of them were cut off. She and the other

wives of these prisoners were every day before the lords, weeping
and kneeling and beseeching them with clasped hands to have pity
and mercy and hear them and set their husbands free. One of the
lords that was about the king, fearing not God nor His justice, but
even as a cruel and felon tyrant, sent word to this same citizeness,
that if she would yield her to his will, he would without fail deliver
her husband. She answered nothing to this, but besought the messenger for the love of God to bring those that kept her husband in
prison to allow her to see and speak to him. And so it befel, for she
was brought to her husband in prison, and all weeping told him
what she saw or could perceive concerning the others, and also the
prospect of his deliverance, and the foul request that had been made
of her. Her husband bade her that howsoever it was she should
bring about his escape from death, and that she should spare neither
her body, nor her honour, nor aught else, to save and rescue his life.
Then parted they from each other, both weeping. Many of the other
citizen prisoners were beheaded, her husband was set free. And she
is excused in a thing so great, for that even supposing it were true,
there is neither fault nor sin in her, nor hath she committed crime
nor ill, for her husband bade her and she did it to save her husband,
wisely and like a good woman. Nathless now leave I the matter,
which is ill to tell and too outrageous (cursed be the tyrant that did
it!) and return to my theme that one should obey one's husband, and
I will leave the great matters and come to little things of desport.

In God's name, I believe that when two good honest folk be wed,
all other loves be put afar off, destroyed and forgotten, save the love
of each other; meseems that when they are in each other's presence
they look upon each other more than upon others, they press each
other, they hold each other, and they do not willingly speak or make
sign save to each other. And when they be parted they think of each
other, and say in their hearts, 'When I see him, I shall do thus, I
shall say this to him, I shall beseech him concerning this or that.'
And all their special pleasures, their chief desires and their perfect
joys be to do pleasure and obedience unto each other, and if they
love each other, they care naught for obedience and reverence beyond the common, which is too small for many.

And in this matter of games and desport between husbands and
wives, by God, I have heard tell by the bailly of Tournai[18] that he
hath been in divers companies and dinners with men that were long

time wedded, and with them hath made divers parties and wagers to pay for the dinner, on condition that all the parties to the wager went thence to the house of each of the married men, one after another, and he among them that should have a wife so obedient that he could, without warning and without fail, make her count up to four without stay, or contradiction, or mockery, or reply, should be free of the scot, and those whose wives should be rebellious and answer and mock or deny, they should pay the scot, or each a share thereof. And when it was thus accorded, they went forth in true merriment and sport to Robin's house, who called his wife Marie, that was a vain woman, and said to her before all the husbands, 'Marie, say after me what I am about to say.' 'Willingly, sire.' 'Marie, say one.' 'One.' 'And two.' 'And two.' 'And three.' Then quoth Marie a little proudly, 'And seven, and twelve and fourteen! Come, do you mock me?' So Marie's husband lost. After this, they went to Jehan's house and he called to his wife Agnes, who well knew how to play the lady, and said to her, 'Say after me what I am about to say – one.' Then disdainfully quoth Agnes, 'And two.' So he lost. Tassin said to Dame Tassine, 'One.' Tassine out of pride quoth aloud, 'Here's something new!' or quoth she, 'I am not a child to learn how to count,' or she said, 'Come now, in God's name, are you become a tradesman?' and the like. And so he lost; and all those that had wedded young and well bred and well taught women won and were right glad.

Look you even what God, Who is wise above all wisdom, did because that Adam, disobeying and despising God's commandment and prohibition, ate the apple (and, sure, an apple was a small thing enough) and how wrath He was; He was not wrath for the apple, but for the disobedience and the small account that Adam made of Him. See how He loved the Virgin Mary for her obedience. Look you at the obedience and the deeds of Abraham, who at a mere command did such great and dreadful things without asking why. Look you at Griselda, what things she bore and endured in her heart without demanding the reason thereof, though there seemed no cause nor colour of a cause, no profit to come and no need therefor, save only that dread and terrible will, and how she asked naught nor said one word, wherefore she won such praise that now, five hundred years after her death, we still read of her goodness.

And the doctrine that women must be obedient to their husbands beginneth not now. It is written in Genesis in the twenty-ninth chapter that Lot and his wife set forth from a city and Lot forbade his wife to look behind her. For a while she obeyed and afterwards she despised his commandment and looked. Forthwith God changed her into a pillar of salt and thus is she still and shall she be. It is the very word of the Bible and we must believe it, else we be not good Christians. For see you, God thus assayed his friends and servants in full small things, as the one for an apple, the other for looking backward, and so it is no marvel that husbands, who of their bounty have set all their heart and all their joy and delight in their wives and have put all other loves behind them, should take pleasure in their obedience, and in loving jests and other ways not harmful should assay them.

Wherefore, returning to what is above said concerning how the husbands assayed the obedience of their wives, though it were but in jest, nathless the hearts of those that were disobeyed and thereupon lost were wounded by the mockery and the loss, and however much they feigned not to be, they were all shamefast and less well loved they their wives, who were not humble and fearful and obedient to them, as they should have been even in so small a thing, unless there had been great reason against it, which they should have told their husbands secretly and apart. And sometimes young and foolish husbands be so wicked that without reason, because of small and trivial matters, the beginnings whereof be arisen out of jests and nothings, and because of continual disobedience by their worthy wives, they amass and heap up a secret and covert wrath in their hearts, whereby worse cometh to both of them. And sometimes they bestow their embraces upon evil and dishonest women who obey them in all things and honour them more than they be honoured of their worthy wives; then those husbands cleave unto those evil women, who know how to keep their peace and honour and obey them in all things and do their pleasure. For doubt not, there is no husband so bad that he would not be obeyed and pleased by his wife, and when husbands find themselves better obeyed elsewhere than they were wont to be aforetime in their homes, then foolishly and neglectfully leave they their wives, that be haughty and disobedient, the which wives be afterwards wroth, when they see that in all gatherings they be not held in such honour as those that be accompanied by their husbands, or their own like fools are held so firmly by their hearts that they may not be drawn away. And it is not so easy to catch a bird that hath escaped from its cage as to keep it well, so that it fly not away; so these women cannot bring back their husband's hearts, when those husbands have sought and found better obedience elsewhere, and they lay upon their husbands the blame which truly is upon themselves.

Dear sister, see you that that which is said concerning men and women may likewise be said concerning wild beasts, and not wild beasts alone, but beasts which be wont to ravish and devour, as bears, wolves and lions: for these same beasts be fed and attracted by doing them pleasure, and afterwards they come and follow those that care for them and go with them and love them; and the bears be made to ride, the monkeys and other beasts to leap and dance and tumble and do all that their master wishes; and so for this reason may I show you how your husband will cherish, love and protect you if you think to do his pleasure. Wherefore concerning what I have spoken (and I have spoken truth) about wild beasts that be fed, etc., I say also the contrary, and you shall find that not only your husband, but your father and mother and your sisters shall grow strange to you if you be fierce to them and be not debonnair and obedient.

Now wot you well that your principal dwelling, your principal labour and love and your principal company is that of your husband, for whose love and company you be rich and honoured, and if he flee, or depart, or be afar from you by reason of your disobedience, or any other cause whatsoever, rightly or wrongly, you will remain alone and disparaged, and the blame thereof will be laid upon you and you will be held in the less honour, and if but once he have this evil of you, 'twill be hard for you ever to appease him, so that the stain of the misdeed dwell not so portrayed and written upon his heart, that howbeit he showeth and saith nought, 'twill not be wiped out and effaced for a long while. And if there cometh a second disobedience, beware of the vengeance spoken of in this same chapter and article at § 'And worse still', etc. (p. 107). Wherefore I beseech you love, serve and obey your husbands, even in very small and jesting matters, for sometimes very little things, full small and in jest, which seem of little worth because disobedience thereto doth little harm, be done for a trial, and by these it is known whether obedience or disobedience shall be looked for in great things; in sooth say I that you should straightway obey, even in full strange and wild things that your husband layeth upon you in jest or in earnest.

This matter I illustrate by a tale which saith thus: Three abbots and three married men were met together and one of them posed a question, asking which were the better obedient, wives to their husbands or monks to their abbot; whereupon they had much talk and argument and ensamples told on both sides. Whether the ensamples were true, I know not; but in the end they were still disagreed, and it was ordained that a proof should be made, loyally and secretly sworn between them by faith and oath, to wit that each of the abbots should order each of his monks that without the knowledge of the others he should leave his room open and a rod beneath his pillow, and await the discipline that his abbot was in mind to give him; and that each of the husbands should secretly order his wife, when they were abed and without letting any of their household or any save their two selves know aught about it, to set and leave a broom behind the door of their room all night long. And within a week the abbots and the husbands were to meet together again, and they swore to carry out their trial before then and faithfully and loyally, without any fraud, to report what had befallen; and whichever had been least well obeyed, the abbots or the husbands, should pay a scot of ten francs. Thus it was accorded and done. The report of each of the abbots was that, upon their souls, they had given the order to each of their monks, and at midnight each had visited every room and had found the order obeyed. Then the husbands told their tales, one after the other. The first said that before going to bed, he secretly gave the order to his wife, who full oft asked him what was the good thereof and what it was for, but he would not tell her. Then she refused to obey and he then feigned him to be wrath, whereupon she promised him that she would do it. At eve they went to bed and dismissed their folk, who carried away the lights. Then he made his wife rise and heard well that she set up the broom. He was full pleased with her, and slept for a little and soon afterwards awoke and was aware that his wife slept; then rose he softly and went to the door and found not the broom, and crept secretly to bed again and woke up his wife and asked her if the broom were behind the door, and she answered, 'Yea.' He replied that it was not there and that he had looked. Then quoth she, 'By God, if I were to lose the best dress I have, I would not leave it there, for when you were asleep, my hair began to stand up on my head, and I began to shiver and I could not have slept while that 'twas in the room; so I flung it through the window into the road.' The second husband said that after they were abed he had made his wife rise, and, full of displeasure and wrath, she had set the broom behind the door, but she had straightway clad herself again and gone from the room, saying that she would not sleep in the room where it was, and that in truth the devils of hell might come; and she went all clad to sleep with her chambermaid. The third said that his wife had answered that she was not born or sprung from wizards and sorcerers, and that she knew not how to play at midnight conjuring, nor at broomsticks, and if she were to die she would not do it or consent to it, nor ever would she stay in the house if it were done.

Thus the monks were obedient in a greater thing to their abbots, which is a marvel; but it is natural, for they be men; and the wedded women were less obedient in a less thing and to their own husbands, that should have been their special care, for 'twas their nature, since they were women; and thus the husbands lost ten francs by them and were disappointed in their outrageous boasts, for they had boasted of their wives' obedience. But I beseech you, fair sister, be not as these were, but be more obedient to your husband that shall be, both in small things and in strange ones, whether in earnest, in game, in jest or otherwise; for all are good.

By God, a full strange thing saw I at Melun,[19] one day where the Sire d'Andresel[20] was captain of the town; for the English were lodged in several places round about and the men of Navarre were lodged within the castle. And one day after dinner the said Sire d'Andresel was at the gate, and he was bored and complaining that he knew not where to go and desport him to pass the day. A squire said to him, 'Sire, will you go and see a damsel dwelling in this town that doth all that her husband commands?' The Sire d'Andresel answered him, 'Yea, let us go.' Then they set forth and on the way a squire was pointed out to the Sire d'Andresel as the damsel's husband. The Sire d'Andresel called him and asked him whether his wife would do as he ordered. And the aforesaid squire replied, 'By God, sir, yes, however great villainy it be.' And the Sire d'Andresel said to him, 'I will wager you a dinner that I will counsel you to make her do something wherein there shall be nought of villainy and she shall not do it.' The squire replied, 'Certes, sir, she will do it and I shall win; and I could win a wager with you more honourably in several other ways and have thereby greater honour in losing and paying for the dinner; so I beseech you, do you wager that she will do it, and I will wager that she will not.' The Sire d'Andresel said, 'I order you to wager even as I have said.' Then the squire obeyed and accepted the wager. The Sire d'Andresel wished to be present together with all that were there and the squire said that he was full willing. Then the Sire d'Andresel, who was holding a stick, said, 'My will is that as soon as we be arrived and without saying anything else, you bid your wife in our presence to leap over this stick in front of us all, and that it be done without frown, or grimace, or any other sign.' Thus it was done and they all entered the squire's house together and straightway the damsel came to meet them. The squire set the stick on the ground and held it there saying, 'Madam, jump over this.' Forthwith she jumped. 'Jump again,' quoth he. She jumped again. 'Jump!' She jumped thrice, without saying a single word save 'Willingly.' The Sire d'Andresel was astounded and said that he had lost and would pay the dinner next day in his house. And straightway they all set out to go thither and when he entered the door of his house, the Lady d'Andresel came to meet him and saluted him. And straightway when the Sire d'Andresel had dismounted, still holding the stick over which the damsel had leapt at Melun, he set the stick to the ground and thought to make the Lady d'Andresel jump over it, the which she refused to do; wherefore the Sire d'Andresel was full sore enangered. And for the rest I will be silent and with reason; but this much I may well say, and well do I know it, that had she accomplished her lord's command, that made it rather for a joke and a trial than for profit, she would the better have upheld his honour and have been the better prized by him for it; but to some women good cometh not, and to others so doth it.

And again on this subject I can tell another full strange thing, how that once on a summer's day, I was riding from Chaumont in Bassigny to Paris and one eve at vespers I stopped to lodge in the town of Bar-sur-Aube. Several young men of the town that were wedded there and had some acquaintance with me, came to pray me to sup with them, as they said, and they said that they were in this case: there were several young men, but lately wedded and to young wives, that had been met together, without other wise folk with them, and they had asked concerning each other's estate and had found by each man's speech, that each of them thought that his own wife was the best and most obedient in all manner of obedience, be it to do or not to do, in great things or small. Wherefore they had plotted together, as they said, to go all together to the house of each one of them and there the lord was to ask his wife for a needle, or a pin, or a pair of scissors, or the key of their coffer, or something of the sort; and if the wife said, 'What for?' or 'What are you going to do with it?' or 'Are you in earnest?' or 'Do you mock me?' or 'I have none,' or if she made any other reply or delay, the husband should pay a franc for the supper; and if without argument or delay she forthwith delivered her husband that for which he asked, the husband should be held happy in possessing so wise and obedient a wife, and wise in maintaining and keeping her in the same obedience, and he should be seated at the head of the table and should pay nought.

And albeit there be some women that cannot and deign not to submit to such small and strange things, but disdain and despise them, and all that thus behave, nathless, fair sister, you may wot well that it is needful for human nature to take pleasure in something; even the poor, the impotent, the sick or languid and those that be upon their deathbed take and seek pleasure and joy, and for more reason still those that be in health. All the delight of some is in hunting or hawking, of others in playing upon instruments, of others in swimming, or dancing, or singing, or jousting; even you seek your own diversely in divers ways; so, if your husband imagine that he would fain take pleasure in your service or obedience, as above, serve him and bear with him, and know that God will give you this great grace that your husband will take greater pleasure in you than in any other thing; for if you be the key to his pleasure, he will serve you and follow you and love you therefore, and if he has pleasure in something else he will follow it and you will be set aside. So I counsel and admonish you to do his pleasure in full small things and full strange ones and in all, and if thus you do, his children and you yourself shall be his minstrels and his joys and pleasures, and he will not seek his joys elsewhere, and it shall be a great good and a great peace and honour for you.

And if it befal that there be some business which your husband remembered not when he left you and therefore spake not to you, nor bade or forbade you concerning it, nathless you should do according to his pleasure, whatsoever pleasure you might have to do otherwise, and you should set aside your pleasure and put it behind you, and ever set his pleasure first. But if the business be important and such that you may have time to make it known unto him, write to him that you believe it would be his will to do thus, etc., and therefore you wish to do his pleasure, but because that such and such an inconvenience may come of doing it, and such and such a loss and damage likewise, it seemeth to you better and more honourable to do thus and thus, etc., the which thing you dare not do without his leave, may it please him to send you his wishes thereupon and you will carry out his orders with a ready heart and with all your power, etc.

All women do not so, wherefore evil cometh to them in the end, and when they be less valued and see the good and obedient wives that be well honoured, companioned and loved by their husbands, these wicked ones that be not so are at war with fate and say that fate hath o'erridden them thus, and the wickedness of their husbands that in no wise set their trust in them; but they lie, fate hath not done it; their own disobedience and disrespect towards their husbands hath done it, for after these husbands have often times failed towards their wives, that have disobeyed them and shown them no respect, they dare no longer trust in them and so they have sought and found obedience, wherein they set their trust, elsewhere.

And I remember, by God, that I saw one of your cousins, that loveth well you and me, and so doth her husband, and she came to me, saying 'Cousin, we have such and such an affair to do, and me-seems it would be well done thus and thus, and 'twould please me so. What think you?' And I said to her, 'The first thing is to know your husband's advice and pleasure; have you not spoken to him?' And she answered me, 'By God, cousin, nay; for by divers ways and strange words I felt that he was in mind to do so and so, and not as I have said. And you know, cousin, that it is less blame to do a thing without one's lord's leave than after he hath forbidden it, and sure am I that he will forbid me and I know well that he loves you and holds you for a good man, and if I did as I say by your advice, whatsoever came thereof, if I excused myself by your advice, he would be easily appeased, so much doth he love you.' And I said to her, 'Since he loves me, I must love him and do his pleasure, wherefore I counsel you to act according to his pleasure and set your own aside.' And naught else might she have of me and she departed full wroth for that I did not help her to do her will, that was all against the will of her husband; and she cared not for her husband's wrath, for she would have been able to say, 'You bade me not otherwise to do, etc., your cousin counselled me to do this.' Now see you her mind, and how anxious the woman is to do great pleasure to her husband and what obedience she giveth him!

Dear sister, other women there be that when they desire to do a thing in one way, but such a one suspecteth that her husband would not have it thus, she resisteth not nor resteth, but fretteth and fumeth, and when she perceiveth that she and her husband be alone and talking of their business, affairs and pleasures, the woman by certain words that be close to a certain matter, subtly enquireth and feeleth, concerning this business, that her husband is in mind to do and follow another way than she wisheth; then doth the woman lead her husband to speak of other things, that he may not say openly concerning this one, 'In this matter do thus'; and quietly she passeth it over and setteth her husband upon other talk and they end upon a business far from that matter. And as soon as this woman knoweth her position, then causeth she the first matter to be done according to her pleasure, nor careth she for her husband's pleasure, which she setteth at nought and thinketh to excuse herself by saying, 'You said naught to me about it,' for she careth not for the wrath and dis-pleasure of her husband, but only that her own be assuaged and her will done. And meseems that it is ill done thus to trick and deceive and try one's husband; but many there be that make such trials and many others, which is ill done, for a woman ought ever to seek to do her husband's pleasure when it is wise and reasonable; and when she tries her husband, covertly and quietly, under strange and mali-cious concealments, if it be the better to manage him, that is ill done, for with one's husband ought one never to act by guile or malice, but openly and roundly, heart to heart.

And worse still is it when the woman hath a husband that is an honest man and debonnair, and she leaveth him, in the hope of hav-ing pardon and excuse for ill-doing, as it is written in the book of the *Seven Sages of Rome*[21] that there was in the city a wise widower, of great age and full rich in lands and of good renown, that had been wedded to two wives that were dead. His friends counselled him to take another wife and he answered that they should find him one and that he would gladly wed her. They found him one that was fair and young and ready of her body, for never shall you see man so old that he doth not willingly take a young wife. He married her and the lady was with him for a year without his once doing that which you wot of. Now this lady had a mother; one day she was at church with her mother, and whispered unto her that she had no solace of her lord and therefore she was in mind to love. 'Daughter,' said the mother, 'if thou do so, he will hold thee in great despite, for certes there is no revenge so great as that of an old man, wherefore believe me and do it not, for never wilt thou be able to appease thy husband.' The daughter replied that she would do it. Then quoth the mother, 'Since otherwise it may not be, I would thou shouldst make trial of thy husband first.' 'Willingly,' replied the daughter, 'I will make trial of him thus. He hath a fruit tree grafted in his garden, which is full fair and which he loveth more than all his other trees. I will cut it down, and so shall I see if I may appease him easily.' Thus they were accorded and forthwith left the church.

The young dame returned to her house and found that her lord was gone to desport him in the fields. Then took she an axe, and began to strike to right and to left, until she felled the tree, and had it cut up by a varlet, and carried to the fire. And at the moment that this man was bringing it, the lord entered his house and saw him bringing the logs of the fruit tree in his hand; and the lord asked, 'Whence cometh this firewood?' The lady answered, 'I came of late from the church and they told me that you were gone into the fields, and I feared, for that it had rained, lest you should return wet and take cold, wherefore went I into the orchard and cut down this fruit tree, for there was no firewood in the house.' 'Lady,' said the lord, 'it is my good fruit tree!' 'Certes, sire,' quoth the lady, 'I know not.' The lord went forth into his orchard and he was full wroth, albeit he showed no sign thereof, but returned and found the lady making the fire with the fruit tree, as though she did it in good will to warm him. When the lord was come, he spake thus to her: 'Now, dame, it is my good fruit tree that you have cut down!' 'Sire,' quoth the lady, 'I marked it not, for certes I did it because I knew well that you would come in all wet and damp with the rain, and I feared lest you should be cold and take harm thereby.' 'Dame,' said the lord, 'I will let it be, since you say that you did it for my sake.'

The next day the lady returned to the church and found her mother and said to her, 'I made trial of my lord and cut down the fruit tree, but he showed me no sign that he was very wroth, and therefore, wot you, mother, that I shall love.' 'Do it not, fair daughter,' quoth the mother. 'Let it be.' 'Certes,' quoth the daughter, 'I will do it: no longer can I restrain myself.' 'Fair daughter,' saith the mother, 'if it be even as thou sayest and thou canst not restrain thyself, then make trial once again of thy husband.' Quoth the daughter, 'Willingly, I will make trial of him again thus. He hath a greyhound that he loveth marvellously well; he would take no money for it, so good it is, and he will suffer none of his varlets to drive it from the fire and none to give it to eat save himself only. I will slay it before him.' Then they parted.

The daughter returned to her house; it was late and cold, the fire was fair and bright and the beds were well arrayed and covered with fair counterpanes and rugs, and the lady was clad in a new pelisse. The lord came from the fields. The lady rose to meet him; she took off his cloak and then would have unbuckled his spurs, but the lord would not suffer her and bade one of his varlets take them off. Much show did the lady make of serving him; she ran and brought in a new-lined mantel and set it on his shoulders and arranged an armchair and set a cushion thereon, and made him sit by the fire, and bespake him thus: 'Sire, certainly you are all pale with cold, warm yourself and be well at your ease.' When she had spoken thus, she sat down close to him and lower than he, upon a footstool, and spread out the skirt of her pelisse, looking ever upon her husband. When the greyhound saw the fine fire, it came by mischance and lay down upon the edge of the lady's dress, and the lady saw close to her a varlet with a big knife, and snatched it and ran it through the body of the aforesaid greyhound, which began then to beat with its paws and died in front of the husband. 'Dame,' quoth he, 'how are you so bold as to slay in mine own presence my leveret that I loved so well?' 'Sire,' said the lady, 'see you not every day how we be troubled? There are no two days that we have not to clean up here after your dogs. And now look at my pelisse that I had never worn before, see how it is spoilt! Did you think that I should not be wroth?' The wise old man answered, 'By God, it is ill done, and I take it full ill of you, but now I will speak of it no more.' The lady said, 'Sire, you may do your will with me, for I am yours, and wot well that I am sorry for what I have done, for I know well that you loved it dearly; I am in grief for that I have angered you.' When she had spoken thus she made great show of weeping. When the lord saw this, he let it pass.

The next day she went to the church and found her mother and told her all that had befallen and how in good sooth, since all had befallen so well and she had so well escaped, she would fain love. 'Ha, fair daughter,' quoth the mother, 'do not so, thou mayst well forbear!' 'Certes, lady, I will not.' Then said the mother, 'Fair daughter, all my life I bore me well unto thy father, and never did such folly nor desired to.' 'Ha, lady,' replied the daughter, ''tis not with me as with you, for you and my father came together as young folk, and you had your pleasures together, but I have no pleasure nor solace of mine; so behoveth me to procure it.' 'Now, fair daughter, if love you must, whom wilt thou love?' 'Mother,' quoth the daughter, 'I will love the chaplain of this town, for priests and monks fear to be shamed, and are more secret. Never would I love a knight, for they would soon boast and brag about me and ask of me my jewels to pledge them.' 'Now, fair daughter, do once more as I counsel, and again make trial of thy lord.' Quoth the daughter, 'Try so much and so much and again and again, there will be no end of this!' 'By my head,' said the mother, 'thou shalt try him once more, by my advice, for never shalt thou see vengeance so foul nor so cruel as an old man's vengeance.' 'Well, lady,' said the daughter, 'I will willingly do your behest yet once again and I will try him thus: Thursday will be Christmas Day and my lord will hold a great feast for his kinsmen and other friends, for all the vavasours of this town will be there and I shall be seated at the head of the table in a chair; and as soon as the first course is served, I shall entangle my keys in the fringe of the cloth, and when this is done, I shall rise of a sudden and drag everything after me, and I shall scatter and spill all that is on the table; and then I will calm all once more. Thus shall I have tried my lord thrice by three great trials and lightly appeased him again, and by this you shall wot well that thus lightly I shall appease him concerning more dark and hidden things, that he can speak of only in suspicion.' 'Well, fair daughter,' said the mother, 'God grant thou do well.'

Then they parted; each went to her house. The daughter cared for her husband cordially, in all semblance, and full eagerly and well and full fairly, until Christmas Day came. The vavasours of Rome and the damsels thereof were come, the tables were arrayed and the cloths laid, and all sat down; and the lady played the mistress and housewife, and sat at the head of the table in a chair, and the servants brought in the first meats and brewets and set them on the table. And when the trencher men had begun to carve, the lady entangled her keys in the fringes at the edge of the tablecloth, and when she perceived that they were well entangled, she rose suddenly and took a long step backward, as though she had staggered as she rose; and she dragged at the cloth, and bowls full of brewet, hanaps full of wine and sauces were spilt and all that was on the table was upset. When the lord saw this he was shamed and full wroth and bethought him of the things that had happened before. At once the lady drew out her keys that were entangled in the cloth. 'Dame,' said the lord, 'you have done ill!' 'Sire,' quoth the lady, 'I could not help it. I was going to seek your carving knives that were not on the table and I was troubled.' 'Dame,' said the lord, 'now fetch us other cloths!' The lady bade fetch other cloths, and other dishes were brought in again. They ate merrily and the lord showed no sign of wrath nor anger, and when they had eaten enough and the lord had shown them great honour, they departed thence.

The lord suffered the night to pass until the next day was come. Then quoth he, 'Dame, you have thrice displeased me and made me full wroth, and you shall not do it a fourth time, if I can help it; and I know well that it is bad blood that hath made you so to do; it behoveth to bleed you.' He sent for the barber and had the fire made ready. The lady said to him, 'Sire, what would you do? Never have I been bled.' 'So much the worse,' quoth the lord, 'it behoveth you now to begin; these three evil tricks that you have played upon me, you have played by reason of bad blood.'

Then he bade her right arm to be warmed at the fire and when it was warmed, he bade bleed her; and she was bled until the thick red blood came forth.[22] Then the lord bade staunch her, and then bade her draw her other arm from out her dress. The lady began to cry mercy. Nought availed it, for he had the second arm warmed and bled, and they took so much that she swooned and lost all speech and became in hue as one dead, and when the lord saw this, he caused her to be staunched and carried to her bed in her room. When she came out of her swoon then began she to cry and weep and sent for her mother, who came forthwith; and when she came into her presence, all went from the room and left these two alone together. When the lady saw her mother she said to her, 'Ha! Mother, I am dead; my lord hath bled me so hard that I trow well that never shall I enjoy my body.' 'Now, daughter, well I wist that bad blood was consuming thee; now tell me, my child, dost thou still desire to love?' 'Certes, lady, nay.' 'Daughter, did I not in troth tell thee that never shouldst thou see vengeance so cruel as that of an old man?' 'Lady, yea; but, for the love of God, help me to recover and be restored to health, and by my soul, Mother, never will I love.' 'Fair daughter,' quoth the mother, 'thou wilt do wisely. Thy lord is a good worthy man and wise, love him and serve him, and wot that naught but good and honour shall come thereby.' 'Certes, Mother, well know I now that you gave me and give good counsel, and I will henceforth believe it and honour my husband and never try him nor anger him.'

Dear sister, this will suffice concerning this matter. For in this matter of obedience we have heretofore spoken and what is to be done if the husband order small things in jest, in earnest, or otherwise, and then of what is to be done when the husband has bidden or forbidden naught, because he has not bethought him thereof, and thirdly of the long way that women will go to accomplish their own will beyond and above the will of their husbands. And now at the last let us say that they should not do what their husbands forbid, in small things or great, for so to do is to act ill. And begin with small matters, in which obedience should just as well be shown; I prove it even by the judgements of God, for you know, dear sister, how that by the disobedience of Adam, who against the command of God ate an apple the which is a small thing, all the world was cast into servitude . . .

But some women there be, that think too slyly to escape, for when their husband hath forbidden them to do something that it liketh them to do and they be full fain to do, they delay and wait and let time go by until that the husband forget that he hath forbidden it, or until he be gone away, or until he be so busy with other and weighty matters that he remembereth not. And thereupon, straightway, at once and hastily, the woman doth the thing according to her pleasure and against the will and command of her lord, or causeth it to be done by her people, saying, 'Do it boldly! My lord will not notice it, he will know naught about it.' Now see you that this woman, in her headstrong will, is in truth a rebel and disobedient, and her malice and wickedness, that naught can withstand, make her case the worse and show clearly her evil mind. And wot that there is naught that will not be made known in the end and when the husband shall see it and shall perceive that she separateth their united wills, that should be one, as is aforesaid, that husband will peradventure be silent, as was the wise man of Rome, of whom it is written before in this article; but his heart will be so deeply wounded thereby, that never will it heal, but every time that he remembereth it, new sorrow will spring thereof.

So I beseech you, dear sister, that you watch and beware very specially against making such trials and attempts upon another husband than I, if you have one, but let your mind and his be one, as you and I are at present; and that will suffice for this article.

THE SEVENTH ARTICLE

The seventh article of the first section showeth how you should be careful and thoughtful of your husband's person. Wherefore, fair sister, if you have another husband after me, know that you should think much of his person, for after that a woman has lost her first husband and marriage, she commonly findeth it hard to find a second to her liking, according to her estate, and she remaineth long while all lonely and disconsolate and the more so still if she lose the second. Wherefore love your husband's person carefully, and I pray you keep him in clean linen, for that is your business, and because the trouble and care of outside affairs lieth with men, so must husbands take heed, and go and come, and journey hither and thither, in rain and wind, in snow and hail, now drenched, now dry, now sweating, now shivering, ill-fed, ill-lodged, ill-warmed and ill-bedded. And naught harmeth him, because he is upheld by the hope that he hath of the care which his wife will take of him on his return, and of the ease, the joys and the pleasures which she will do him, or cause to be done to him in her presence; to be unshod before a good fire, to have his feet washed and fresh shoes and hose, to be given good food and drink, to be well served and well looked after, well bedded in white sheets and nightcaps, well covered with good furs, and assuaged with other joys and desports, privities, loves and secrets whereof I am silent. And the next day fresh shirts and garments.

Certes, fair sister, such services make a man love and desire to return to his home and to see his goodwife, and to be distant with others. Wherefore I counsel you to make such cheer to your husband at all his comings and stayings, and to persevere therein; and also be peaceable with him, and remember the rustic proverb, which saith that there be three things which drive the goodman from home: to wit a leaking roof, a smoky chimney and a scolding woman.[23] And therefore, fair sister, I beseech you that, to keep yourself in the love and good favour of your husband, you be unto him gentle, and amiable, and debonnair. Do unto him what the good simple women of our country say hath been done to their sons, when these have set their love elsewhere and their mothers cannot wean them therefrom. Sure it is that when fathers and mothers be dead and stepfathers and stepmothers that have stepsons rail at them and scold them and repulse them and take no thought for their sleeping, nor for their food and drink, their hose and their shirts, nor for their other needs or affairs, and these same children find elsewhere a good refuge and counsel from some other woman, that receiveth them unto herself and taketh thought to warm them by some poor gruel with her, to give them a bed and keep them clean and mend their hosen, breeches, shirts and other clothes, then do these same children follow her and desire to be with her and to sleep and be warmed between her breasts, and they be altogether estranged from their mothers and fathers, that before took no heed of them, and now be fain to get them back and have them again; but it may not be, for these children hold more dear the company of strangers that think and care for them, than of their kinsfolk that care no whit for them. Then they lament and cry and say that these same women have bewitched their children and that the lads be spellbound and cannot leave them and are never at ease save when they are with them. But, whatever they may say, it is no witchcraft, but it is for the sake of the love, the care, the intimacies, joys and pleasures that these women show unto them in all things and, on my soul, there is none other enchantment. For whoever giveth all its pleasure to a bear, a wolf, or a lion, that same bear, wolf, or lion will follow after him, and so the other beasts might say, could they but speak, that those thus tamed must be bewitched. And, on my soul, I trow that there is none other witchcraft than well doing, and no man can be better bewitched than by giving him what pleaseth him.

Wherefore, dear sister, I beseech you thus to bewitch and bewitch again your husband that shall be, and beware of roofless house and of smoky fire, and scold him not, but be unto him gentle and amiable and peaceable. Have a care that in winter he have a good fire and smokeless and let him rest well and be well covered between your breasts, and thus bewitch him. And in summer take heed that there be no fleas in your chamber, nor in your bed, the which you may do in six ways, as I have heard tell. For I have heard from several that if the room be strewn with alder leaves, the fleas will be caught thereon. *Item*, I have heard tell that if you have at night one or two trenchers [of bread] slimed with glue or turpentine and set about the room, with a lighted candle in the midst of each trencher, they will come and be stuck thereto. The other way that I have tried and is true: take a rough cloth and spread it about your room and over your bed, and all the fleas that shall hop thereon will be caught, so that you may carry them away with the cloth wheresoe'er you will. *Item*, sheepskins. *Item*, I have seen blanchets [of white wool] (p. 208, III¹) set on the straw and on the bed, and when the black fleas hopped thereon, they were the sooner found upon the white, and killed. But the best way is to guard oneself against those that be within the coverlets and the furs, and the stuff of the dresses wherewith one is covered. For know that I have tried this, and when the coverlets, furs or dresses, wherein there be fleas, be folded and shut tightly up, as in a chest tightly corded with straps, or in a bag well tied up and pressed, or otherwise put and pressed so that the aforesaid fleas be without light and air and kept imprisoned, then will they perish forthwith and die. *Item*, I have sometimes seen in divers chambers, that when one had gone to bed they were full of mosquitoes, which at the smoke of the breath came to sit on the faces of those that slept, and stung them so hard, that they were fain to get up and light a fire of hay, in order to make a smoke so that they had to fly away or die, and this may be done by day if they be suspected, and likewise he that hath a mosquito net may protect himself therewith.

And if you have a chamber or a passage where there is great resort of flies, take little sprigs of fern and tie them to threads like to tassels, and hang them up and all the flies will settle on them at eventide; then take down the tassels and throw them out. *Item*, shut up your chamber closely in the evening, but let there be a little opening in the wall towards the east, and as soon as the dawn breaketh, all the flies will go forth through this opening, and then let it be stopped up. *Item*, take a bowl of milk and a hare's gall and mix them one with another and then set two or three bowls thereof in places where the flies gather and all that taste thereof will die. *Item*, otherwise, have a linen rag tied at the bottom of a pot with an opening in the neck, and set that pot in the place where the flies gather and smear it within with honey, or apples, or pears; when it is full of flies, set a trencher over the mouth and then shake it. *Item*, otherwise, take raw red onions and bray them and pour the juice into a bowl and set it where the flies gather and all that taste thereof will die. *Item*, have whisks[24] wherewith to slay them by hand. *Item*, have little twigs covered with glue on a basin of water. *Item*, have your windows shut full tight with oiled or other cloth, or with parchment or something else, so tightly that no fly may enter, and let the flies that be within be slain with the whisk or otherwise as above, and no others will come in. *Item*, have a string hanging soaked in honey, and the flies will come and settle thereon and at eventide let them be taken in a bag. Finally meseemeth that flies will not stop in a room wherein there be no standing tables, forms, dressers or other things whereon they can settle and rest, for if they have naught but straight walls whereon to settle and cling, they will not settle, nor will they in a shady or damp place. Wherefore meseemeth that if the room be well watered and well closed and shut up, and if nought be left lying on the floor, no fly will settle there.

And thus shall you preserve and keep your husband from all discomforts and give him all the comforts whereof you can bethink you, and serve him and have him served in your house, and you shall look to him for outside things, for if he be good he will take even more pains and labour therein than you wish, and by doing what I have said, you will cause him ever to miss you and have his heart with you and your loving service and he will shun all other houses, all other women, all other services and households. All will be as naught to him save you, who think for him as is aforesaid, and who ought so to do, by the ensample that you see of horsemen riding abroad, for you see that as soon as they be come home to their house from a journey, they cause their horses to be given fresh litter up to their bellies; these horses be unharnessed and made comfortable, they be given honey and picked hay and sifted oats, and they be better looked after in their own stables on their return than anywhere else. And if the horses be thus made comfortable, so much the more ought the persons, to wit the lords, to be so at their own expense on their return.

Hounds returning from the woods and from the chase be littered
before their master and he maketh their fresh litter himself before
the fire; their feet be greased at the fire with soft grease, they be
given sops and be well eased, for pity of their labour; and likewise,
if women do thus unto their husbands, as men do unto their horses,
dogs, asses, mules, and other beasts, certes, all other houses, where
they have been served, will seem to them but dark prisons and
strange places, compared with their own, which will be then a paradise of rest unto them. And so on the road husbands will think of
their wives, and no trouble will be a burden to them for the hope
and love they will have of their wives, whom they will be fain to see
again with as great longing as poor hermits and penitents are fain to
see the face of Jesus Christ; and these husbands, that be thus looked
after, will never be fain to abide elsewhere nor in other company,
but they will withhold, withdraw and abstain therefrom; all the rest
will seem unto them but a bed of stones compared with their home;
but let it be unceasing, and with a good heart and without pretence.

But there be certain old hags, which be sly and play the wise
woman and feign great love by way of showing their heart's great
service, and naught else; and wot you, fair sister, that the husbands
be fools if they perceive it not; and when they perceive it, if the husband and wife be silent and pretend one with another, it is an ill
beginning and will lead to a worse end. And some women there be,
that in the beginning serve their husbands full well, and they trow
well that their husbands be then so amorous of them and so debonnair that, trow they, those husbands will scarce dare to be wroth
with them, if they do less, so they slacken and little by little they try
to show less respect and service and obedience, but – what is more
– they take upon themselves authority, command and lordship, at
first in a small thing, then in a larger, and a little more every day.
Thus they essay and advance and rise, as they think, and they trow
that their husbands, the which because they be debonnair or peradventure because they set a trap, say nought thereof, see it not because they suffer it thus. And certes, it is an ill thought and deed,
for when the husbands see that they cease their service, and mount
unto domination, and that they do it too much and that by suffering
ill good may come, then those women be all at once, by their
husband's rightful will, cast down even as Lucifer was, that was the
chief of the angels of paradise, and that our Lord so loved that He

allowed and suffered him to do his will, and he grew puffed up with overweening pride. He did and undertook so much that he went too far, and displeased our Lord that long had dissimulated and suffered him without a word, and then all at once He bethought him of all. So He cast him forth into the nethermost depths of hell, because that he continued not the service whereunto he was ordained and for the which he had in the beginning won the full great love of our Lord. Wherefore you should be obedient in the beginning and ever persevere therein, by this ensample.

THE EIGHTH ARTICLE

The eighth article of the first section saith that you should be silent or at least temperate in speech and wise to keep and to hide your husband's secrets. Upon which, fair sister, wot you that he that groweth hot in speech is not temperate of mind, and know that it is a sovereign virtue to know how to set a rein to the tongue and many dangers be come of too much talk, and especially if it be with arrogant or hot-headed folk or courtiers. And do you above all take heed that you hold not speech with such people, and if perchance they should speak to you, do you make an end and leave them wisely and courteously and it shall be a sovereign good sense in you, and know that to do thus is verily necessary; and though it befall that your heart be hot within you, yet must you sometimes master it, and no man is wise who cannot do so; for there is a rustic proverb that saith how that none is worthy to have rule or lordship over any other who cannot rule himself.

Wherefore in this matter and in all others, you should so be master of your heart and tongue that they may be subject to your head, and take good heed before whom and to whom you shall speak; and I pray and charge you that, whether in company or at table, you do take heed that you speak not too much, for from too many words ill must needs sometimes arise, and sometimes there be joking words spoken in desport and in jest, which be afterwards remembered to the great scorn and mockery of those that have spoken. Wherefore take heed before whom and concerning what you speak and in what manner, and do you say what you have to say simply and to the point, and in speaking take thought that nothing cometh from your lips that ought not to come forth and that a bridle be in your mouth to keep you from too much speech. And be a good keeper of secrets and take heed ever to guard the secrets of your husband that shall be; first his misdeeds, vices or sins, if you know of any, do you conceal and cover them, even without his knowledge, that he be not shamed; for hardly ever will you find any man that hath a friend who perceiveth his sin, but henceforth he will look upon his friend less lovingly than before and will be shamed before him and hold him in fear. And likewise I counsel you that you never reveal those things which your husband saith unto you in discussion, to any person however privy with you, and in this you shall conquer your woman's nature, which is such (so it is said) that they – to wit the bad and wicked ones – can hide nothing. Concerning which a philosopher called Macrobius tells in the book of *Scipio's Dream* how that there was in Rome a child, a young boy, hight Papirius, who went one day with his father that was a senator of Rome into the hall of the senators, in which room the Roman senators held counsel together. And there they made oath that none should be bold to reveal their counsel on pain of losing his head. And when they had held counsel and the child returned home, his mother asked him whence he came and he replied that he had been at the meeting of the Senate with his father. His mother asked him what had there passed, and he answered that he dared not say, on pain of death. Then had the mother full great longing to know, and she began first to flatter and then to threaten her son, that he should tell. And when the child perceived that he could not withstand his mother, he bade her first to promise that she should tell it to no man, and she promised him. Then he told her this lie, to wit that the senators had taken counsel together whether a husband should have two wives or a wife two husbands. When the mother heard this, she forbade him to tell it to any other, and then sped she to her gossips and told them the counsel in secret, and each told it to another, until at last they all knew the matter, each as her own secret.

So it befel in a short while that all the women of Rome came to the senate house, where the senators were assembled together, and cried oftentimes and full loudly that rather would they that a woman should have two husbands than a man two wives. The senators were all astonied and knew not what might be the meaning thereof, and looked at one another, asking whence it had arisen, until the child

Papirius told them the story. And when the senators heard it, they were full of wrath and they made him a senator and ruled that nevermore should a child be of their company.

Thus appeareth it by this ensample that the boy child that was young knew how to hide and be silent and evade, and the woman that was of meet age to have sense and discretion knew not how to be silent and conceal that which she had sworn and promised on her oath to hide, albeit a secret which touched the honour of her husband and her son.

And again the worst of it is that when women tell a thing one to the other, always the last addeth a little more and increaseth the falsehood and setteth somewhat of her own thereto, and the next still more. And concerning this there is a country tale of a good woman that was accustomed to rise early. One morning she rose not as early as was her wont, and her gossip feared lest she were ill, and went to her bedside and asked her ofttimes how she did. The good woman was shamed that she had sported long with her husband and knew not what to say save that she was very heavy and ill, and in such plight that she might not tell it. The gossip besought and prayed her for love of her to say, and swore, promised and bound herself never to reveal what she heard for anything in the world, to any living creature, father, mother, sister, brother, husband, confessor and any other. After the which promise and oath the good woman knew not what to say, and at last told her that she had laid an egg. The gossip was full astonied and feigned her to be in great agitation and swore more loudly than ever that not a word thereof should be revealed.

Shortly afterwards this gossip departed and on her way home she met another gossip who asked her whence she came and forthwith she answered that she had been to see a good woman that was ill and had laid two eggs, and prayed her to keep it secret and the other promised. The other met another and told her eight eggs, and so the number grew ever more and more. The good woman rose and learned that all through the town folk were saying that she had laid a whole basket full of eggs. Thus she perceived how that women be ill keepers of secrets, and what is worse make all things worse in the telling.[25]

Wherefore, fair sister, know you to keep your secrets from everyone, save only your husband, and you shall show good sense thereby, for think not that another person shall hide for you that which you yourself have not been able to keep; wherefore be secret and discreet to all save to your husband, for from him ought you to conceal naught, but tell all to him, and he likewise to you. And it is said *ad Ephesios v°: Sic viri debent diligere uxores scilicet ut corpora sua. Ideo ibidem dicitur: Viri diligite uxores vestras,* etc. *Unusquisque uxorem suam diligat sicut se ipsum,* that is to wit, a man should love his wife as his own body, and therefore you two, to wit man and wife, should be as one, and everywhere and in all things take counsel one with the other, and so do and should do all good and wise folk. And I would well that the husbands know they ought likewise to hide and cover the foolish deeds done by their wives, and gently guard against their foolish deeds to come. And thus was a good worthy man of Venice fain to do.

At Venice there was a wedded pair that had three children in marriage. Afterwards the woman lay upon her deathbed and confessed, among other things, that one of the children was not her husband's. The confessor at the end said to her that he would advise him what counsel to give her and would return to her. This confessor went then to the physician that tended her and asked the state of her illness and the physician said that she could not recover. Then came the confessor to her and told her how that he had considered her case and that he saw not how God might give her salvation, save if she sought pardon from her husband for the wrong which she had done him. She bade seek her husband, and caused the room to be cleared of all save her mother and her confessor, who set her and supported her upon her knees in the bed, and with hands clasped before her husband, she humbly besought his mercy for that she had sinned against the law of marriage, and had had one of her children by another than he; and she would have said more, but her husband cried out and said, 'Ho! ho! ho! say no more!' Whereupon he kissed her and pardoned her, saying, 'Never say you more, nor tell you to me nor to any other which of your children it is, for I would love them all with so equal a love that neither during your life, nor after your death shall you be blamed, for by your blame should I be shamed and your children and through them others, to wit our parents, should receive foul and perpetual reproach. Wherefore be silent: I wish to know no more, so that it shall never be said of me that I am doing ill by the other two. Whichever he be, I give him in

free gift henceforward during my life, all that would come to him by
the law of succession.'

Fair sister, thus you see how the wise man softened his heart to
save his wife's honour, which touched the honour of himself and his
children, and so may you learn what wise men and wise women
ought to do for each other to save their honour. And concerning this
another ensample may be drawn.

There was once a great and wise man that his wife left to go with
another young man to Avignon, and when this young man was
aweary of her he left her, as such young men are oftentimes wont to
do. She was poor and without comfort and she became a common
woman, because she had not wherewithal to live. Then it came to the
knowledge of her husband and he was in full great distress and set
thereto this remedy. He mounted his wife's two brethren upon horse-
back and gave them money and bade them go seek their sister that
was even as a common woman in Avignon, and bade them clothe her
in sackcloth, and hang her with cockle shells after the custom of
pilgrims coming from St James [of Compostella], and mount her
suitably and when she was a day's journey from Paris, send her to
him. They set forth at once and the wise man spread abroad and told
everyone how that he was full glad of heart because his wife was
returning in good state, gramercy, from the place where he had sent
her, and when they asked him whither he had sent her, he answered
that he had lately sent her to St James in Galicia, to make a pilgrimage on his behalf, that his father had laid upon him on his deathbed.
All were full astonied at his words, seeing what men had hitherto
said of her. When his wife was come to within a day's journey of
Paris, he caused his house to be adorned with branches and green
herbs and called together his friends to ride and meet his wife. He
rode at their head to her, and they kissed, and both fell to weeping,
and had great joy of each other. He caused his wife to be warned
that she should speak gaily and proudly and boldly to all and to himself and before the household, and that when she came to Paris she
should visit all her neighbours one after another and show them all
a joyful countenance. And so the good man came back and kept his
wife's honour.

And in God's name, if a man keep his wife's honour and a wife
blame her husband or suffer him to be blamed, either covertly or
openly, she herself hath blame thereby and with reason; for either

he is wrongly blamed or he is rightly blamed; if he be wrongly blamed, then should she fiercely avenge him; if he be rightly blamed, then ought she graciously to cover and sweetly to defend him, for certain it is that if the blame remain and be not wiped out, the worse her husband is the worse shall be her own report and she shall share the blame because she is married to one so wicked. For even as he that playeth at chess holdeth long time his piece in his hand before he setteth it down, in order that he may advise him that he may set it in a safe place, even so ought a wife to hold her ready to consider and choose and set herself in a good place. And if she doth not so, it shall be a reproach unto her and she must share her husband's blame; and if he be blemished in aught, she should cover and conceal it with all her might. And it behoveth the husband to do as much for his wife, as is said above and shall be said hereafter.

I knew a very famous advocate in Parliament, the which advocate had a daughter that he had got upon a poor woman, who put her out to nurse; and for want of payment, or of visits, or of the courtesies which men know not how to do to nurses in such cases, there was such talk thereof that the advocate's wife heard it, and she heard likewise that I was making the payments for this nurture, for to save the honour of her lord, to whom I was and am much beholden, may God keep him! Wherefore the wife of this same advocate came to me and said that I did great sin to allow her lord to be slandered and ill-famed, and that she was in better position to undertake the difficulty of this nurture than I, and bade me lead her to the place where the child was. And she put the child into the care of a sewing-woman, and caused her to be taught her trade, and then married her, and never did her husband know it by one sign of ill will, or one angry or reproachful word. And thus do good wives bear them to their husbands and good husbands to their wives when they are in error.

THE NINTH ARTICLE

The ninth article showeth how that you shall be wise when your husband beareth him foolishly, as young and simple folk often do, and that you should gently and wisely draw him away from his follies. First, if he is in mind to be wroth and deal ill with you, take heed that by good patience and gentle words you slay his proud cruelty,

and if thus you can do, you will so have vanquished him that he will
rather be dead than do you ill, and he will remember him so often
hereafter of your goodness, howbeit he saith no word thereof to you,
that you shall have him wholly drawn unto you. And if you cannot
move him that he turn his wrath from you, take heed that you make
not plaint thereof to your friends or to others, so that he may perceive it, for he will think the less of you and will remember it another
time; but go you into your chamber and weep gently and softly in a
low voice, and make your plaint to God; and thus do all wise ladies.
And if perchance he be prone to wrath against another person less
near unto him, do you wisely restrain him . . . [26]

Wherefore I say unto you that it behoveth good ladies, subtly,
cautiously and gently, to counsel and restrain their husbands from
the follies and silly dealings whereunto they see them drawn and
tempted, and in no wise to think to turn them aside by lording over
them, nor by loud talk, by crying to their neighbours or in the street,
by blaming them, by making plaint to their friends and parents, nor
by other masterful means. For all this bringeth nought but irritation
and the making of bad worse, for the heart of man findeth it hard to
be corrected by the domination and lordship of a woman, and know
that there is no man so poor nor of so small value that would not be
lord and master when he is wed.

Again will I not be silent concerning an ensample of how to reclaim a husband by kindness, the which ensample I once heard my
late father — God rest his soul — tell; who said that there was a
citizen's wife, dwelling at Paris, hight Dame Jehanne la Quentine,
that was wife to Thomas Quentin. She knew that the aforesaid
Thomas her husband foolishly and lightly desported himself, and
went with and sometimes lay with a poor girl that was a spinner of
wool at the wheel, and for a long time, without seeming to be aware
of it or saying a single word, the said Dame Jehanne bore with it and
suffered it very patiently; and at last she sought to find where this
poor girl lived and sought so that she found out. And she came to
the house and found the poor girl, who had no provisions of any kind,
neither wood, nor tallow, nor candle, nor oil, nor coal, nor anything,
save only a bed and a coverlet, her spinning-wheel and full little
furniture beside. Then she spoke to her saying, 'My dear, I am
bound to keep my husband from blame, and because I know that he
takes pleasure in you and loves you and that he comes here, I pray

you that you speak of him as little as you can in company, to spare
him from blame and likewise me and our children, and that for your
part you hide it; and I swear to you that you and he shall be well
hidden for my part, for since it haps that he loves you, it is my intent
to love you and help you and aid you in all that you have to do, and
you shall perceive it well; but I pray you with all my heart that his
sin be not revealed nor spread abroad. And because I know that he
is of good birth and has been tenderly nurtured, well fed, well
warmed, well bedded and well covered according to my power, and
I see that you have little wherewith to do him ease, rather would I
that you and I together should care for him in health, than that I
alone should care for him in sickness. So I pray you that you love
and keep and serve him so that by you he may be restrained and
kept from leading a light life elsewhere in divers dangers; and without his knowledge I will send you a great pail that you may often
wash his feet, and store of wood to warm him, a fair bed of down,
sheets and coverlets according to his estate, nightcaps, pillows,
and clean hose and linen; and when I shall send you clean ones,
so shall you send me those that be soiled, and he shall know naught
of all that is between you and me, lest he be shamed; for God's
sake bear you so wisely and secretly towards him that he learn not
our secret.' Thus it was promised and sworn and Jehanne la Quentine
departed and carefully sent all things as she had promised.

When Thomas came at eventide to the young girl's house, his
feet were washed and he was laid in a fair bed of down, with great
sheets spread and hanging on each side, very well covered and better
than had been his wont, and on the morrow he had white linen, clean
hose and fair new slippers. Greatly did he marvel at this new thing
and was full of thought and went to hear mass as he had been wont
and returned to the girl and charged her that these things were ill
gotten, and very sharply accused her of evil, so that she in self defence should tell him whence they were come. For well he knew that
he had left her poor two or three days before, and that she could not
have grown so rich in so short a time. When she saw herself thus
accused, and that she must answer in order to defend herself, she
knew enough of this Thomas's conscience to know that he would
believe what she told him; so she lied not but told him the truth
concerning all that is aforesaid.

Then went the said Thomas all shamed to his house, more full of

thought than ever, but no word said he to the said Jehanne his wife,
nor she to him, but she served him very joyously and he and his wife
slept together very sweetly that night, without saying a word to each
other about it. The next day the said Thomas of his own will went
to hear mass and confessed his sins, and soon afterwards returned to
the girl and gave her what she had of his, and vowed continence and
to abstain from all women save only his wife as long as he lived. And
thus did his wife reclaim him by subtlety and very humbly and
cordially loved him thereafter. And thus it behoveth good ladies to
counsel and reclaim their husbands, not by mastery and pride, but
by humility; and bad women know this not nor can their hearts
endure it, therefore their affairs go often worse than before. And
albeit many other ensamples thereof could be set down, the which
would be long to write, nathless this should suffice you concerning
this article, for you have no cause to take heed for this last matter,
and you know well how to avoid the danger.[27]

Second Section

THE FIRST ARTICLE

THE WHICH TELLETH OF THE CARE OF THE HOUSEHOLD

Fair sister, know you that I am in great distress whether to end here my book, or more thereof to set down, for much I fear lest I should weary you. For it might be that I should charge you with so much that you would have cause to hold me unreasonable and that my counsel should lay upon you so many things and so grievous that you would despair of the too great burden, thinking to shame and anger me, because you could neither bear nor perform everything. Wherefore I would here bethink me and consider that I lay not too much upon you and that I counsel you to take upon you only those things which be very necessary and honourable, and as few of these as may be, so that you be in those necessary things the better grounded and well conducted and therefore the more honoured in your words and deeds. For I know that you can do no more than other women, and for this reason I would first consider how much I have laid upon you, and whether more is necessary and whether I must burden you with more and with how much. And if there be more than you can do, I am in mind to give you help; and thus I gather together what I have said to begin with.

First, I have admonished you to praise God at your waking and your rising, and to betake yourself to church, there to hear mass and confess you and put yourself in the love and grace of God. By my soul, it is needful for you, and it is a thing which none may do for you, save only yourself alone. And thereafter, I have counselled you to be continent and chaste, to love your husband, obey him, bethink you that you keep his secrets, and know how to restrain him if he be foolish or desire to do foolish things; and certes this too is needful and very honourable for you, and belongeth to you alone and is not too great a burden; you may well perform it by the help of the aforesaid doctrine, which will much advantage you; for other women never had the like.

Certain it is, to boot, that after the matters aforesaid you must bethink you for yourself, your children and your household, but in these three things you may well have help. So it is meet that I tell you how you may comport yourself therein, what help and what folk you shall take and how you shall set them to work, for in these affairs I would that you should have only the ordering thereof, and the supervision and the care of setting others to perform them at your husband's cost.

Thus you may well see, dear sister, that you ought not to complain and that you are not overburdened, for that you are charged only with that which none other but you can do, a thing in sooth which should be full pleasant to you, as to serve God and take thought for the person of your husband, and that is the sum of all.[1]

THE SECOND ARTICLE

THE WHICH ARTICLE TELLETH OF THE ART OF GARDENING

First, be it noted that whatsoever you sow, plant or graft, you should sow, plant or graft in damp weather and at eve or early morn, before the heat of the sun, and in the wane of the moon, and you should water the stem and the earth and not the leaves.

Item, you should not water in the heat of the sun, but at eve or in the morning; cut not cabbage, parsley, nor other such green things which shoot again, for the heat of the sun will harden and burn the cut, and so the plant will never sprout again at the place of the cut.

Nota that in rainy weather it is good to plant but not to sow, for the seed sticketh to the rake.

From the season of All Saints' [1 November] we have beans, but that they may not be frostbitten, do you plant them towards Christmas and in January and February and at the beginning of March; and plant them thus at divers times, so that if some be taken by the frost others be not. And when they come up out of the ground, so soon as the tops thereof show, you should rake them and break the first shoot; and as soon as they have six leaves you should spread earth over them. And of them all, the first come be the most delicate and they must be eaten the day they are shelled, or else they become black and bitter.

Nota that if you would keep violets and marjoram in winter against the cold, you must not move them of a sudden from cold to heat, nor from damp to cold, for he that keepeth them long time through the winter in a damp cellar and suddenly setteth them in a dry place, loseth them; *et sic de contrariis similibus*.

In winter you should cut off the dead branches of the sage plants. Again let sage, lavender, dittany, mint, clary, be planted in January and February, up to May. Let parsnips be sown broadcast. Let sorrel be sown at the wane of the moon and up to March or later.

Nota that the winter weather of December and January kills the porray or greens,[2] to wit all that be above ground, but in February the roots put forth fresh and tender green again, to wit as soon as the frost endeth, and a fortnight later cometh spinach.

February. Savory and marjoram be as it were of the same savour to eat, and they be sown at the wane and stay only eight days in the earth. *Item*, savory lasteth only until St John's Day [24 June]. *Item*, in the wane you should plant trees and vines and sow white and headed cabbage. *Nota* that layers[3] put out roots from the moment that they be planted.

Spinach comes in February and has a long crenellated leaf like an oak leaf, and grows in tufts like greens and you must blanch them and cook them well afterwards. Beets come later.

Nota that it is good to plant raspberry-bushes and also raspberries.

March. At the wane you should graft; plant house-leek from March to St John's Day. Violets and gillyflowers sown in March or planted on St Remy's Day [28 October]. *Item*, both of these, when the frosts draw near, you should replant in pots, at a season when the moon waneth, in order to set them under cover and keep them from the cold in a cellar, and by day set them in the air or in the sun and water them at such time that the water may be drunken up and the earth dry before you set them under cover, for never should you put them away wet in the evening. Plant beans and break the first shoot by raking them, as is aforesaid. *Nota* that parsley sown on the Eve of Lady Day in March [24 March] is above ground in nine days.

Plant fennel and marjoram at the wane in March or April; and *nota* that marjoram delighteth in a richer soil than violets, and if it be too much in the shade it groweth yellow. *Item*, when it has well taken hold, then must you take it up in tufts and replant it separately in pots. *Item*, branches cut off, set in the earth and watered, put forth roots and grow. *Item,* land manured with cow and sheep dung is better than with horse dung.

March violets and Armenian violets[4] desire neither cover nor shelter; and *nota* that the Armenian violet doth not flower until the second year, but gardeners who have had it in the ground for a year, sell it and replant it elsewhere, and then it flowereth.

Sorrel and basil be sown in January and February and as late as March at the wane of the moon, and if you would transplant sorrel sown the year before, you must transplant it with all the earth which is round its roots. *Item,* there is an art in cooking it, for you should always gather the big leaves and leave the little leaves that be beneath them to grow; and if perchance all have been gathered, it is best to cut the stem down to the ground, and fresh sorrel will grow again.

Sow parsley, weed it and remove the stones, and that which is sown in August is the best, for it doth not grow high and keepeth its goodness all the year long.

Lettuces should be sown, and *nota* that they do not linger in the ground, but come up very thickly, wherefore you must root them up here and there, to give space to the rest that they crowd not. And *nota* that the seed of French lettuce is black, and the seed of Avignon lettuce is whiter, and Monseigneur de La Rivière[5] caused it to be introduced, and the lettuces be better and somewhat tenderer than those of France; and the seed is gathered from one head after the other, as each head puts out its branch thereof.

Nota that lettuces be not planted, and likewise when you would have them to eat, you must pull them up root and all.

Pumpkins. The pips are the seed and they must be soaked for two days and then sown; and you must let them grow without moistening them until they show above ground, and then moisten the foot only and the earth, without wetting the leaves, and in April water them gently and transplant them from one place to another, about four inches or half a foot in the earth, each pumpkin half a foot away from the next, and keep the stem ever moist, by hanging a pot with a hole therein on a stick, and in the pot a straw and some water, etc., or a strip of new cloth.[6]

Sow beets in May and when they be ready for eating, let them be cut down close to the root, for they always shoot forth and grow again and become porray.

Borage and orach as above.

White cabbage and headed cabbage be the same;[7] and they be sown in the wane of March, and when they have five leaves, then must they be pulled up gently and planted half a foot each from each, and they must be set in earth up to the eye and their roots watered; and they be eaten in June and July.

Cabbage hearts be sown in March and transplanted in May. Roman cabbages be of the same nature as these and of the same sort of seed, for in both the seed groweth upon the stem, and from the seed that cometh from the midmost stalk and is topmost groweth the heart of cabbage and from the seed that cometh from below grow the Roman cabbages. Lenten sprouts be the second growth of the cabbage and they last until March and those March sprouts be of stronger taste in eating, wherefore should they be longer boiled, and at this time the stalks must be pulled up from the ground. *Nota* that cabbages should be planted in July when it raineth.

Nota that ants abound in a garden and if you cast sawdust of oaken planks upon their heap, they will die or depart at the first rain that falleth, for the sawdust retaineth the moisture.

Nota that in April and May each month you shall sow the porray or greens for eating in June and July. Summer greens must be cut down and their roots left in the ground and after winter the roots put forth green again and it is meet to cover them with earth and rake the earth round them and there sow the new ones which be to come and gather the green put forth by the old. *Nota* that it is meet to sow porray from April to St Mary Magdalen's Day [22 July] and the Lenten greens be sown in July and up to St Mary Magdalen's Day and no later and they be called beets. *Item*, spinach. *Item*, the aforesaid beets, when they show above the ground, must be transplanted in rows. *Item*, in April and May it behoves to plant out white cabbages and cabbage hearts that were sown in February and March. In May come new beans, turnips and radishes.

Nota that you must sow parsley on St John's Eve in June [23 June] and also on the eve of mid-August.

August and mid-August. Sow hyssop. Cabbages for Eastertide be sown at the wane of the moon and parsley too, for it groweth not high.

Nota that porray or greens that be in the ground put forth new greens five or six times, like unto parsley, and you can cut them above the stump up to mid-September and thereafter cut them not, for the stump will decay, but strip off the outer leaves with your hands and not those that be midmost.

At this season it is meet to cut down all greens that be run to seed, for the seed cannot ripen by reason of the coldness of the weather, and if the seed be cut and cast away the stump beareth new greens. *Item*, at this time it behoveth not to cut parsley, but to pluck it leaf by leaf.

After the Nativity of Our Lady in September [? *la Septembresse*, 8 September] let peony, dragonwort [*serpentine*], lily bulbs, rose trees and currant bushes be planted.

October. Peas, beans, a finger deep in earth and four inches apart and let them be the largest beans possible, for when they be new they look larger than the little ones and you should plant but a few, and at each wane that followeth a few, so that if some be shrivelled in the frost, others be not.

If you would sow pierced peas, sow them in a dry fine weather and not in rain, for if the rain water should enter within the opening of the pea, it would rot and split in half and would not germinate.

Up to All Saints' cabbages may always be transplanted and when they be too much eaten by caterpillars, so that no leaf remaineth save only the veins, if they be transplanted they all bear sprouts; and it is meet to strip off the lower leaves and replant them up to the topmost eye. The stumps from which all the leaves have been stripped should not be transplanted, but should be left in the earth, for they will bear sprouts.

Nota, that if you plant in summer in dry weather, you should water the holes, but not so in damp weather.

Nota, that if the caterpillars eat your cabbages, spread cinders beneath the cabbages when it rains and the caterpillars will die. *Item*, you may look under the leaves of the cabbages and there you shall find a great host of white grubs and know that it is from these that the caterpillars be born, wherefore you should cut off the leaves whereon is this seed and cast them afar off.

Let leeks be sown in season and then transplanted in October and November.

If you would have grapes without pips, take at the waxing of the moon in the time when vines be planted, to wit in February, a vine plant with its root, and slit the stock right through the midst unto the root, and draw out the pith from each side. Then prune the stock and bind it all the length thereof with black thread, then plant the stock and manure it with good manure, and fill up the hole with earth above the join of the stock.[8]

If you would graft a cherry or a plum upon a vine stock, prune the vine, then in March cut it four fingers' breadth from the end and draw out the pith from each side, and there make place for the kernel of a cherry stone, and put it and enclose it within the cut, and bind with thread the stock joined as is aforesaid.

If you would graft a vine stock upon a cherry tree, do you prune the vine stock, which shall be planted a long time and rooted near to the cherry, and in March, round about Lady Day [25 March] pierce your cherry tree with a wimble of the size of the said stock, and push the aforesaid stock into the hole in the aforesaid cherry, so that it enters for a foot's length at least, then stop up the hole on both sides of the cherry, to wit with clay and moss, and bind it round with cloths so that no rain may touch the opening. *Item*, the bark should be stripped off the vine stock that is within the trunk of the cherry and it should be peeled down to the green, for if this be done thus and the bark be peeled and cast away, the pith of the stock will join the pith of the cherry and they will become one, which would be prevented by the bark of the stock if it remained. Having done this, do you leave them together for two years, and afterwards cut the stock behind and below the juncture with the cherry.

Item, you can graft ten or twelve trees upon the trunk or stump of an oak; to wit in the month of March, round about Lady Day, furnish yourself with as many grafts and divers fruits as you be minded to have for grafting, and cause the oak or tree on which you would make your graft to be sawn asunder; and having sharpened your grafts on one side only in the manner of a blind corner, even thus ◣, in such a way that the bark of the aforesaid graft is whole on the one side, without being stripped or cut, then slip your grafts between the bark of the oak and the wood, with the pith of the graft towards the wood or pith of the oak. Then stop it up and cover it with clay and moss and cloths, that neither rain, snow nor frost may harm it.

If you would keep roses in winter, take from the rose tree little buds that be not full blown and leave the stems thereof long, and set them within a little wooden cask like unto a compost cask, without water. Cause the cask to be well closed and so tightly bound up that

naught may come in or out thereof, and at the two ends of the aforesaid cask tie two great and heavy stones and set the aforesaid cask in
a running stream.

Rosemary. Gardeners say that the seed of rosemary groweth
never in French soil, but whosoever shall pluck little branches of
rosemary and shall strip them from the top downwards and take
them by the ends and plant them, he shall see them grow again; and
if you would send them far away, you must wrap the aforesaid
branches in waxed cloth and sew them up and then smear the parcel
outside with honey, and then powder with wheaten flour, and you
may send them wheresoever you will.

I have heard Monseigneur de Berry say that in Auvergne the
cherries be larger than in France, because they layer their cherry
trees.

THE THIRD ARTICLE

THE WHICH TELLETH OF THE CHOICE OF VARLETS, SERVANTS AND CHAMBERMAIDS, ETC.

Concerning which matter, dear sister, if haply you should desire to
become a good housewife, or to help thereto some lady among your
friends, know you that serving folk be of three kinds. Some there be
that be hired as workmen for a fixed time, to perform some short
piece of work, as porters who carry burdens on their backs, wheel-
barrow men, packers and the like; or for one day or two, a week or
a short season, to perform some necessary, or difficult, or laborious
work, as reapers, mowers, threshers, vintagers, basket bearers, wine
pressers, coopers and the like. Others [be hired] for a time and for
a special craft, as dressmakers, furriers, bakers, butchers, shoemakers and the like, who work by the piece upon a particular task.
And others be taken to be domestic servants, serving by the year and
dwelling in the house. And of all these none there is that doth not
full readily seek work and a master.

As touching the first, they be necessary for the unloading and
carrying of burdens and the doing of heavy work; and these be commonly tiresome, rough and prone to answer back, arrogant, haughty
(save on pay day), and ready to break into insults and reproaches if
you do not pay them what they ask when the work is done. So I pray

you, dear sister, that when it behoveth you to order this matter, you
bid Master Jehan the Dispenser[9] or other of your folk to seek out,
choose and take, or cause to be sought out, chosen and taken, the
peaceable ones; and always bargain with them before they set hand
to the work, that there may be no dispute afterwards, nathless most
often they wish not to bargain, but desire to fall upon the task without bargain made, and they say gently, 'Milord, it is naught – there
is no need; you will pay me well, and I shall be content with what
you think fit.' And if Master Jehan take them thus, when the work
is finished they will say, 'Sir, there was more to do than I thought;
there was this and that to do, and here and there to go'; and they will
not take what is given them and will break out into shouting and foul
words. So bid Master Jehan not to set them to work, nor suffer them
to be set to work, without first making terms with them, for those
that desire to earn be your subjects before the work is begun, and for
the need that they have to earn they fear lest another should take it
before them and fear to lose the work and the wage thereof to
another. Wherefore they bear themselves more reasonably. And if
perchance Master Jehan were to believe in them and put too great
faith in their fair words, and it befel therefore that he suffered them
to begin work without bargaining, they know well that after they
have set their hand to it, none other for shame will meddle with it, and
so you will be in their power afterwards and they will ask more;
and if then they be not paid according to their will, they will cry and
shout foul and outrageous blame upon you; and they have no shame
and spread abroad evil report concerning you, which is worst of all.
Wherefore it is better to bargain with them plainly and openly before
the work, to avoid all argument. And certes, this do I beg of you, that
if need be you cause enquiry to be made, how those whom you would
set to work have borne them towards others, and also that you
have naught to do with folk who answer back and be arrogant, proud
and scornful, or give foul answers, however great profit or advantage
it seemeth to be and however cheaply they be minded to come; but
do you graciously and quietly send them away from you and from
your work, for if once they begin thereon, you shall not escape without slander and wrangling. Wherefore cause your people to engage
servants and workmen that be peaceful and debonnair, and pay them
more, for all of peace and rest lieth in having to deal with worthy
servants; for which reason there is a saying, 'he that hath to do with

good servants, he hath peace'; and likewise one might well say that he that hath to do with grumblers layeth up sorrow for himself.

Item, concerning others, such as vintagers, threshers, labourers and the like, or such as tailors, clothmakers, shoemakers, bakers, farriers, tallow-candlemakers, spicers, blacksmiths, wheelwrights, and others like unto them, dear sister, I counsel and pray you ever to bear in mind that you bid your people to have quiet folk to work for them and to make bargain beforehand and to reckon and make payment often, without long credit by tally or on paper. Nathless better it is to keep tally and paper than to keep all things in the memory, for creditors think ever that the sum is more and debtors that it is less, and thereby is born wrangling, hatred and foul reproach; and cause your good creditors to be paid readily and often that which is owing to them and bear yourself lovingly towards them, that they change not towards you; for it is not always possible to find others that be peaceable folk.

Item, as to chambermaids and house varlets, who are called domestics, know, dear sister, that in order that they may obey you better and fear the more to anger you, I leave you the rule and authority to have them chosen by Dame Agnes the Béguine,[10] or whichever other of your women you please, to receive them into our service, to hire them at your pleasure, to pay and keep them in our service as you please, and to dismiss them when you will. Nathless you should privily speak with me about it and act according to my advice, because you are too young and might be deceived by your own people. And know that of those chambermaids that be out of a place, many there be who offer themselves and clamour and seek urgently for masters and mistresses; and of these take none until you first know where their last place was, and send some of your people to get their character, to wit whether they chattered or drank too much, how long they were in the place, what work they have been wont to do and know how to do, whether they have homes or friends in the town, from what manner of folk and what part of the country they come, how long they were there and why they left; and by their work in the past you shall find out what hope or expectation you may have of their work in the future. And know that oftentimes such women from distant parts of the country have been blamed for some vice in their own district and this it is that bringeth them into service at a distance. For if they were without fault they would be mistresses

and not servants; and of men I say the same. And if you find from
the report of her master and mistress that a girl is what you need,
find out from her and cause Master Jehan to register in his account
book in her presence, on that same day whereon you engage her, her
name and the names of her father and mother and some of her kinsfolk, and the place where they live and her birthplace and her references. For servants will fear the more to do wrong if they know that
you are recording these things, and that if they leave you without
permission, or be guilty of any offence, you will write and complain
to the justice of their country and to their friends. And notwithstanding bear in mind the saying of the philosopher called Bertram
the Old, who saith that if you engage a maid (or man) of high and
proud answers, you shall know that when she leaveth she will miscall
you if she can; and if, on the contrary, she be flattering and full of
blandishments, trust her not, for she seeketh in some other way to
trick you; but if she blushes and is silent and shamefast when you
correct her, love her as your daughter.

Next wot you well, dear sister, that after your husband, you
should be mistress of the house, the giver of orders, visitor, ruler and
sovereign administrator, and it is for you to keep your maidservants
in subjection and obedience to you, teaching, correcting and chastis-
ing them; wherefore forbid them all excess and gluttony of life.

Also forbid them to quarrel with each other or with your neighbours; forbid them to speak ill of others, save only to you and in
secret, and in so far only as the misdeed concerneth your profit, and
to save harm from befalling you and not otherwise; forbid them to
lie, to play at forbidden games, to swear foully and to utter words
that smell of villainy, unseemly words and ribald, like to certain evil
or ill-bred persons, who curse upon 'bloody bad fevers, the bloody
bad week, the bloody bad day'.[11] It seemeth that they know well
what is a bloody day and a bloody week, but that know they not,
nor should they know what a bloody thing is, for honest women
know it not, for it is abominable to them to see the blood but of a
lamb or a pigeon, if it be slain before them. And certes, women
should utter no foulness . . . *Item*, there be foul-mouthed women,
who say sometimes of a woman that she is a whore or light, and so
saying it seemeth that they know well what is a whore or a light
woman, and honest women know naught of this; wherefore forbid
such language to them, for they know not what they say. Forbid

revenge to them and teach them in all patience by the ensample of Melibeus, of whom I have told you, and for you yourself, dear sister, be you such in all that you do, that in you they may find an ensample of all goodness.

Now it behoveth me to speak of setting your folk and your servants to work at times meet for work and of giving them rest likewise at due times. Concerning the which matter, dear sister, know that you and Dame Agnes the Béguine (who is with you to teach you wise and ripe behaviour and to serve and lesson you, and to whom in particular I give the charge of this matter) must devise and order and lay one duty upon one and another upon the other, according to the work which has to be done and the fitness of your folk to one sort of labour or another. And if you bid them to do something now and these your servants answer, 'There is plenty of time,' 'It shall be done soon,' or 'It shall be done early tomorrow morn,' consider it to be forgot; all must be done again, it goes for naught. And likewise concerning that which you order all in general to do, know that each waiteth for the other to do it, and it is as before.

So be you warned, and bid Dame Agnes the Béguine see that which you desire to be done at once begun before her eyes; and first, let her bid the chambermaids very early to sweep out and clean the entrances to your house, to wit the hall and other places whereby people enter and stay to speak in the house, and let them dust and shake out the covers and cushions which be on the benches; and afterwards let the other rooms be likewise cleaned and tidied for the day, and so daily, as beseemeth our estate.

Item, through the said Dame Agnes do you chiefly and carefully and diligently take thought for your chamber animals, as little dogs and birds; and also do you and the Béguine take thought for other domestic birds, for they cannot speak, and therefore must you speak and think for them, if you have any.

And also I bid Dame Agnes the Béguine, when you are in the country, to order those whose business it is to take thought for the other beasts; as Robin the shepherd, to look to his sheep, ewes and lambs and Josson the oxherd to his oxen and bulls, Arnould the cowherd and Jehanneton the dairymaid to take thought for the kine, the heifers and the calves, the sows, pigs and piglings, Eudeline the farmer's wife to look to the geese, goslings, cocks, hens, chickens, doves and pigeons, and the carter or the farmer to take thought for our horses, mares and the like. And the said Béguine and you your-self, likewise, ought to show your folk that you know about it all and care about it, for so will they be the more diligent. And, if you remember, cause your people to remember to feed these beasts and birds, and Dame Agnes ought to lay this work upon those men and women that be best suited thereto. And hereupon be it observed that it behoves you to cause Dame Agnes the Béguine to inform you of the tale of your sheep, ewes and lambs, and to have them con-stantly visited and to make enquiry concerning their increase and decrease and how or by whom they be cared for, and she should report it to you, and between the two of you you should cause it to be written down.

And if you be in a part where there be wolves, I will teach Master Jehan, the steward of your household, or your shepherds and ser-vants how to kill them without striking a blow, according to the recipe which followeth. RECIPE FOR A POWDER TO KILL WOLVES AND FOXES. [Let him] take the root of black hellebore (it is the hellebore that hath a white flower) and dry the root thoroughly and not in the sun, and clean the earth therefrom; and then make it into powder in a mortar and with this powder mix a fifth part of glass well ground and a fourth part of lily leaf, and let it all be mixed and pounded together, so that it can be passed through a sieve. *Item*, [let him] take honey and fresh fat in equal part and mix them with the afore-said powder, and make it into a hard and stiff paste, rolling it into round balls of the size of a hen's egg, and cover the aforesaid balls with fresh fat and lay them upon stones and shards, in the places where he knoweth that wolves and foxes will come. And if he wish to use an old dead beast as a decoy, he may do so two or three days beforehand. *Item*, he may also scatter the powder upon the carrion, without making it into balls.

Thus do you and the Béguine set some of your folk to do the work that is proper to them, and also bid Master Jehan the Dis-penser send or cause to be sent others to visit your barns, to move and dry your grain and your other stores; and if your household beareth word that the rats be harming your corn, bacon, cheese and other provisions, tell Master Jehan that he may destroy them in six ways: First, by having good array of cats, second, by ratcatchers and mousecatchers, third, by traps made of little planks upon sticks, which good servants make, fourth, by making cakes of paste and toasted cheese and powdered aconite and setting these near to their holes, where they have naught to drink, fifth, if you cannot keep them from finding water to drink, it is meet to cut up little pieces of sponge, and then if they swallow these and drink afterwards, they will swell up and die, sixth, take an ounce of aconite, two ounces of fine arsenic, a quarter of pig's fat, a pound of fine wheaten meal and four eggs, and out of these make bread and cook it in the oven and cut it into strips and nail them down with a nail.

Now let me return to my subject of how you shall set your folk to work, you and the Béguine, at fit times and shall cause your women to air and go over your sheets, coverlets, dresses and furs, fur cover-lets and other things of the sort. Concerning which know you and tell you your women, that in order to preserve your fur coverlets and your stuffs, it is meet often to air them, in order to prevent the dam-age which moths may do unto them; and because such vermin gather when the cold weather of autumn and winter groweth milder and be born in the summer, at such time it behoves you to set out furs and stuffs in the sun in fair and dry weather; and if there come a dark and damp mist and clingeth to your dresses and you fold them in such condition, that mist folded and wrapped up in your dresses will shelter and breed worse vermin than before. Wherefore choose a fine dry day and as soon as you see heavier weather coming, before that it reacheth you cause your dresses to be hung up under cover and shaken to get rid of most of the dust, then cleaned by beat-ing them with dry rods. And the Béguine knoweth well that if there be any spot of oil or other grease, this is the remedy: Take wine and heat it until it is warm and set the stain to soak therein for two days, and then wring out the stuff in which the stain is, without squeezing it too hard, and if the stain be not gone, let Dame Agnes the Béguine have more wine prepared and mix ox-gall therewith and do as before. Or you shall do this: cause fuller's earth to be taken and soaked in lye and then put upon the stain and allow it to dry and then rub it; if the earth cometh not off easily, cause it to be moistened with lye and allow it to dry again and rub until it goeth; or if you have no fuller's earth, set ashes to soak in lye and when they be well moistened lay them upon the stain; or take very clean feathers of chickens and steep them in very hot water, in order that any grease upon them may remain therein, and rinse them again in clean water, full hot: rub well and all stains will go.

If a blue robe be in any way stained or faded, take a sponge and soak it in clean and clear lye, and then squeeze it out and wipe the dress therewith, rubbing the stain, and the colour will return. And if on stuffs of any other colours there be faded places, cause full clean lye, which hath not been used upon drapery, to be taken and mixed with ashes upon the stain and allow it to dry, and then cause it to be rubbed and the original colour will return.

To take stains out of dresses of silk, satin, camlet, damask or other such, steep and wash the stain in verjuice and the stain will depart, and even though the dress be faded, yet will its colour return (this do I not believe).

Verjuice. *Nota* that at that season wherein fresh verjuice is made, it is meet to take a flask thereof without salt and keep it, for it serveth to take stains from dresses and restore their colour, and it is always good, whether new or old.

Item, if any of your fur coverlets or furs have been damp and have grown hard, take the fur off the garment, and sprinkle the fur which is hard with wine, and let it be sprinkled with the mouth, even as a dressmaker sprinkles with water the lappet of a dress that wrinkleth, and cast flour upon it thus watered, and allow it to dry for a day; then well rub the fur, until it returneth to its first state.

Now let me return to what I was saying before, and let me say that your steward ought to know that each week he must examine and taste your wines, verjuice and vinegar and look at the grain, oil, nuts, peas, beans and other stores. And as to wines, know that if they fall sick, their sickness must be cured in the following manner:

First, if the wine should go bad, he must set the barrel in winter in the midst of a courtyard upon two trestles, so that the frost catches it, and it will be cured.

Item, if the wine be too tart, he must take a basket full of black grapes very ripe, and put it into the barrel through the bung-hole, and the wine will improve.

Item, if the wine smell ill, he must take an ounce of powdered elder wood and an equal quantity of grain of paradise [cardamom] powdered and put each of the powders aforesaid in a little bag and pierce it with a stick, and then hang both the bags inside the cask on cords and stop up the bung-hole firmly.

Item, if the wine be muddy, take twelve eggs and set them to boil in water till they be hard, and then cast away the yolks and leave the whites and the shells together, and then fry them in an iron frying-pan and put them, still hot, into a bag pierced with a stick as above, and hang them in the cask by cords.

Item, take a big new pot and set it above an empty tripod, and when it is well baked, break it into pieces and throw them into the cask and they will cure the muddiness.

Item, to take the redness out of white wine, take a basket full of holly leaves and cast them into the cask through the bung-hole.

Item, if the wine be bitter, take a crock of water and pour it in, that it may separate the wine from the dregs, and then take a dish full of corn and set it to soak in water, and then throw away the water and set it in fresh water to boil, and boil it therein until the grain is on the point of bursting and then take it out; and if therein there be burst grains, cast them away, and then pour the hot corn into the cask. And if the wine refuseth to clear for this, take a basket full of sand well washed in Seine water and cast it into the cask through the bung-hole and it will clear.

Item, to make a strong wine of the vintage do not fill up the cask with more than about two gallons of wine, and rub all round the bung and then it cannot drip out and it will thereby be stronger.

Item, to tap a cask of wine without letting air into it, bore a little hole with a drill near the bung-hole, and then take a little wad of tow of the size of a silver penny[12] and set it thereon, and take two little sticks and put them crosswise over the aforesaid wad, and set another wad upon the sticks. And to clear thick wine, if it be in a cask, empty two quart pots of it, then stir it up with a stick or otherwise, until the dregs and all are well mixed, then take a quarter of a pound of eggs, and beat up the yolks and the whites for a long while until the whole is fine and clear like water, and then cast in a quarter of pounded alum and immediately thereon a quart of clear water and stop it up, otherwise it will run away by the bung-hole.

And after this and with this, fair sister, bid Master Jehan the Dispenser to order Richard of the kitchen to air, wash and clean and do all things that appertain to the kitchen, and see you that Dame Agnes the Béguine for the women and Master Jehan the Dispenser for the men, set your folk to work on all sides: the one upstairs, the other downstairs, the one in the fields, the other in the town, the one in the chamber, the other in the solar,[13] or the kitchen, and send one here and the other there, each after his place and his skill, so

that these servants all earn their wages, men and women according
to what they know and have to do; and if they do so, they will do
well, for know you that laziness and idleness be the root of all evil.

Nathless, fair sister, at times fitting cause them to be seated at
table, and give them to eat one kind of meat only, but good plenty
thereof, and not several varieties, nor dainties and delicacies; and
order them one drink nourishing but not intoxicating, be it wine or
something else, and not several kinds. And do you bid them to eat
well and drink well and deeply, for it is reasonable that they should
eat at a stretch, without sitting too long over their food and without
lingering over their meat, or staying with their elbows on the table.
And so soon as they shall begin to tell tales and to argue and to lean
upon their elbows, order the Béguine to make them rise and remove
their table, for the common folk have a saying: 'When a varlet holds
forth at table and a horse grazes in the ditch, it is time to take them
away for they have had their fill.' Forbid them to get drunk, and
never allow a drunken person to serve you nor approach you, for it
is perilous; and after they have taken their midday meal, when it is
due time, cause your folk to set them to work again. And after their
afternoon's work, and upon feast days, let them have another meal,
and after that, to wit in the evening, let them be fed abundantly and
well as before, and if the weather be cold let them warm themselves
and take their ease.

After this, let your house be closed and shut up by Master Jehan
the Dispenser or by the Béguine, and let one of them keep the keys,
so that none may go in or out without leave. And every evening ere
you go to bed cause Dame Agnes the Béguine or Master Jehan the
Dispenser to go round with a lighted candle, to inspect your wines,
verjuice and vinegar, that none be taken away, and bid your farmer
find out from his men whether your beasts have fodder for the
night. And when you have made sure by Dame Agnes or Master
Jehan that the fires on the hearths be everywhere covered, give to
your folk time and space for the repose of their limbs. And make you
certain beforehand that each hath, at a distance from his bed, a
candlestick with a large foot wherein to put his candle, and that they
have been wisely taught how to extinguish it with mouth or hand
before getting into bed, and by no means with their shirts. And do
you also have them admonished and told, each separately what he
must begin to do on the morrow, and how each must rise up on the

morrow morn and set to work on his own task, and let each be informed thereon. And nathless there be two things I would say unto you: the one is that if you have girls or chambermaids of fifteen to twenty years, since they be foolish at that age and naught have seen of the world, do you cause them to sleep near to you, in a closet or chamber, where there is no dormer window or low window looking on to the road, and let them go to bed and arise at your own time, and do you yourself (who, if God please, will be wise ere this time) be near to guard them. The other thing is that if one of your servants fall ill, do you lay all common concerns aside, and do you yourself take thought for him full lovingly and kindly, and visit him and think of him or her very carefully, seeking to bring about his cure. And thus you will have fulfilled this article.

Now I am in mind in this place to let you rest, or disport you, and no more to speak to you; and while you enjoy yourself elsewhere, I shall speak to Master Jehan the Dispenser, who ruleth our household, so that he shall know a little of what he should do if any of our horses, as well carthorses or steeds for riding, be out of action, or if it be necessary to buy or exchange a horse . . .[14]

THE FOURTH ARTICLE

THE WHICH TEACHETH YOU HOW YOU,
AS SOVEREIGN MISTRESS OF YOUR HOUSEHOLD,
MUST KNOW HOW TO ORDER AND DEVISE
DINNERS AND SUPPERS WITH MASTER JEHAN,
AND HOW TO DEVISE DISHES AND COURSES

And at the beginning I will set certain terms, how they be used, the which shall be an introduction or at least an amusement unto you.

First, since it is meet that you send Master Jehan to the butcheries, hereafter follow the names of all the butcheries of Paris and their deliveries of meat.[15]

At the Porte-de-Paris there be nineteen butchers who by common estimation sell weekly, taking them all together and the busy season with the empty season, 1,900 sheep, 400 oxen, 400 pigs and 200 calves.

Sainte-Geneviève: 500 sheep, 16 oxen, 16 pigs and 6 calves.

Le Parvis: 80 sheep, 10 oxen, 10 calves and 8 pigs.

At Saint-Germain there be thirteen butchers; 200 sheep, 30 oxen, 30 calves and 50 pigs.

The Temple, 2 butchers; 200 sheep, 24 oxen, '28 calves, 32 pigs.

Saint-Martin: 250 sheep, 32 oxen, 32 calves, 22 pigs.

Sum of all the butcheries of Paris, weekly, without counting the households of the king and the queen and other our lords of France, 3,080 sheep, 514 oxen, 306 calves and 600 pigs. And on Good Friday there be sold from 2,000 to 3,000 salted porks.

As to what has been said before concerning butchers' meat and poultry, the king's household consumeth in butchers' meat weekly at least 120 sheep, 16 oxen, 16 calves and 12 pigs; and 200 salted porks a year.

In poultry daily, 600 chickens, 200 pairs of pigeons, 50 kids and 50 goslings.

The queen and the children: butchery, weekly, 80 sheep, 12 calves, 12 oxen, 12 pigs; and 120 salted porks a year. In poultry, daily, 300 chickens, 36 kids, 150 pairs of pigeons and 36 goslings.

[The Duke of] Orleans likewise. [The Duke of] Berry likewise.

Monseigneur de Berry's folk say that on Sundays and great feasts they require 3 oxen, 30 sheep, 160 dozen of partridges and coneys in proportion, but I doubt it. (Since verified). And certainly 'tis so on divers great feasts, Sundays and Thursdays, but most commonly on the other days 'tis 2 oxen and 20 sheep. *Nota* again that at the court of Monseigneur de Berry the varlets and pages have livery of the ox cheeks, and the muzzle of the ox is carved asunder, and the mandibles be left for the livery, as is aforesaid. *Item*, the neck of the ox is also given in livery to the aforesaid varlets. *Item*, and that which cometh next to the neck is the best part of the beef, for that which is betwixt the front legs is the breast and that which is above is the shoulder.

[The Duke of] Burgundy [is] to the king as Paris money is to money of Tournai.[16] [The Duke of] Bourbon's household uses half as much as the queen's.

Item, without spending or paying out your money every day you may send Master Jehan to the butcher and order meat by tally.

After these things it behoveth to tell and speak of certain general terms that be used in the feat of cookery, and afterwards to show how you may know and choose the viands wherewith the cook worketh, as followeth:

First, in all sausages and thick pottages, wherein spices and bread be brayed, you should first bray the spices and take them out of the mortar, because the bread which you bray afterwards requires that which remaineth from the spices; thus naught is lost that would be lost if 'twere done otherwise.

Item, spices and bindings put into pottages ought not to be strained; nathless do so for sauces, that the sauces may be clearer and likewise the more pleasant.

Item, wot you well that pea or bean pottages or others burn easily, if the burning brands touch the bottom of the pot when it is on the fire. *Item,* before your pottage burns and in order that it burn not, stir it often in the bottom of the pot, and turn your spoon in the bottom so that the pottage may not take hold there. And *nota* as soon as thou shalt perceive that thy pottage burneth, move it not, but straightway take it off the fire and put it in another pot.

Item, nota that commonly all pottages that be on the fire boil over, and fall on to the said fire, until salt and grease be put into the pot, and afterwards they do not so.

Item, nota that the best caudle there is, is beef's cheek washed twice in water, then boiled and well skimmed.

Item, one may know whether a coney be fatted, by feeling his sinew or neck betwixt the two shoulders for there you may tell if there be much fat by the big sinew; and you can tell if he be tender by breaking one of his back legs.

Item, nota that there is a difference among cooks between 'sticking' and 'larding', for sticking is done with cloves and larding with bacon-lard.

Item, in pike the soft-roed are better than the hard, save when you would make rissoles thereof, for rissoles be made of the hard roes, *ut patet in tabula.* Of pike one speaketh of a hurling pike, a pickerel, a pike, a luce.[17]

Item, fresh shad cometh into season in March.

Item, carp should be very well cooked, or otherwise it is dangerous to eat it.

Item, plaice be soft to the touch and dab the contrary.

Item, at Paris the cooks of roast meat fatten their geese with flour, neither the fine flour nor the bran, but that which is between the two which is called the pollen; and as much of this pollen as they take, they mix an equal amount of oatmeal therewith, and mix with a little water, and it remaineth of the thickness of paste, and they put this food in a dish on four feet, and water beside and fresh litter every day, and in fifteen days [the geese] be fatted. And *nota* that their litter maketh them to keep their feathers clean.

Item, to give the flavour of game to capons and hens, it behoveth to bleed them by cutting their throats and straightway put them and cause them to die in a bucket of very cold water, and they will be as high on the same day as though two days killed.

Item, you may tell young mallards from old ones, when they be the same size, from the quills of the feathers, which be tenderer in the young birds than in the old. *Item*, you may tell the river mallard, because they have sharp black nails and they have also red feet and the farmyard ducks have them yellow. *Item*, they have the crest or upper part of the beak green all along, and sometimes the males have a white mark across the nape of the neck, and they have the crest feathers very wavy.

Item, ring-doves be good in winter and you may tell the old ones for that the mid-feathers of their wings be all of a black hue, and the young ones of a year old have the mid-feathers ash coloured and the rest black.

Item, you may know the age of a hare from the number of holes that be beneath the tail, for so many holes, so many years.

Item, the partridges whose feathers be close set and well joined to the flesh, and be orderly and well joined, as are the feathers of a hawk, these be fresh killed; and those whose feathers be ruffled the wrong way and come easily out of the flesh and be out of place and ruffled disorderly this way and that, they be long killed. *Item*, you may feel it by pulling the feathers of the belly.

Item, the carp which hath white scales and neither yellow nor reddish, is from good water. That which hath big eyes standing forth from the head and palate and tongue joined, is fat. And *nota* if you would carry a carp alive the whole day, wrap it up in damp hay and carry it belly upmost, and carry it without giving it air, in a cask or bag.

The season for trout begins in [*blank*] and lasts until September. The white trout be good in winter, and the red [salmon-]trout in summer. The best part of the trout is the tail and of the carp it is the head.

Item, the eel which hath a small head, loose mouth, shining skin, undulating and glistening, small eyes, big body and white belly, is fresh.[18] The other has a big head, yellow belly and thick brown skin.

Hereafter follow divers dinners and suppers of great lords and others and notes, whereupon you may choose, collect and learn whatsoever dishes it shall please you, according to the seasons and to the meats which are native to the place where you may be, when you have to give a dinner or a supper.

I Dinner for a Meat Day served in Thirty-one Dishes and Six Courses

First course. [Wine of] Grenache[19] and roasts, veal pasties, pimpernel[20] pasties, black-puddings and sausages.

Second course. Hares in civey[21] and cutlets, pea soup [lit., strained peas], salt meat and great joints (*grosse char*), a *soringue* of eels (p. 175) and other fish.

Third course. Roast: coneys, partridges, capons, etc., luce, bar, carp (p. 177) and a quartered pottage.[22]

Fourth course. River fish *à la dodine*,[23] savoury rice (p. 182), a bourrey[24] with hot sauce and eels reversed (p. 178).

Fifth course. Lark pasties, rissoles, larded milk (p. 185), sugared flawns.[25]

Sixth course. Pears and comfits, medlars and peeled nuts. Hippocras[26] and wafers.

II Another Meat Dinner of Twenty-four Dishes in Six Courses

First course. Pasties of veal well minced with fat and marrow of beef, pimpernel pasties, black puddings (p. 163), sausages (p. 202), stuffed straws (*pipefarces*) (p. 187) and Norwegian pasties (p. 185).

Second course. Hares in civey and eel broth; bean soup [lit., strained beans], salt meat, great joints, to wit beef and mutton.

Third course. Capons, coneys, veal and partridges, fresh- and salt-water fish, some *taillis*[27] with glazed meats.[28]

Fourth course. River mallard *à la dodine*, tench with sops[29] and bourreys with hot sauce, fatted capon pasties, with gravy[30] of the fat and parsley.

Fifth course. A larded broth, savoury rice, eels reversed, some roast sea or freshwater fish, crisps[31] and old sugar.

The sixth and last course for Issue. Sugared flawns and larded milk, peeled nuts, cooked pears and comfits. Hippocras and wafers.

III Another Meat Dinner

First course. Beef pasties and rissoles, black purée, lampreys with cold sage (p. 182), a meat brewet of Almaign,[32] a white fish sauce and a herbolace,[33] great joints of beef and mutton.

Second course. Freshwater fish, salt-water fish, a meat *cretonnée*,[34] *raniolles*,[35] a rosee[36] of young rabbits and bourreys with hot sauce, Pisan bird tarts (i.e. Pisa in Lombardy and they be called Lombard tarts and there are little birds in the stuffing and henceforth in divers places they be called Lombard tarts).

Third course. Tench with sops, blankmanger[37] decorated, larded milk, croûtes, boar's tail (p. 192) with hot sauce, bream and salmon pasties, boiled plaice and leches fried [fritters][38] and darioles.[39]

Fourth course. Frumenty (p. 180), venison, roast fish, cold sage, eels reversed, fish jellies, capon pasties with hasty gravy.[40]

IV Another Meat Dinner

First course. Norwegian pasties (p. 185), a cameline[41] meat brewet, beef marrow fritters, *soringue* of eels, loach in water and cold sage, great joints and salt-water fish.

Second course. The best roast that may be had and freshwater fish, a larded broth, a meat tile (p. 174), capon pasties and crisps, bream and eel pasties and blankmanger.

Third course. Frumenty, venison, lamprey with hot sauce, leches fried, roast bream and darioles, sturgeon and jelly.

V Another Meat Dinner

First course. Beef and marrow pasties, hare in civey, great joints, a white coney brewet (p. 173), capons and venison with sops, white porray (p. 165), turnips, salt ducks and chines.

Second course. The best roast, etc., a rosee of larks, a blank-manger, umbles[42] and boar's tail with hot sauce, fat capon pasties, fritters and Norwegian pasties.

Third course. Frumenty, venison, various sorts of glazed meats, fat geese and capons *à la dodine*, cream darioles and leches fried and sugared, bourreys of hot *galentine* (p. 190), capon jelly (p. 183), coneys, young chickens, rabbits and piglings.

Fourth course. Hippocras and wafers for Issue.

VI *Another Meat Dinner*

First course. Frizzled beans (p. 165), a cinnamon brewet (p. 172), a hare in black civey, a green eel brewet, red herring, great joints, turnips, tench with sops, salt geese and chines, rissoles of beef marrow, hastelettes of beef.[43]

Second course. The best roast that may be had, fresh- and salt-water fish, boiled plaice, bourreys with hot sauce such as lampreys, a gravy (p. 170) of shad the colour of peach blossom, a party blank-manger (p. 216[22]), Lombard tarts, pasties of venison and small birds, Spanish *cretonnée*, fresh herring.

Third course. Frumenty, venison, glazed meats, fish jellies, fat capons *à la dodine*, fish roast, leches fried and darioles, eels reversed, crayfish, crisps and stuffed straws.

VII *Another Meat Dinner*

First course. White porray, beef hastelettes, great joints, veal in civey, some garnished (*houssié*) brewet (p. 172).

Second course. Roast meat, salt- and freshwater fish, Lombard *raniolles*, a Spanish *cretonnée*.

Third course. Lampreys, shad, a rosee, larded milk and [sugared] croûtes in milk, Pisan, i.e., Lombard tarts, cream darioles.

Fourth course. Frumenty, venison, glazed meats, bream and gurn-ard pasties, eels reversed, fat capons *à la dodine*.

Issue is hippocras and wafers.

Sally-forth (*Boute-hors*): wine and spices.

VIII *Another Meat Dinner*

First course. Great joints, Norwegian pasties, beef marrow fritters, cameline meat brewet, *soringue* of eels, loach in water, salt-water fish and cold sage.

Second course. The best roast that may be had, freshwater fish, a meat tile, goat's flesh boiled and larded, capon pasties, bream and eel pasties and blankmanger.

Third course. Frumenty, venison, glazed meats, lampreys with hot sauce, leches fried and darioles, roast bream, broth with verjuice, sturgeon and jelly.

IX Another Meat Dinner

First course. White leeks, beef pasties, ducks and chines, hares and coneys in civey, a *geneste* (p. 174) of larks, great joints.

Second course. Roast; boar's tail with hot sauce, a party blankmanger, goose *dodines*, larded milk and [sugared] croûtes, venison, glazed meats, jellies, [sugared] crusts in milk *à la dodine*, capon pasties, cold sage, cow's flesh pasties and talemouse.[44]

X Another Meat Dinner

First course. Pea soup, herrings, salted eels, oysters in black civey, an almond brewet, a tile, a broth of pike and eels, a *cretonnée*, a green brewet of eels, silver pasties.[45]

Second course. Sea-water and freshwater fish, bream and salmon pasties, eels reversed, a brown herbolace, tench with larded broth, a blankmanger, crisps, lettuces, losenges, *orillettes*[46] and Norwegian pasties, farced luce and salmon.

Third course. Frumenty, venison, glazed *pommeaulx*,[47] Spanish puffs and chastletes,[48] a roast of fish, jelly, lampreys, congers and turbot with green sauce (p. 189), leches fried, darioles and a great entremet.

XI Another Dinner

First course. Beef pasties and rissoles, black porray (p. 167), lamprey gravy, a meat brewet of Almaign, a meat brewet garnished (*georgé*) (p. 172), a white fish sauce, a herbolace.

Second course. Roast meat, salt-water and freshwater fish, *raniolles*, a rosee of little rabbits and birds, bourreys with hot sauce, Pisan tarts.

Third course. Tench with sops, a party blankmanger, larded milk and [sugared] croûtes, boar's tails with hot sauce, capons *à la dodine*, bream and salmon pasties, plaice in water, leches fried and darioles.

Fourth course. Frumenty, venison, glazed meats, a fish roast, cold sage, eels reversed, fish jelly, capon pasties.

XII Another Dinner

First course. Frizzled beans, a cinnamon brewet, hare in black civey, or a green brewet of eels, red herrings, great joints, turnips, tench with sops, salt geese and chines, rissoles of beef marrow.

Second course. The best roast that may be had, fresh- and salt-water fish, plaice in water, bourreys with hot sauce, a gravy of shad the colour of peach blossom, party blankmanger, Lombard tarts, pasties of venison and small birds, Spanish *cretonnée*, fresh herrings.

Third course. Frumenty, venison, glazed meats, fish jelly, fat capons *à la dodine*, a fish roast, leches fried and darioles, eels reversed, crayfish, crisps and stuffed straws.

XIII Another Meat Dinner

First course. A brewet of Almaign, cabbages, a *soringue* of eels, turnips, beef pasties, great joints.

Second course. The best roast that may be had, fatted ducks *à la dodine*, freshwater fish, blankmanger, a herbolace, Norwegian pasties, crisps, larded milk, milk tarts.

Third course. Capon pasties *à la dodine*, savoury rice, boar's tail with cold sauce, leches fried and sugared darioles.

Fourth course. Frumenty, venison, glazed meats, eels reversed and a roast of breams.

The boar's head for the entremet.

XIV Another Meat Dinner

First course. White leeks with capons, duck with chines and roast chitterlings, leches of beef and mutton, a garnished brewet (*george*) of hares, veals and coneys.

Second course. Capons, partridges, coneys, plovers, farced pigs,[49] pheasants for lords, fish and meat jelly.

Entremet borne on high: swan (p. 176), peacocks, bitterns, herons and other things.

Issue. Venison, savoury rice, capon pasties, cream flawns, darioles, eels reversed, fruit, wafers, *estriers*[50] and clarry.[51]

XV Another Dinner in Twenty-four Dishes in Three Courses

First course. Pea soup, salted eels and herrings, leeks with almonds, great joints, a yellow brewet (p. 174), a *salemine*,[52] salt-water fish, oysters in civey.

Second course. Roast freshwater and salt-water fish, a Savoy brewet (p. 174), a larded brewet of skinned eels.

Third course. Roast breams, *galentine*, chine, peregrine capons,[53] jelly, party blankmanger, boiled plaice, turbot *à la soucie*, cream darioles, lampreys with hot sauce, glazed meats, savoury rice, etc.

SUPPERS

XVI Meat Supper in Four Courses
First course. *Seymé* (p. 170), *pullet aux herbes*, brewet of verjuice and poultry, an *espinbesche* (p. 175) of meat boiled and larded, pickerells and loach in water, salted roach and *chastelongnes*.[54]

Second course. The best roast that may be had of meat and fish, and titbits of parsley and vinegar, *galentine* of fish, a white sauce on fish and meat livers.

Third course. Capon pasties, biscuit[55] of pike and eels, lettuces, and a herbolace, fish, crisps and stuffed straws.

Fourth course. Jelly, crayfish, plaice in water, whitebait and cold sage, umbles with hot sauce, pasties of cow's flesh and talemouses. Pottage for an Issue, called jelly.

XVII Another Meat Supper
First course. Capons *aux herbes*, a *comminée* (p. 171), peas *daguenets*,[56] loach *au jaunet* (p. 175), venison with sops.

Second course. The best roast that may be had, jelly, party blankmanger, cream flawns well sugared.

Third course. Capon pasties, cold sages, stuffed shoulder of mutton, pickerells *à un rebouly*,[57] venison *à la* boar's tail, crayfish.

XVIII Another Meat Supper
First course. Three sorts of pottage, capons whole in white brewet, a chawdon of salmon,[58] venison with sops, loach with sliced eels thereon.

Second course. Roast capons, coneys, partridges, plovers, blackbirds, small birds, kids; a blankmanger standing, etc.; luce, carp and bar, etc.; eels reversed – pheasants and swans as entremets.

Third course. Venison *à la* frumenty, pasties of doves and larks, tarts (p. 183), crayfish, fresh herring, fruit, clarry, pastries,[59] medlars, pears, peeled nuts.

XIX A Fish Dinner for Lent
First course and service. Cooked apples, large Provençal figs roast, with bay-leaves thereon, cress and sorrel with vinegar, pea soup, salted eels, white herring, gravy on fried salt- and freshwater fish.

Second course. Carp, luce, soles, roach, salmon, eels.

XX Another Fish Dinner for Lent

First course. Cooked apples, etc., as above.

Second course. Carp, luce, soles, roach, salmon, eels reversed *à la boe* (i.e. with thick sauce) (p. 178) and a herbolace.

Third course. Roast pimpernels, fried whiting, powdered porpoise with water and frumenty, crisps and Norwegian pasties.

Issue. Figs and raisins, hippocras and wafers as aforesaid.

XXI Another Fish Dinner

First course. Pea soup, purée, civey of oysters, white sauce of broach and perch, a cress porray, herrings, salted whale,[60] salted eels, loach in water.

Second course. Fresh- and salt-water fish, turbot *à la soucie*, *taillis*, a biscuit, eels in *galentine*.

Third course. The fairest and best roast that may be had, white pasties, loach *au waymel*, crayfish, perches with parsley and vinegar, tench with sops, jelly.

XXII Another Fish Dinner

First course. Pea soup, herrings, purée, salted eels, oysters, a *salemine* of broach and carp.

Second course. Freshwater fish, a *soringue* of eels, Norwegian pasties and party blankmanger, a herbolace, pasties, fritters.

Third course. The best roast, etc., savoury rice, tarts, leches fried and darioles, salmon and bream pasties, a chawdon.

Fourth course. *Taillis*, crisps, stuffed straws, skirrit roots, fried pike, glazed dishes, congers and turnip *au soucié*, Lombard tarts, eels reversed.

XXIII Another Fish Dinner

First course. Cooked apples, ripe figs, [wine of] Grenache, cress and pennyroyal, pea soup, chad, salted eels, herrings and salted whale, white brewet on perches and cuttle fish in a gravy on fritters.

Second course. The best freshwater fish that can be found and salt-water fish, skinned eels, bourreys with hot sauce, tench with sops, crayfish, pasties of bream and plaice in water.

Third course. Frumenty of porpoise, Norwegian pasties and roast mackerel, roast pimpernels and crisps, oysters, fried cuttle fish, with a biscuit of pickerells.

XXIV Another Fish Dinner

First course. Pea soup, herring, salt eels, a black civey of oysters, an almond brewet, a tile, a broth of broach and eels, a *cretonnée*, a green brewet of eels, silver pasties.

Second course. Salt- and freshwater fish, bream and salmon pasties, eels reversed, a brown herbolace, tench with a larded broth, a blankmanger, crisps, lettuces, losenges, *orillettes*, and Norwegian pasties, stuffed luce and salmon.

Third course. Porpoise frumenty, glazed *pommeaulx*, Spanish puffs and chastletes, roast fish, jelly, lampreys, congers and turbot with green sauce, breams with verjuice, leches fried, darioles and entremet. Then Dessert, Issue and Sally-Forth.

*Hereinafter follow divers incidents
likewise appertaining to the same matter*

The arrangements which M. [the abbé] de Lagny made for the dinner which he gave to Monseigneur de Paris, the president, the *procureur* and the *avocat du roi* and the rest of the council[61] amounting to eight covers [i.e. sixteen persons].[62]

First, preparation of tablecloths, vessels for the dining hall and the kitchen, branches, greenstuff to set on the table, ewers and hanaps[63] with feet, two comfit dishes, silver salt cellars, bread two days old for toast and trenchers.[64] For the kitchen: two large pails, two washing tubs and two brooms.

Nota that Monseigneur de Paris had three esquires of his own to serve him and he was served apart with covered dishes. And monseigneur the president had one esquire and was served apart, but not with covered dishes. *Item*, at the bidding of monseigneur the president, the *procureur du roi* was seated above the *avocat du roi*.

The courses and dishes follow: two quarts of [wine of] Grenache, to wit [allowing] two persons to the half-pint (but that is too much, for a half-pint between three suffices, and let the seconds[65] have some). Hot cracknels and ruddy apples[66] roast with white comfits thereon, a quarter [lb.]; ripe figs roast, five quarters; sorrel, cress and rosemary.

Pottages, to wit a *salemine* of six salmon[67] and six tench, green porray (p. 167) and white herring, a quarter [lb.]; six freshwater eels salted the day before, and three stockfish soaked for a night.

For the pottages: almonds, 6 lbs.; ginger powder, ¼ lb.; saffron, ½ oz.; small spices, 2 oz.; cinnamon powder, ¼ lb.; comfits, ½ lb.

Sea-fish: soles, gurnard, congers, turbot, salmon; freshwater fish: luce, two Marne carps, bream.

Entremets: plaice, lamprey *à la boe*.

Roast: (and more towels be needed and likewise sixteen oranges), porpoise in its sauce, mackerel, soles, bream, chad *à la* cameline, or with verjuice, rice with fried almonds thereon; sugar for rice and apples, 1 lb.; little napkins.

For dessert: compost[68] with white and red comfits spread thereon; rissoles, flawns, figs, dates, raisins, filberts.

Hippocras and wafers are the Issue. Hippocras two quarts (and this is too much, as is aforesaid concerning the [wine of] Grenache), two hundred wafers and *supplications*. And note that for each cover one allows eight wafers, four *supplications* and four *estriers* and that is generous allowance; and the cost thereof is 8d. per cover.

Wine and spices are the Sally-Forth. Wash, grace and go to the withdrawing room; and then the servants dine and immediately afterwards [serve] wine and spices; and so farewell.

> *The arrangements for the wedding feast*
> *that Master Helye shall give on a Tuesday in May;*
> *a dinner only for twenty covers [i.e. 40 persons]*

Service: butter, none, because it is a feast day. *Item*, cherries, none, because none were to be had; and for this course nought.

Pottages: capons with blankmanger, pomegranates and red comfits thereon.

Roast: on each dish a quarter of a kid; a quarter of kid is better than lamb; a duckling, two spring chickens and sauce thereto; oranges, cameline, verjuice and fresh towels and napkins therewith.

Entremets: crayfish jelly, loach, young rabbits and pigs.

Dessert: frumenty and venison.

Issue: hippocras and wafers.

Sally-Forth: wine and spices.

The ordering of the supper that is to be had on the same day is thus for ten covers [twenty persons]:

Cold sage of the halves of chickens, little ducklings, and a vinaigrette of the same meats for the said supper in a dish. A pasty of two young hares and two peacocks (although some say that at the bridals of free folk there ought to be darioles), and in another dish minced kids with the heads halved and glazed.

Entremets: jelly as above.

Issue: apples and cheese without hippocras, because it is out of season.

Dancing, singing, wine and spices, and torches for lighting.

Now it behoveth [to set down] the quantity of the things above-said and their appurtenances and the price thereof and who shall purvey and bargain for them.

From the baker: ten dozen flat white loaves, baked the day before and for a penny piece. Trencher bread, three dozens, half a foot wide and four inches high, baked four days before and let it be brown – or let Corbeil bread be got from the market.

Wine cellar: three cauldrons of wine.

From the butcher: half a mutton, to make sops[69] for the guests and a quarter of bacon to lard them; the master bone of a leg of beef to cook with the capons, so as to have the broth to make blank-manger; a fore-quarter of veal to serve for blankmanger. The seconds a hind quarter of veal or calves feet, to have liquid for the jelly. Venison, a foot quartered.

From the wafer-maker[70] it behoves to order: first, for the bride's service, a dozen and a half of cheese *gauffres*, 3s.; a dozen and a half of *gros bastons*, 6s.; a dozen and a half of *portes*, 18d.; a dozen and a half of *estriers*, 18d.; a hundred sugared *galettes*, 8d.

Item, it was bargained with him [that he should provide for] twenty covers for the wedding dinner and six covers for the servants and that he should have 6d. per cover and serve each cover with eight wafers, four *supplications* and four *estriers*.

From the poulterer: twenty capons at 2s. *Parisis* [i.e. Paris money] apiece; five kids, 4s. *Parisis*; twenty ducklings, 3s. *Parisis* apiece; fifty chickens, 12d. *Parisis* apiece; that is to wit forty roasts for the dinner, five for the jelly and five at supper for the cold sage. Fifty young rabbits, to wit forty for the dinner, which shall be roast, and ten for the jelly and they shall cost 12d. *Parisis* apiece. A lean pig for the jelly, 4d. *Parisis*; twelve pairs of pigeons for the supper, 10d. *Parisis* the pair. (It behoves to ask him concerning the venison.)

In the market: bread for trenchers, 3 dozen [loaves]. Pomegranates for blankmanger, three, which will cost [*blank*]. Oranges, fifty, which will cost [*blank*]. Six green cheeses and one old cheese and three hundred eggs.

And wot you that each cheese should furnish six tartlets and also three eggs must be allowed to each cheese.

Sorrel to make verjuice for the chickens, sage and parsley to make the cold sage, two hundred blaundrel apples.[71]

Two brooms and a pail for the kitchen and some salt.

From the sauce-maker: three half pints of cameline for dinner and supper and a quart of sorrel verjuice.

From the spicer: 10 lbs. of almonds, 14d. the lb.; 3 lbs. of hulled corn, 8d. the lb.; 1 lb. of powdered colombine ginger,[72] 5s.; ¼ lb. of ground cinnamon, 5s.; 2 lbs. of ground rice, 2s.; 2 lbs. of lump sugar, 16s.; 1 oz. of saffron, 3s.; a quarter [lb.] of cloves and grain [of paradise] mixed, 6s.; ½ a qr. [lb.] of long pepper, 4s.; ½ a qr. [lb.] of galingale, 5s.; ½ a qr. [lb.] of mace, 3s. 4d.; ½ a qr. [lb.] of green bay-leaves, 6d.; 2 lbs. of large and small candles, 3s. 4d. the lb., which amounteth to 6s. 8d.; torches of 3 lbs. apiece, six; flambeaux of 1 lb. apiece, six; to wit, 3s. a lb. when purchased and the ends to be taken back at 6d. less per lb.

From him spices for the chamber, to wit candied orange peel, 1 lb., 10s.; citron, 1 lb., 12s.; red anise, 1 lb., 8s.; rose-sugar,[73] 1 lb., 2s.; white comfits, 3 lbs., 10s. the lb. From him hippocras, 3 quarts, 10s. the quart, and he will find all.

Sum total of this spicery came to twelve francs, counting what was burnt of the torches, and little was left of the spices; thus half a franc can be allowed per cover.

At the Pierre-au-Lait [milk market]: a sester of good milk, neither curdled nor watered, to make frumenty.

In the [Place de] Grève: a hundred Burgundy faggots, 13s.; two sacks of coal, 10s.

At the Porte-de-Paris: branches, greenery, violets, chaplets, a quart of white salt, a quart of coarse salt, a hundred crayfish, a half pint of loach, two earthenware pots, one of a sester for the jelly, the other of two quarts for the cameline.

Now have we first the service in general and secondly where the things be to be found. Now behoveth it, thirdly, to know the ordainers and officers needful thereto.

First, there is needed a clerk or varlet to purchase greenery, violets, chaplets, milk, cheese, eggs, logs, coal, salt, vats and washing tubs both for the dining hall and for the butteries, verjuice, vinegar, sorrel, sage, parsley, fresh garlic, two brooms, a shovel and other small things.

Item, a cook and his varlets, who will cost two francs in wages without other perquisites, but the cook will pay varlets and porters, and there is a saying 'the more covers, the more wages'.

Item, two knife-bearers, whereof one is to cut up bread and make trenchers and salt-cellars of bread and they shall carry the salt and the bread and the trenchers to the tables and shall make for the hall two or three receptacles, wherein to throw the large scraps, such as sops, cut or broken bread, trenchers, pieces of meat and other things; and two buckets for casting away and receiving broth, sauce and liquid things.

Item, one or two water-carriers be needed.

Item, a big and strong *sergent* to guard the portals.

Item, two esquires of the kitchen and two helpers for the service of the kitchen, one of whom shall go bargain for the kitchen things, pastry and linen for six tables; for the which there be needed two large copper pots for twenty covers, two boilers, four strainers, a mortar and a pestle, six large cloths for the kitchen, three large earthenware pots for wine, a large earthenware pot for pottage, four wooden basins and spoons, an iron pan, four large pails with handles, two trivets and an iron spoon. And he shall likewise purvey the pewter vessels; to wit ten dozen bowls, six dozen small dishes, two dozen and a half large dishes, eight quart [pots], two dozen pint [pots], two almsdishes.[74]

Item, concerning the house; wherein be it known that the *hôtel de* Beauvais[75] cost Jehan Duchesne[76] four francs; tables, trestles *et similia* five francs; and the chaplets cost him fifteen francs.

And the other esquire of the kitchen or his helper shall go with the cook to the butcher, the poulterer, the spicer, etc., to purvey and choose the things, have them borne home and pay for the carriage thereof; and they shall have a hutch shutting with a key, wherein they shall keep the spices, etc., and they shall distribute all things according to reason and measure. And afterwards they or their helpers shall gather up that which remaineth and put it away safely in baskets in a closed hutch, to prevent waste and excess by the meynie.

Two other esquires be needed for the service of the dining hall, and they shall give out spoons and collect them again, give out hanaps, pour out whichsoever wine be asked for by the guests at table and collect the vessels again.

Two other esquires be needed for the wine cellar, who shall give out wine to be carried to the dresser, the tables and elsewhere, and they shall have a varlet to draw the wine.

Two of the most honest and skilled [esquires] shall accompany the bridegroom and shall go with him before the dishes.

Two stewards to seat the guests and make them rise, and a sewer[77] and two servants for each table, who shall serve and take away, throw the remnants into the baskets and the sauces and broths into the buckets and pails and receive and bring the dessert dishes to the esquires of the kitchen or others that be ordained to keep them and they shall carry nought elsewhere.

The office of steward is to purvey salt-cellars for the high table; hanaps, four dozen; covered gilt goblets, four; ewers, six; silver spoons, four dozen; silver quart [pots], four; alms dishes, two; comfit dishes, two.

Item, a woman chaplet-maker, who shall deliver garlands on the wedding eve and on the wedding day.

The office of the women is to make provision of tapestries, to order and spread them and in especial to dight the chamber and the bed that is to be blessed.[78]

A laundress for folding [? sheets].

And *nota* that if the bed be covered with cloth, there is needed a fur coverlet of half vair; but if it be covered with serge, embroidery, or counterpane of sendal, not so.

The arrangements for the Hautecourt[79] wedding,
for twenty covers [i.e. 40 persons]
in the month of September

Service: raisins and peaches or little pasties.

Pottages: civey, four hares and a veal; or for blankmanger, twenty capons, 2s. 4d. apiece, or pullets.

Roast: five pigs, twenty young capons, 2s. 4d. apiece; forty partridges, 2s. 4d. apiece. Mortrews[80] or [*line blank in MS*].

Jelly: ten chickens, 12d.; ten young rabbits, one pig; crayfish, a hundred and a half.

Frumenty, venison, pears and nuts. *Nota* that for the frumenty three hundred eggs be needed.

Tartlets and other things, hippocras and wafers, wine and spices.

Supper: gravy of twelve dozen small birds or ten ducks, or a larded broth of fresh venison. Pasties of forty young hares, twenty chickens, forty pigeons; forty darioles or sixty tartlets.

Nota that three small birds to a cover sufficeth; nathless when one has capon gizzards *vel similia*, one allows three small birds and half a gizzard therewith to a cover.

The Quantity of the Things Aforesaid

From the baker: *ut supra* concerning the preceding wedding [feast].

From the pastrymaker: *ut supra*.

Wine cellar: *ut supra*.

From the butcher: three quarters of mutton to make the sops for the guests, a quarter of bacon for larding, a forequarter of veal for the blankmanger; for the servants, venison.

From the wafer maker: a dozen and a half of ready-made cheese wafers, to wit made of flour kneaded with eggs and leches of cheese rolled therein, and eighteen other wafers kneaded with eggs and without cheese. *Item*, a dozen and a half of *gros bastons*, to wit flour kneaded with eggs and ginger powder beaten in with it and made in the shape and size of a chitterling, and then set between two irons on the fire. *Item*, a dozen and a half of other *bastons* and as many *portes*.

Item, on the aforesaid wedding eve behoveth it to send (over and above the things that be made by the aforesaid wafer-maker) fifty blaundrell apples, the chaplets and the minstrels.

Item, from the aforesaid wafer-maker, the provision for the wedding day, *ut supra* concerning the preceding wedding.

From the poulterer: the roasts, poultry and venison, *ut supra*.

In the market at the Porte-de-Paris: the things appertaining thereto, *ut supra*.

From the sauce-maker: a quart of cameline for the dinner and for the supper two quarts of mustard.

From the spicer: spices for the chamber: comfits, rose-sugar, sugared nuts, citron and *manus-christi*;[81] 4 lbs. in all. *Item*, hippocras. Kitchen spices: white powder, 1 lb.; fine powder, ½ lb.; cinnamon powder, ½ lb. for blankmanger. Small spices, 2 oz. Lump sugar, 3 lbs.; three pomegranates; white and red comfits, ¼ lb.; almonds, 6 lbs.; flour of rice, 1 lb.; a quart of hulled wheat.

From the wax chandler were bought torches and flambeaux at 3s. the lb., and at 2s. 6d. for the returned ends.

Item, for the hire of linen, to wit, for six tables: three large copper pots, for sixteen bowls, two boilers, two strainers, a mortar, a pestle, six large cloths for the kitchen, three large earthenware pots for wine, a large earthenware pot for pottage, four basins, four wooden spoons, an iron pan, four large pails with handles, two trivets and a spoon of pierced iron; for this 56s. *Parisis*.

Pewter vessels: ten dozen bowls, six dozen small dishes, two dozen and a half large dishes, eight quart [pots], two dozen pint [pots], two alms dishes; for all this 16s.

In [the Place de] Grève *ut supra* concerning the other wedding.

Nota that because they were widowed they were wedded in the early morn in their black robes and then put on others.

Nota concerning the extra payments for Jehan Duchesne's wedding. To the cook 4¼ francs and helpers and porters 1 franc; in all 5¼ francs. To the concierge of Beauvais, 4 francs; for tables, trestles, *et similia*, 5 francs. To the chaplet maker, 15 francs. Water, 20s. Minstrels 8 francs, without the spoons and other gratuities; and they will play on the wedding eve and the acrobats [likewise]. *Sergents*, 2 francs. Greenery, 8s. Flambeaux and torches, 10 francs. Kitchen vessels, cloths, towels and glasses, 7 francs. Pewter pots, 4 francs.

THE FIFTH ARTICLE

THE WHICH TELLETH OF ORDERING, DEVISING AND CAUSING TO BE MADE ALL MANNER OF POTTAGES, CIVEYS, SAUCES AND ALL OTHER VIANDS[82]

Now behoveth it to show how to prepare the viands named above, but first it behoves thee to know divers general terms, the which thou mayst collect more fully by means of certain additions thereto, that be here and there throughout this book, to wit concerning binding for pottages, as bread, eggs, *amidon*, flour, etc., and throughout the thick soups.

Item, to prevent thy pottage from burning, thou must move it in the bottom of the pot and look that the logs touch not the bottom and if already it have begun to burn, thou must forthwith change it into another pot.

Item, to keep milk from turning.

Item, that the pot boil not over on to the fire.

Into pottages the spices should be put very well brayed and not strained and at the last moment. In sauces and in jelly the contrary.

Item, TO KILL PIGS. It is said that the males should be killed in the month of November, and the females in December; and such is their season, and for example we speak of 'a shrovetide hen'.

Item, to make black puddings, have the blood of a pig collected into a fair basin or pan, and when you have had your pigling cleaned out and the haslet very well washed and set to cook, and while it is cooking, do you take the clots of blood out of the bottom of the basin and throw them away; and afterwards have onions peeled and minced to the amount of half the blood, with half of the fat which is betwixt the intestines, minced as small as dice, together with a little brayed salt, and put it into the blood. Then take ginger, cloves and a little pepper and bray all together. Then take the small intestines, wash them well, reverse them and wring them out in running water, and to get rid of the moisture, set them in a pan on the fire and stir; then add salt, and do it a second and a third time. Then wash them, and then turn them and wash them and set them to dry on a towel; and rub and wring them to dry them. (These be the big intestines, that have fat within them, and that be cut out with a knife.) After you have put in and measured in equal portions and quantities, for so much blood half as much of onions and for so much blood a quarter as much of fat, and when your black puddings have been filled therewith, cook them in a pan in the pot water of the haslet, and prick them with a pin when they swell, or else they will burst.

Nota, that the blood keepeth well for two days, in sooth for three, after the spices be therein. And some instead of spices take pennyroyal, the large savory, hyssop, marjoram, gathered when they be in flower and then dried and brayed instead of spices. And as to the haslet, set it in a copper pot to cook on the fire, whole and without salt, and put the length of the throat outside the pot; and when it is cooked take it out and keep it to make pottage.

Quaeritur how the intestines shall be reversed to wash them; *responsio:* by a linen thread and a brass wire as long as a gauger's rod.

Nota, that some hang their pigs at Eastertide and the air yellows them; wherefore it is best to keep and salt them as they do in Picardy, although the flesh be not as firm, it seemeth; nathless bacon which is fair and white is much better to be served up than that which is yellow, for however good be the yellow, it is too much condemned and discourages one to look upon it.

VENISON OF STAG OR ANY OTHER. He that would salt it in summer, it behoves him to salt it in a wash tub or a bath tub [with water and] coarse brayed salt, and then dry it in the sun. The haunch which is salted ought to be cooked first in water and wine to get rid of the salt, and then throw away the wine and water and afterwards set it to cook slowly in meat broth and turnips, and serve it in strips with water in a dish and venison.

Item, he that hath young and small turnips should cook them in water and without wine for the first boiling and then throw away the water and then cook slowly in water and wine with chestnuts therein, or if he have no chestnuts, sage; then serve as above.

In June and July, beef and mutton salted in pieces and well cooked in water with shallots; salted from morn to eve, or a day at most.

Common Pottages Thin and Unspiced

And first POTTAGE OF OLD PEAS (POTAGE DE POIS VIELZ). Behoveth to shell them and to find out from the people of the place the nature of the peas of that place (for commonly peas cook not well in well water; and in some places they cook well in spring water or river water, as in Paris, and in others they will not cook in spring water, as at Béziers) and when you have found this out it behoves to wash them in a pail of warm water, then set them in a pot of warm water on the fire and boil them till they burst. Then drain off the liquid and set it aside, and fill the pot with the peas with warm water and set it on the fire and boil and pour off a second time, if you will; then put them back without water, for they will give out enough and boil in that; and it behoves not to put the spoon into the pot after the purée is made, but shake the pot and the peas together and little by little drop warm water into them, or hotter than warm and not cold, and boil and cook them thoroughly before you add anything other than hot water, be it meat or anything else; do not put in salt or bacon or any seasoning until they be quite cooked. You may add sewe[83] of bacon or meat, but not salt and the spoon ought not to be put in until they be well cooked; nathless they may be well moved about in the pot.

On a meat day it behoveth after that they be drained, to add sewe of bacon or meat, and when they be nearly cooked, you may put bacon therein; and when you take the bacon out of the peas, you ought to wash it in the sewe of the meat, so that it be fairer to set in strips on the meat, and be not covered with bits of the peas.

On a fish day, when the peas be cooked, you should have onions, which have cooked for as long as the peas in one pot and the bacon in another pot, and right as you pour and add the sewe of meat to the peas, so on a fish day, when you have put your peas on the fire in a pot, you must set aside your onions sliced in another pot, and pour and add the pot-water of the onions to the peas; and when all is cooked, fry the onions and put half of them with the peas and the other half in the purée, which is spoken of hereafter, and then add salt. And if on a fish day or in Lent there be whale-flesh (*craspois*) (p. 219[60]), you ought to use it as you use bacon on a meat day.

As to new peas, sometimes they be cooked with sewe of meat and brayed parsley to make a green pottage and that is for a meat day; and on a fish day, they be cooked in milk with ginger and saffron therein; and sometimes *à la cretonnée* as will be shown hereafter.

Item, BEANS may be frizzled (*frasées*) at Eastertide in this manner, to wit if you would have *fèves frasées*, it behoves you to shell and wash them and put them without soaking them, skin and all, into a pot of boiling water on the fire and let them boil until the skin be all wrinkled and cooked; then take it off the fire and put in a spoon and skin them and frizzle them in their own heat, one spoonful after another, and cast them into cold water. After this, it behoves to wash them in warm water like peas, and set them to boil in cold water and when they be boiled till they burst, drain them; and throw away the pot water and fill up with meat broth on a flesh day, or with some other liquid on a fish day; and season with oil and onion well cooked and then fried, or with butter, and they can be made green again with bean leaves fresh brayed, moistened with warm water and strained; then do as with the others [the peas], either with bacon on a meat day, or as for a fish day.

PORRAY OR GREENS (PORÉE). There be three sort of porray, according to the saying of cooks, who call them white, green and black.

White porray is so called because it is made of the white of leeks, chines, chitterlings and ham, in the autumn and winter seasons on meat days; and know that no other fat save pigs' fat is good therewith. And first you pick over, wash, slice and blanch the leeks, to wit in summer when they be young; but in winter, when the aforesaid leeks be older and harder, it behoves you to parboil[84] them, instead of blanching them, and if it be a fish day, after what has been said, you must put them in a pot of hot water and so boil them, and also boil sliced onions and then fry the onions, and afterwards fry the leeks with the onions that have been fried already; then put all to cook in a pot of cow's milk, if it be out of Lent and on a fish day; and if it be in Lent one puts milk of almonds therein. And if it be a meat day, when these summer leeks be blanched, or the winter leeks parboiled as aforesaid, do you set them to cook in a pot of sewe of salt meat or pork, with some bacon therein.

Nota that sometimes for leeks one makes a thickening of bread.

Item, white porray of beets is made as above in mutton and beef sewe mixed, but not in sewe of pork; and on a fish day with milk of almonds or cows' milk.

Item, CRESS IN LENT WITH MILK OF ALMONDS. Take your cress and set it to parboil, with a handful of beets cut up, and fry them in oil, then set to boil in milk of almonds; and when it is not Lent fry it in lard and butter until it be cooked, then dilute it with sewe of meat; or do it with cheese and serve it quickly or it will turn brown. Nathless, if you put parsley therein it should not be blanched.

There is a kind of porray called spinach and it has longer leaves, thinner and greener than common porray and it is eaten at the beginning of Lent.

Porray of beets that is washed, then cut up and parboiled, keeps greener than that which is first parboiled and then sliced. But still greener and better is that which has the outer leaves removed and is then washed and cut up very small, and blanched in cold water; then the water is changed and it is set to soak in fresh water, then well drained and set in a pot with bacon and mutton sewe and brought to the boil once; and when it has boiled for a little and you would serve it, set therein some parsley, picked over, washed and cut up, and a little green fennel and boil once only.

All considered, porray that is least boiled and not parboiled is the greenest and parsley ought not to be boiled, or only very little, for in boiling it loses its savour.

Green porray on a fish day. Let it have the outer leaves removed and be cut up and then washed in cold water without parboiling it and then cooked with verjuice and a little water, and put some salt therein and let it be served boiling and very thick, not clear; and put at the bottom of the bowl, underneath the porray, salt butter, or fresh if you will, or cheese, or old verjuice.

Porray of sprouts is in season from January to Easter and afterwards.

Black porray is made with spiced strips of bacon; to wit the porray is picked over, washed, then cut up and blanched in boiling water, then fried in the fat of bacon slices; then do you moisten it with boiling water (and some say that if it be washed in cold water it is darker and more black) and you must set upon each bowl two slices of bacon.

CABBAGES be of five sorts; the best be those that have been frost-bitten and they be tender and soon cooked; and in frosty weather they must not be parboiled, but in rainy weather they must.

White cabbages come at the end of August.

Cabbage hearts at the end of the vintage. And when the heart of the cabbage, which is in the midst, is plucked off, you pull up the stump of the cabbage and replant it in fresh earth, and there will come forth from it big spreading leaves; and the cabbage takes a great deal of room and these cabbage hearts be called Roman cabbages and they be eaten in winter; and when the stumps be re-planted, there grow out of them little cabbages which be called sprouts and which be eaten with raw herbs in vinegar; and if you have plenty, they are good with the outer leaves removed and then washed in warm water and cooked whole in a little water; and then when they be cooked add salt and oil and serve them very thick, without water, and put olive oil over them in Lent. Then there be cabbages which be called Easter cabbages, because they be eaten at Eastertide, but they be served from August; and when after sowing they are half a foot above the ground, they must be pulled up and transplanted.

And first concerning the cabbage hearts, to wit when the leaves be plucked off, and picked over and cut up, it behoves to parboil them very well and for much longer than the other cabbages, for Roman cabbages require to have the green of the leaves torn into pieces and the yellow, that is to wit the veins, crushed in a mortar, then all blanched together in hot water, then drained and put in a pot of warm water, if you have not enough meat sewe; and serve with very greasy pot-water and some brayed bread therein.

And know that cabbages require to be put on the fire very early in the morning and cooked for a very long time, much longer than any other pottage, and on a good, strong fire, and they should be diluted with beef fat and none other, whether they be hearts or early cabbages, or whatever they be save sprouts. Know also that the greasy pot-water of beef and mutton is proper thereto, but in no wise that of pork, which is only good for leeks.

Then on a fish day you may parboil cabbages and set them to cook in warm water and add oil and salt.

Item, therewith some put oatmeal. *Item*, instead of oil some put butter thereto.

On a meat day you may put therewith pigeons, sausages and hare, coots and plenty of bacon.

TURNIPS be hard and ill to cook until they have been in the cold and frost; you cut off the head and tail and other hairs or roots, then scrape and wash them in two or three cauldrons of hot – very hot – water, then cook them in hot meat sewe, be it of pig, beef or mutton.

Item, in Beauce after cooking them, they cut them up into slices and fry them in a pan and cast spice powder over them.

HANDY OR IMPROVISED SOUP[85] (SOUPE DEPSOURVUE). Take parsley and fry it in butter, then pour boiling water on to it and boil it and add salt, and serve your sops as in the purée.

Aliter, if you have some cold beef, cut it up very small and then bray a little bread moistened with verjuice and run it through the strainer and set it in a dish with spice powder over it. Warm it on the coal.[86] It is good for three people.

Aliter, on a meat day, take water and set it to boil with almonds in it; then peel and bray the almonds, moisten them with warm water, strain them and set them to boil with powder of ginger and saffron and serve in bowls; and in each bowl a slice of fried fish.

Aliter, on a fish day, take meat broth and bread soaked in thin pot-water of meat, then bray it with six eggs, strain and put in a pot with greasy water, spices, verjuice, vinegar and saffron; bring it up to the boil once and serve in bowls.

Aliter, boil a little bacon in a pot and when it is half cooked take a fresh mackerel and cut it into pieces and set them to cook with the bacon and then take it all out and set minced parsley to boil until it bubbles once and serve.

TO KNOW A GOOD CHEESE. Good cheese has six qualities: *Non Argus, nec Helena, nec Maria Magdalena, sed Lazarus et Martinus, respondens pontifici.*[87]

Non mie blanc comme Helaine,
Non mie plourant com Magdalaine,
Non Argus, mais du tout avugle,
Et aussi pesant comme un bugle [boeuf]:
Contre le poulce soit rebelle,
Et qu'il ait tigneuse cotelle [cotte].
    Sans yeulx, bien plourer, non pas blanc.
    Tigneulx, rebelle, bien pesant.

Not white as snow, like fair Helen,
Nor moist, like tearful Magdalen,
Not like Argus full of eyes,
But heavy, like a bull of prize.
Well resisting thumb pressed in,
And let it have a scaly skin.
    Eyeless and tearless, in colour not white.
    Scaly, resisting and weighing not light.

Pottages Thin and Spiced

First, *nota* that all spices that be for putting into pottages must be well brayed and not strained, save it be for a jelly; and into all pottages behoveth it to put the spices as late as may be, for the sooner they be put in, the more they lose their savour; and the bread crumbs should be strained.

MUTTON COLOURED YELLOW (MOUTON AU JAUNET). Cut it into pieces all raw and let it be from the leg, cook it in water, then bray thereon a head of ginger and some saffron and moisten it with verjuice, wine and vinegar.

CAPON BREWET (BROUET DE CHAPONS). Cook you capons in water and wine, then dismember them and fry them in grease, then bray the guts and livers of your capons with almonds and moisten them with your sewe and boil; then take ginger, cinnamon, clove, galingale, long pepper and grain of paradise and moisten them with

vinegar and boil; and to serve it forth, put the solid part out into
bowls and pour the pottage on to it.

GRAVY (GRAVÉ OU SEYMÉ) is a winter pottage. Peel onions and
boil them in slices, then fry them in a pot. Now behoveth it to have
your chicken cleft across the back and grilled on the grill over a coal
fire, or if it be veal the same; and let the veal be put in in gobbets
and the chicken in quarters and put them with the onions in the pot;
then have white bread toasted on the grill and steeped in the sewe of
another meat; and then bray ginger, clove, grain [of paradise] and
long pepper, moisten them with verjuice and wine (but strain them
not) and set them aside; then bray the bread and run it through the
strainer and put it in the brewet and let all strain together and boil;
then serve it forth.

ROSEE OF YOUNG RABBITS (ROSÉ DE LAPPEREAUX [etc.]), larks and
small birds or chickens. Let the rabbits be skinned, cut up, parboiled, done again in cold water and larded; let the chickens be
scalded for plucking, then done again, cut up and larded, and let
larks and little birds be plucked only for parboiling in sewe of meat;
then have bacon lard cut up into little squares and put them into a
frying pan and take away the lumps but leave the fat, and therein fry
your meat, or set your meat to boil on the coal, often turning it, in
a pot with fat. And while you do this, have peeled almonds and
moisten them with beef broth and run it through the strainer, then
have ginger, a head of clove, cedar otherwise hight *alexander* [red
cedar], make some gravy and strain it and when the meat is cooked
set it in a pot with the broth and plenty of sugar; then serve in bowls
with glazed spices thereon.

Red cedar is a wood that is sold by the spicers, and it is called
'cedar whereof the sheaths of knives be made'.

Other Thick Meat Pottages

CRETONNÉE of NEW PEAS OR BEANS (CRETONNÉE DE POIS NOUVEAULX
OU FÈVES NOUVELLES). Cook them until they become a purée and
then pour away the liquid, then take cows' milk very fresh — and
say to the woman who shall sell it to you that she give it not to you
if she have put water therein, for often they add to their milk and
it is not fresh if there be water in it, it will turn. And first boil this
milk before putting anything into it, for again it will turn [if you do
not]; then bray first ginger to give appetite, and saffron to colour it

yellow; nathless if you would thicken it with yolks of eggs dropped slowly therein, the same yolks of eggs will suffice to colour it and also to thicken it, but milk turneth more quickly with yolks of eggs than with a thickening of bread and saffron for colouring. Wherefore, if you would thicken it with bread, it must be white bread and not risen and it must be put to soak in a bowl with milk and broth of meat, then brayed and run through a strainer. And when your bread is strained and your spices not so, set all to boil with your peas; and when all be cooked, add thereto your milk and some saffron. Again you may use another thickening, to wit peas or beans, brayed and then strained; and do you take whatsoever thickening best pleaseth you. When the thickening is of yolk of eggs, it behoveth to beat them, put them through the strainer and run them very slowly into the milk, after it hath been well boiled with the new peas or beans and the spices, and hath been taken off the fire. The safest way is to take a little milk and moisten the eggs in the bowl and then [do so] again and again, until the yolks be well mixed with plenty of milk by the spoon; then put it into a pot away from the fire and the pottage will not turn. And if the pottage is thick moisten it with the sewe of the meat. This done, behoveth it to have chickens quartered, or veal, or a gosling boiled and then fried and do you put two or three pieces in each bowl and the pottage over them.

CRETONNÉE for a fish day, let the fried meats be of tench, pike, soles or dab fried.

POULTRY FLAVOURED WITH CUMMIN (COMMINÉE DE POULAILLE). Cut it into pieces and put it to cook in water and a little wine, then fry it in fat; then take a little bread dipped in your broth and take first ginger and cummin, moisten them with verjuice, bray and strain and put all together with meat or chicken broth, and then colour it either with saffron or with eggs or yolks run through a strainer and dropped slowly into the pottage, after it is taken off the fire. *Item*, best it is to make it with milk as aforesaid and then to bray your bread after your spices, but behoveth it to boil the milk first lest it burn, and after the pottage is finished let the milk be put into wine (*meseemeth that this is not needful*)[88] and fry it. Many there be that fry it not, nathless it tastes best so.

(*Bread is the thickening and afterwards he saith eggs, which is another thickening, and one should suffice, as is said in the chapter concerning the* cretonnée.)

Verjuice and wine. If you would make your pottage with milk behoveth not to use wine or verjuice.)

COMMINÉE FOR A FISH DAY. Fry your fish, then peel almonds and bray them and dilute with purée or fish broth and make milk of almonds; but cows' milk is more appetising, though not so healthy for the sick; and for the rest do as above. *Item*, on a meat day, if you cannot have cows' milk, you may make the dish of milk of almonds and meat as above.

CINNAMON BREWET (BROUET DE CANELLE). Break up your poultry or other meat and stew it in water, putting wine therewith, and [then] fry it; then take raw dried almonds in their shells unpeeled and great plenty of cinnamon and bray them very well and moisten them with your broth or with beef broth and boil them with your meat; then bray ginger, cloves and grain [of paradise] etc., and let it be thick and red.

GARNISHED BREWET (BROUET GEORGÉ, BROUET HOUSSIÉ). Take poultry broken into quarters, or veal or such meat as you will broken into gobbets and boil it with bacon; and beside this have onions minced small, cooking and frying in a pan with some fat. Have, likewise, bread toasted on the grill and set it to soak in the broth of your meat with some wine therein; then bray ginger, cinnamon, long pepper, saffron, cloves and grain [of paradise] and the livers and bray them so well that needeth not to strain them, and moisten them with verjuice, wine and vinegar. And when the spices be taken out of the mortar, bray your bread and moisten it with that in which it hath been soaking, and run it through the strainer and add leaves of parsley if you will and set all to boil with fat and onions and then fry your meat. And this pottage ought to be the brown hue of fat and as thick as a *soringue*.

(*I do not believe that it behoveth [to use] wine or vinegar.*)

Nota that because of the parsley only is it called 'garnished' (*houssié*) brewet, for just as one saith 'fringed' (*frangié*) with saffron, so doth one say garnished with parsley; and it is the manner of speaking of cooks.

RED BREWET (BROUET ROUSSE) is made like Brewet *Georgé* above, save that one putteth not saffron therein, nor wine nor vinegar, but putteth therein greater plenty of cinnamon and onions cut into rounds.

A VINEGAR DISH (UNE VINAIGRETTE). Take the spleen of a pig and let it be well washed and scalded and then half roasted on the grill;

then mince it into gobbets and put them in an earthenware pot, with fat and onions cut into rounds, and set the pot on the fire and move it often. And when all is well fried or cooked, add thereto beef broth and boil all together, then bray toasted bread, ginger, grain [of paradise], saffron, etc., and moisten with wine and vinegar, and boil it, and it ought to be brown.

WHITE BREWET (BROUET BLANC). Take capons, pullets or chickens killed the due time beforehand, either whole or in halves or quarters, and slices of veal and cook them with bacon in water and wine and when they be cooked take them off, and then take almonds and peel and bray them and moisten them with sewe from your birds, and let it be as clear as may be, with no dregs nor any thickness, and then run it through the strainer; then take white ginger, pared or peeled, with grain of paradise moistened as above, and run them through a very fine sieve and mix with milk of almonds. And if it be not thick enough, then run in flour of *amidon* or rice boiled and add a drop of verjuice and put therein great plenty of white sugar. And when you have served it forth, powder thereon a spice that is hight red coriander and set pomegranate seeds with comfits and fried almonds round the edge of each bowl. See hereafter concerning this under blankmanger.

BLANKMANGER (BLANC MANGIER) of capons for sick folk. Cook it in water until it is well done, then bray great plenty of almonds and capons' guts and let them be well brayed and moistened with your broth and run through the strainer. Then set it to boil well, until it is well thickened; then bray pared white ginger and the other spices contained heretofore under white brewet.

GERMAN BREWET (BROUET D'ALEMAIGNE). Take meat of coneys, poultry and veal and break it into pieces; then boil it in water until it is half cooked and then fry it in bacon lard; then have some onions minced small in a pot on the fire, and in the pot some fat, and move the pot often; then bray ginger, cinnamon, grain of paradise, nutmegs and roasted livers in a brochette on the grill, and some saffron diluted with verjuice, and let it be of a yellow hue and thick. And first [have] bread toasted on the grill and strained; and let it all be set together to boil with some leaves of parsley in the aforesaid pot and let there be sugar therein; and to serve it forth, set two or three pieces of your meat in the bowl and some broth over it and sugar on the top of the broth.

(Note what is required; for some cooks say that German broth ought not to be yellow, and this one saith that it should. So if it ought to be yellow the saffron ought not to be passed through the strainer, but it ought to be well brayed and moistened and put thus into the pottage; for that which is strained is to give colour; that which is sprinkled on the top is said to be 'fringed' (frangié).)

DELICATE ENGLISH BREWET [SOUBTIL BROUET D'ANGLETERRE]. Take peeled and cooked chestnuts and as much or more of hard yolks of eggs or pork liver: bray all together, moisten with warm water, then run through the strainer; then bray ginger, cinnamon, cloves, grain [of paradise], long pepper, galingale and saffron to give colour and set them to boil together.

SAVOY BREWET (BROUET DE SAVOIE). Take capons or pullets and boil them with very lean bacon and livers; and when they be half cooked, take them off and put in breadcrumbs soaked in the sewe, then bray ginger, cinnamon, and saffron and take them out; then bray the livers with plenty of parsley, strain and afterwards bray and strain the bread and boil all together.

GENESTE is called *geneste* because it is as yellow as the flowers of broom (*geneste*)[89] and it is yellowed with yolk of eggs and saffron and this is done in summer instead of civey and it is done as is said hereafter, save that there be no onions therein.

HARE CIVEY (CIVÉ DE LIÈVRE). First, cleave the breast of the hare, and if it be fresh taken, as one or two days since, wash it not, but set it to toast upon the grill, i.e. to grill on a good coal fire or on the spit; then have cooked onions and fat in a pot and put your onions in with the fat and your hare by gobbets, and fry them on the fire, moving the pot very often, or fry them in a frying pan. Then toast and burn some bread and soak it in the sewe of the meat with vinegar and wine; and beforehand have brayed ginger, grain [of paradise], clove, long pepper, nutmegs and cinnamon and let them be brayed and moistened with verjuice and vinegar or meat broth; pour it out again and set it aside. Then bray your bread, moisten it with broth and strain the bread (and not the spices) through the strainer, and put the broth, onions and fat, spices and toasted bread all to cook together, and the hare likewise; and take care that the civey is brown, sharpened with vinegar, tempered with salt and spices.

A TILE OF MEAT (TUILE DE CHAR). Take cooked crayfish and remove the flesh from the tails; and the rest, to wit tails and carcase, must be brayed for a very long time; and afterwards take unpeeled almonds, and let them be shelled and washed in hot water like peas, and let them be brayed with the shell in what is abovesaid and with them bray breadcrumbs browned on the grill. Now you should have capons, chickens and pullets broken all raw into quarters, or veal broken into gobbets, and cooked, and with their sewe wherein they be cooking you should moisten and dilute what you have brayed and then pass it through a strainer; then bray the dregs left [in the strainer] once more and strain again; then add ginger, cinnamon, clove and long pepper, moistened with verjuice without vinegar, and boil all together. Now let your meat be cooked in pork's fat in gobbets or quarters, and serve it forth in bowls and pour pottage over it and on the pottage, in each bowl, set four or five crayfish tails, with powdered sugar over all.

More Thick Pottages Without Meat

SORINGUE OF EELS (SORINGUE D'ANGUILLES). Skin and then cut up your eels; then have onions cooked in slices and parsley leaves and set it all to fry in oil; then bray ginger, cinnamon, clove, grain [of paradise] and saffron, and moisten with verjuice and take them out of the mortar. Then have toasted bread brayed and moistened with purée and run it through the strainer, then put in the purée and set all to boil together and flavour with wine, verjuice and vinegar; and it must be clear.

ESPINBESCHE OF ROACHES (ESPINBESCHE DE ROUGETS). Parboil and roast your roaches; then take verjuice and powder, cameline and parsley; boil them together and pour over.

YELLOW POTTAGE OR YELLOW SAUCE (POTAGE JAUNET OU SAUSSE JAUNETTE) on cold or hot fish. Fry in oil, without any meal, pike, skinned perch or other fish of this sort, then bray almonds and dilute them with wine and verjuice and strain and set on the fire; then bray ginger, clove, grain [of paradise] and saffron and moisten them with your broth and when the pottage boils, put in your spices; and to serve put in sugar and let it be thick.

Roast Meats

STUFFED PIGLING (POURCELET FARCI). Let the pig be killed by cutting his throat and scalded in boiling water and then skinned; then take the lean meat and throw away the feet and entrails of the pig and set him to boil in water; and take twenty eggs and boil them hard and chestnuts cooked in water and peeled. Then take the yolks of the eggs, the chestnuts, some fine old cheese and the meat of a cooked leg of pork and chop them up, then bray them with great plenty of saffron and ginger powder mixed with the meat; and if your meat becometh too hard, soften it with yolks of eggs. And open not your pig by the belly but across the shoulders and with the smallest opening you may; then put him on the spit and afterwards put your stuffing into him and sew him up with a big needle; and let him be eaten either with yellow pepper sauce or with cameline in summer.

(Nota, that I have indeed seen stuffed pig and it is very good. And that is how it is now done and pigeons likewise.)

BOAR'S UMBLES (BOURBELIER DE SANGLIER). First behoveth to put it in boiling water and soon have it forth and stick it all over with cloves; set it to roast and baste it with sauce made of spices, to wit ginger, cinnamon, clove, grain [of paradise], long pepper and nutmegs, moistened with verjuice, wine and vinegar and baste therewith without boiling; and when it is roasted boil all together. And this sauce is called Boar's Tail and you will find it hereafter *(and there it is thickened with bread and here not)*.

SWAN. Pluck him like a chicken or a duck and scald or do again [in hot water]; put him on a spit skewered in four places and roast him whole with beak and feet and pluck not his head; eat with yellow pepper sauce.

Item, who will may glaze him.

Item, in killing, split him from head to shoulders.

Item, they be sometimes skinned and clad again in their feathers.

Pasties

CHICKENS be set in a pasty on their backs with the breast upward and large slices of bacon on the breast, and then covered.

Item, in the Lombard manner, when the chickens be plucked and prepared, take beaten eggs (to wit yolks and whites) with verjuice and spice powder and dip your chickens therein; then set them in the pasty with strips of bacon as above.

MUSHROOMS of one night be the best and they be little and red within and closed at the top; and they must be peeled and then

washed in hot water and parboiled and if you wish to put them in a
pasty add oil, cheese and spice powder.

Item, put them between two dishes on the coals and then add a
little salt, cheese and spice powder. They be found at the end of
May and June.

PASTIES OF FRESH VENISON. You must parboil and scour venison,
then lard it and make pasties; and pasties of all sorts of fresh venison
be made thus; and it must be cut into big slices like faggots and so
it is called *pasté de bouly lardé*.

BEEF PASTIES. Take good, young beef and remove all the fat and
set the lean to cook in pieces until it boil once, and then take it to the
pastry cook to be minced; and the fat with beef marrow.

The meat of a beef's cheek cut into slices and set in a pasty; then
when the pasty is cooked, the sauce of a young duckling (*halebran*)
(p. 191) must be cast therein.

MUTTON PASTIES. Well minced up small with shallots.

Freshwater Fish

CARP. Some prefer the soft-roed to the hard *et e contrario*. And *nota*
that the sterile be better than either.

Item, to prepare it, remove the gall that is right at the back of the
throat, and this done you may put the head to cook whole and it will
cook well and fairly; and if the gall were not taken out the head
would always be bloody and bitter. Wherefore when the gall cometh
not out whole without breaking, you should forthwith wash the
place and rub in salt, and if the gall cometh out whole you should
not wash the head nor anything else, but it behoveth to put the head
to boil first and soon afterwards the tail, and then afterwards the
remnant, all on a slow fire. Boiled carp is eaten with green sauce and
if any be left over it is put in *galentine*.

Item, STEAMED CARP (CARPE A L'ESTOUFFÉE). First, put minced
onions in a pot to boil with water and when the onions be well
cooked, cast in the head and soon afterwards the tail, and soon afterwards the pieces [of the body] and cover it well over, so that no
steam cometh forth. And when it is cooked, have ready your seasoning of ginger, cinnamon and saffron, moistened with wine and a
little verjuice, to wit the third part, and set all to boil together well
covered up; and then serve forth in bowls.

Nota that the Germans say of the French that they put themselves in great danger by eating their carp so underdone. And it hath been observed that if French and Germans have a French cook who cooketh carps for them, those carps being cooked after the French fashion, the Germans will take their portion and will have it cooked somewhat more than before and the French not so.

EEL REVERSED (ANGUILLE RENVERSÉE). Take a large eel and steam it, then slice it along the back the length of the bone on both sides, in such manner that you draw out the bone, tail and head all together, then wash and turn it inside out, to wit the flesh outwards, and let it be tied from place to place; and set it to boil in red wine. Then take it out and cut the thread with a knife or scissors, and set it to cool on a towel. Then take ginger, cinnamon, cloves, flour of cinnamon, grain [of paradise], nutmegs, and bray them and set them aside. Then take bread toasted and well brayed, and let it not be strained, but moistened with wine wherein the eel hath been cooked and boil all together in an iron pan and put in verjuice, wine and vinegar and cast them on the eel.

LAMPREYS. Be it known that some bleed the lamprey before they steam it and some steam it before they bleed or scald it. To bleed it, first wash your hands very well, then split its mouth in the midst of the chin and put your finger in and pull out the tongue, and bleed the lamprey into a dish, and put a little spit into its mouth to make it bleed the better. And if your fingers or hands be covered in blood, wash them and likewise the cut with vinegar and run it into the dish and keep this blood, for it is the fat.

As to steaming, have hot water on the fire, boiling, and steam it like an eel; and with a blunt knife peel away the inside of the throat and throw away the skin and roast it to a turn. And to make the thick sauce (*boe*, i.e. *boue*) take ginger, cinnamon, long pepper, grain [of paradise] and a nutmeg and bray them and set them on one side; then take bread toasted until it is quite black and bray it and moisten it with vinegar and run it through the strainer; then set the blood, the spices and the bread to boil all together and bring them to the boil once only, and if the vinegar be too strong, temper it with wine or verjuice; and then it is muddy; and it is black and just thick enough and not too thick, and the vinegar is slightly the strongest taste and it is a little salt; then pour it hot on to the lamprey and let it simmer.

Item, another and quicker sauce may be made. Take the blood and some vinegar and salt and when the lamprey is roasted to a turn, boil the sauce, bring it once to the boil only, and pour it over your lamprey and leave it to simmer between two dishes.

CRAYFISH cooked in water and wine and eaten with vinegar.

Sea-fish Round and Flat[90]

Round sea-fish in winter, flat in summer. *Nota* that no sea-fish is good when it is taken in rainy or damp weather.

COD. When it is taken in the far seas and it is desired to keep it for ten or twelve years, it is gutted and its head removed and it is dried in the air and sun and in no wise by a fire, or smoked; and when this is done it is called stockfish. And when it hath been kept a long time and it is desired to eat it, it behoves to beat it with a wooden hammer for a full hour, and then set it to soak in warm water for a full two hours or more, then cook and scour it very well like beef; then eat it with mustard or soaked in butter. And if any remain in the evening, let it be fried in small pieces like shreds and spice powder thereon.

FRESH COD prepared and cooked like gurnard with white wine and eaten *à la jance*; and the salt fish eaten with butter or mustard. If the salt fish is too little soaked it tastes too salty, and if too much it is not good; wherefore whoever is buying it ought to taste it by eating a little.

FRESH MACKEREL is in season in June, albeit it is found from the month of March. Clean it out by the ear, then dry with a clean rag and set it to roast without washing it at all, and it is eaten with cameline or fine salt; and if salted, with vinegar and shallots. And it is also put in pasties with spice powder thereon.

RAY (or SKATE) is cleaned out through the navel and keep the liver, and cut it into small pieces and cook it like plaice, then skin it and eat it with cameline garlic sauce. Ray is good in September and better in October, for then it eats fresh herrings.

GALENTINE FOR RAY in summer. Bray almonds and moisten them with boiling water and run through the sieve; then bray ginger and garlic and moisten this with almond milk and strain it and boil all together and spread it over the pieces of ray.

Ray that has been cooked may be fried without flour in oil and eaten hot with cameline sauce and that is better than cold *galentine*.

Divers Ways of Preparing Eggs

ONE HERBOLACE (ARBOULASTRE) or two of eggs. Take of dittany two
leaves only, and of rue less than the half or naught, for know that it
is strong and bitter; of smallage, tansey, mint and sage, of each some
four leaves or less, for each is strong; marjoram a little more, fennel
more, parsley more still; but of porray, beets, violet leaves, spinach,
lettuces and clary, as much of the one as of the others, until you have
two large handfuls. Pick them over and wash them in cold water,
then dry them of all the water, and bray two heads of ginger; then
put your herbs into the mortar two or three times and bray them
with the ginger. And then have sixteen eggs well beaten together,
yolks and whites, and bray and mix them in the mortar with the
things abovesaid, then divide it into two, and make two thick om-
elettes, which you shall fry as followeth. First you shall heat your frying pan very well with oil, butter, or such other fat as you will, and
when it is very hot all over and especially towards the handle, mingle
and spread your eggs over the pan and turn them often over and
over with a flat palette, then cast good grated cheese on the top; and
know that it is so done, because if you grate cheese with the herbs
and the eggs, when you come to fry your omelette, the cheese at the
bottom will stick to the pan; and thus it befalls with an egg omelette
if you mix the eggs with the cheese. Wherefore you should first put
the eggs in the pan, and put the cheese on the top and then cover the
edges with eggs; and otherwise it will cling to the pan. And when
your herbs be cooked in the pan, cut your herbolace into a round or
a square and eat it not too hot nor too cold.

Entremets, Fried Dishes and Glazed Dishes
(Doreures)

FRUMENTY (FROUMENTÉE). First it behoves you to hull your wheat as
is done for peeled barley, then know that for ten bowls there is
needed a pound of hulled wheat, the which is sometimes to be had
from the spicers already hulled for a silver penny [5d.] a pound. Peel
and cook it in water until the evening, and leave it all night covered
by the fire in warm water, then take it out and peel. Then boil milk
in a pan and do not stir it, for it would turn; and straightway without
delay set it in a pot so that it smell not of brass; and also, when it is
cold, skim off the cream on the top so that this cream may not make
the frumenty turn, and once more boil the milk and a little of the

wheat with it, until there is no more wheat; then take yolks of eggs and break them into it, to wit for each sester [8 pints] of milk a hundred eggs, then take the boiling milk and beat the eggs with the milk, then take off the pot and throw in the eggs and take it off; and if you see that it is likely to turn, put the pot in a pailful of water. On a fish day one takes milk, or a meat day, meat broth; and it is meet to put in saffron if the eggs do not make it yellow enough; *item*, two heads of ginger.

FAULX GRENON. Cook the livers and gizzards of chickens, or some veal or a leg of pork or of mutton in water and wine, then mince it very small and fry it in lard; then bray ginger, cinnamon, clove, grain [of paradise], wine, verjuice, beef broth or its own, and a great store of yolks of eggs, and pour on to your meat and make all boil well together. Some add saffron, for it should be of a yellowish colour, and some add bread toasted, brayed and strained, for it should be thickened with eggs and bread and likewise it should be sharpened with verjuice. And when you serve it cast powdered cinnamon on to each bowl.

MORTREWS (MORTREUL) is made in like manner to *faulx grenon*, save that the meat is brayed in a mortar with cinnamon spice; and there is no bread but cinnamon powder over it.

TAILLIS to serve in Lent. Take fine raisins, boiled milk of almonds, cracknels, *galettes* and crusts of white bread and apples cut into little squares and boil your milk and add saffron to colour it and sugar and put all in together until it is thick enough to be cut. It is served in Lent, instead of rice.

STUFFED POULTRY (POULAILLE FARCÉE). Take your chickens and cut their throats, then scald them and pluck them, and be careful when you pluck them not to tear the skin; then do them again in water, then take a quill, and insert it betwixt the skin and the flesh and blow the bird up; then open it betwixt the two shoulders and see that you make not too large a hole, and draw out the intestines, and leave in their skin the legs, the wings, the neck and all the head and the feet.

And to make the stuffing, take mutton, veal and pork and chicken livers and mince them all up together raw, then bray them in a mortar with raw eggs and cheese and good spice powder and a very little saffron and just enough salt. Then fill your chickens and sew up the hole, and with the rest of your stuffing make balls like to the pastilles of woad[91] and set them to cook in beef broth or in fair boiling water with great plenty of saffron and let it not boil too much lest they fall to pieces; then spit them on a very thin spit. And to glaze them take great plenty of yolks of eggs and beat them with a little saffron brayed therein, and glaze therewith; and if you would have a green glaze, bray greenstuff and then great plenty of yolks of eggs well beaten and passed through a strainer for the greenstuff, and therewith glaze your poultry when it is cooked and your balls likewise. And put your spit into the vessel wherein is your glaze and run your glaze all along it, and set it back at the fire twice or thrice, so that your glaze may take hold; and have a care that your glaze come not before too hot a fire lest it burn.

SAVOURY RICE (RIS ENGOULÉ) for a meat day. Peel it and wash it in two or three lots of cold water until the water be quite clear, then half cook it, run off the purée and set it on flat trenchers to dry before the fire; then cook it until it is very thick, with beef dripping and saffron, if it be a meat day; and if that it be a fish day, put not therein dripping but instead put in almonds well brayed and unstrained; then sugar it and add not saffron.

TO MAKE A COLD SAGE (UNE FROIDE SAUGE). Take your chicken and quarter it and set it to cook in salt and water, then set it to get cold. Then bray ginger, cinnamon powder, grain [of paradise] and cloves and bray them well without straining; then bray bread dipped in chicken broth, parsley (the most), sage and a little saffron in the leaf to colour it green and run it through a strainer (and some there be that run therewith yolk of egg) and moisten with good vinegar, and when it is moistened set it on your chicken, and with and on the top of the aforesaid chicken set hard-boiled eggs cut into quarters and pour your sauce over it all.

Aliter, take the chicken and pluck it, then set it to boil with salt until it be cooked, then take it off and put in quarters to get cold; then put hard-boiled eggs to cook in water, and put some bread to soak in wine and verjuice or vinegar, as much of one as of the other; then take parsley and sage then bray ginger and grain [of paradise] and run it through the strainer and run in yolks of eggs and set the hard-boiled eggs in quarters on the chicken and cover it with your sauce.

FLAWNS IN LENT (FLAONS EN KARESME). Prepare and steam eels; cook them afterwards in water so hot that you can remove the flesh without the bones and leave also the head and tail and take only the flesh; and bray saffron in the mortar, then bray it on to the eel's flesh and moisten with white wine and of that make your flawns; and put sugar over them.

Item, flawns have a savour of cheese if made of the roes of luce and carp and of brayed almonds or *amidon*, and of saffron moistened with wine and plenty of sugar thereon.

Item, they be made with the meat of tench, luce or carp, and *amidon* and saffron, moistened with white wine and sugar thereon.

TO MAKE A TART (TOURTE), take four handfuls of beets, two handfuls of parsley, a handful of chervil, a sprig of fennel and two handfuls of spinach, and pick them over and wash them in cold water, then cut them up very small; then bray with two sorts of cheese, to wit a hard and a medium, and then add eggs thereto, yolks and whites, and bray them in with the cheese; then put the herbs into the mortar and bray all together and also put therein some fine powder. Or instead of this have ready brayed in the mortar two heads of ginger and on to this bray your cheese, eggs and herbs and then cast old cheese scraped or grated on to the herbs and take it to the oven and then have your tart made and eat it hot.

TO MAKE FOUR DISHES OF MEAT JELLY (GELÉE DE CHAR), take a pig and four calves' feet and have two chickens plucked and two thin young rabbits skinned, and you must cut away the fat, and let them be cut right along when they be raw, save the pig which is in gobbets; then put into a pan three quarts of white wine or clarry, a pint of vinegar, and half a pint of verjuice and boil and skim them well; then put therein a ½oz. of saffron tied up in a little cloth to give it the colour of amber, and boil meat and all together with a little salt; then take 10 or 12 heads of white ginger, or 5 or 6 heads of galingale, ½oz. of grain of paradise, 2 or 3 pieces of mace leaf, 2 silver pennyworths [10d.] of zedoary; cubebs and nard 3 silver pennyworths [15s.]; bay-leaves and 6 nutmegs; then bray them in a mortar and put them in a bag and set them to boil with the meat until it be cooked, then take it out and set it to dry on a clean cloth, then take the feet, groin and ears for the best dish and all the rest for the others. Then take a fair towel on two trestles and pour all your caudle therein, save the spices, which you shall take out, and set to strain for pottage, and do not move it, so that it may rub the clearer. But if it run not well, set fire on each side to keep it hot that it may run better, and run it two or three times until it be quite clear, or through a towel folded three times. Then take your dishes and serve forth your meat thereon and have cooked crayfish to set upon the meat of the legs and tail; and pour as much of your jelly (which you shall have heated up again) over the meat for the meat to lie and be covered therein, for there should only be a little meat. Then set it for a night to get cold in the cellar, and in the morning stick therein cloves and bay-leaves and flour of cinnamon and scatter red anise. *Nota* that to have it ready in two hours, it is meet to have quince seed, fern and cherry gum and crush them and set them in a linen bag to boil with the meat.

Item, on a fish day, jelly is made as above of luce, tench, bream, eels and crayfish and of pike. And when the fish is cooked, you set it to dry on a fair white cloth, and skin it and clean it very well, and throw away the skins and the broth.

Item, TO MAKE BLUE JELLY, take of the aforesaid broth, be it of flesh or fish, and set it in a fair pan and boil it again on the fire, and get from the spicer two ounces of tournsole and set it to boil therewith until it be of a good colour, then take it off; and then take a pint of loach and cook it somewhere else, and spread the loach on your dishes and let the broth run on to it as above and then leave it to cool. *Item*, thus is made a blue jelly. And if you would make armorial bearings on the jelly, take gold or silver, whichsoever pleaseth you best, and trace [your design] with the white of an egg on a feather, and put the gold thereon with a brush.

POMMEAULX. Take the lean part of a leg of mutton, raw, and as much of the leg of a lean pig; and let them be minced together very small; then bray in a mortar ginger, grain [of paradise] and cloves and scatter the powder on your mincemeat, and moisten it with white of egg without the yolk; then knead the spices and the raw meat with your hands into the shape of an apple, then when the shape is well done, set them to cook in water with salt, then take them off, and have skewers of hazelwood and skewer them and set them to roast; and when they be roasted have parsley brayed and passed through a strainer and flour mixed therewith, neither too thin nor too thick, and take your *pommeaulx* off the fire and put a dish under them, and grease your *pommeaulx* by turning the spit over the dish; then put them to the fire as often as need be until the *pommeaulx* be quite green.

FROGS. To catch them have a line and a hook with a bait of meat or a red rag, and having caught the frogs, cut them across the body near the thighs, and take out the foulness from the hindparts, and take the two thighs, cut off the feet, and skin the thighs all raw, then take cold water and wash them; if the thighs remain for a night in cold water, they be so much the better and tenderer. And when they be thus steeped, let them be washed in warm water, then put in a towel and dried; the aforesaid thighs, thus washed and dried, must be rolled in flour and then fried in oil, fat or some other liquid, and let them be served in a bowl with spice powder thereon.

SNAILS that be called *escargols*, must be caught in the morning. Take those snails that be young and small and have black shells off vines and elder bushes, then wash them in water until they put forth no more slime; then wash them once in salt and vinegar and set them to cook in water. Then it behoves you to draw the aforesaid snails out of their shells at the end of a pin or needle, and then you should remove their tail which is black (for that is their turd); and then wash them, and set them to cook and boil in water and then take them out and set them in a dish or bowl, to be eaten with bread. And some say likewise that they be better fried in oil and onions, or other liquid after that they be cooked as aforesaid, and they be eaten with spice powder and be for rich folk.[92]

NORWEGIAN PASTIES (PASTÉS NORROIS) be made of cod's liver and sometimes with fish minced therewith. And you must first parboil them for a little and then mince them and set them in little pasties the size of a threepenny piece, with fine powder thereon. And when the pastry-cook brings them not cooked in the oven, they be fried whole in oil and it is on a fish day; and on a meat day they be made of beef marrow re-cooked, that is to wit the marrow is put in a pierced spoon, and the pierced spoon with the marrow therein is put in the broth of the pot of meat, and left there for as long as you would leave an unplucked chicken in hot water to warm it up; then set it in cold water, then cut up the marrow and round it into big balls or little bullets, then carry them to the pastry-cook, who puts them by fours or threes in a pasty with fine powder thereon. And without putting them in the oven they be cooked in fat.

Other Entremets

LARDED OR SEASONED MILK [LAIT LARDÉ]. Take cows' milk or ewes'

milk and set it to boil on the fire and cast in pieces of bacon and
saffron; and take eggs, to wit whites and yolks, beat them well
and cast them in all at once without stirring and boil all together; and
after this take it off the fire and let it turn; or without eggs you may
make it turn with verjuice. And when it has cooled, wrap it very
tightly in a piece of linen or thin stuff and squeeze it into whatsoever
shape you will, either flat or long, and weight it with a big stone,
and let it cool on the dresser all night; and the next day cut it up and
fry it in an iron pan, and it cooks by itself without other fat, or with
fat if you will; and it is set in dishes or bowls like strips of bacon and
stuck with cloves and pine-kernels.[93] And if you would make it
green, use tournsole.

RISSOLES ON A FISH DAY. Cook chestnuts on a slow fire and peel
them, and take hard-boiled eggs and cheese scraped, and mince
them up together very small; then moisten them with the white of
eggs, and mingle therewith spice powder and a very little moistened
salt, and make your rissoles, and then fry them in plenty of oil and
sugar them.

And *nota*, in Lent instead of eggs and cheese, take stockfish and
skirret roots cooked and cut up very small or the flesh of pike or
eels, figs and dates minced.

Item, commonly they be made of figs, raisins, roast apples and
nuts peeled to counterfeit pine-kernels and powder of spices; and let
the paste be well saffroned and then let them be fried in oil. And if
a binding be necessary *amidon* binds and rice too. *Item*, the flesh of
sea crayfish is good instead of meat.

RISSOLES ON A MEAT DAY be in season from St Remy's Day [1
October]. Take a haunch of pork and remove all the fat until none
remaineth, then set the lean to cook in a pot with plenty of salt; and
when it is nearly done, take it off and have eggs hard boiled and cut
up, both whites and yolks, and likewise cut up your meat very small,
and mix the eggs and the meat together and scatter spice powder
over them, then make it into a paste and fry in its own fat. And *nota*
that it is the right stuffing for a pig; and sometimes cooks buy it
from roasters in order to farce their pigs with it; nathless in stuffing
a pig it is good to put good cheese in it.

Item, at the court of lords like Monseigneur de Berry when they
kill an ox for beef, they make rissoles out of the marrow.

CRISPS OR PANCAKES [CRESPES]. Take flour and moisten it with eggs, as well the yolks as the whites, removing the germ, and dilute it with water, add salt and wine and beat them for a long time together. Then set some fat on the fire in a little iron pan, or half fat and half fresh butter and fry them; and then have a bowl pierced with a hole as big as your little finger and pour some of this liquid into the bowl, beginning with the middle, and let it run all round the pan; then set it in a dish, with powdered sugar thereon. And let the aforesaid iron or copper pan hold three half pints, and let the edge be half a finger high and let it be as wide above as below, neither more nor less; and for a good reason.

PANCAKES IN THE MANNER OF TOURNAI (CRESPES A LA GUISE DE TOURNAY). First, it behoves you to have provided yourself with a copper pan holding a quart, whereof the mouth must be no larger than the bottom, or very little more, and let the edge be of the height of four fingerbreadths, or a good three and a half. *Item*, it behoves to fill it with salt butter and to melt, skim and clean this and then pour it into another pan and leave all the salt and some fresh fat, very clean, in equal quantities. Then take eggs and fry them and take the whites away from half of them and let the remnant be beaten up, whites and yolks together, then take the third or fourth part of warm, white wine and mix all together. Then take the fairest wheaten flour that you can get and beat them together long enough to weary one person or two and let your paste be neither thin nor thick, but such that it may run gently through a hole the size of a little finger. Then set your butter and fat on the fire together, as much of one as of the other, until it boils; then take your paste and fill a bowl or a big spoon of pierced wood and run it slowly into your grease, first in the middle of the pan then turning it about until your pan be full; and then go on beating your paste without stopping, so as to make more crisps. And this crisp that is in the pan must be lifted with a little spit or skewer, and turned upside down to cook it, then taken out and put on a dish and the next must be begun; and all the time let someone be moving and beating up the paste unceasingly.

STUFFED STRAWS (PIPEFARCES). Take the yolks of eggs and flour and salt and a little wine and beat them well together, and cheese cut into strips and then roll the strips of cheese in the paste and fry them in an iron pan with fat therein. One does likewise with beef marrow.

Sauces Not Boiled

MUSTARD. If you would make provision of mustard to keep for a long time, make it in the harvest season and of soft pods. And some say that the pods should be boiled. *Item*, if you would make mustard in the country in haste, bray mustard seed in a mortar and moisten it with vinegar and run it through the strainer and if you would prepare it at once, set it in a pot before the fire. *Item*, if you would make good mustard and at leisure, set the mustard seed to soak for a night in good vinegar, then grind it in a mill and then moisten it little by little with vinegar; and if you have any spices left over from jelly, clarry, hippocras or sauces, let them be ground with it and afterwards prepare it.

SORREL VERJUICE. Bray sorrel very well without the stems and dilute it with old white verjuice and do not strain the sorrel, but bray it well; *vel sic*: bray parsley and sorrel or blades of corn. *Item*, vine shoots, to wit young shoots and tender ones, without stems.

CAMELINE. Note that at Tournai to make cameline they bray ginger, cinnamon and saffron and half a nutmeg moistened with wine, then take it out of the mortar; then have white breadcrumbs, not toasted but moistened in cold water and brayed in the mortar, moisten them with wine and strain them, then boil all together and put in brown sugar last of all; and that is winter cameline. And in summer they do the same, but it is not boiled.

And in truth, to my taste, the winter sort is good, but in [summer] that which followeth is far better; bray a little ginger and a great deal of cinnamon, then take it out and have toasted bread moistened, or plenty of bread raspings in vinegar, brayed and strained.

Nota that three differences there be between string ginger (*gingembre de mesche*) and colombine ginger. For the string ginger has a darker skin and is softer to the knife to cut, and lighter inside than the other; *item*, better and always dearer.

The galingale which has the reddest violet hue when cut is the better. Of nutmegs the heaviest and firmest to cut be the best. And likewise galingale which is heavy and firm to cut, for sometimes it is spoilt, mouldy and light as dead wood; that is not good, but that which is heavy and firm to the knife like a nut, that is good.

GARLIC CAMELINE FOR SKATE. Bray ginger, garlic and crusts of white bread moistened with vinegar; and if you add liver thereto it will be better.

WHITE OR GREEN GARLIC SAUCE FOR DUCKLINGS OR BEEF. Bray a clove of garlic and some white breadcrumbs untoasted, and moisten with white verjuice; and if you would have it green, for fish, then bray also some parsley and sorrel, or one of them, or rosemary.

MUSTY GARLIC (AULX MOUSSUS) FOR FRESH HERRINGS. Bray the garlic without peeling it, and let it be well brayed and moistened with must and serve it with the peel.

GREEN SPICE SAUCE. Well bray ginger, clove, grain [of paradise] and take them out of the mortar; then bray parsley or herb bennet, sorrel, marjoram, or one or two of these four, and white breadcrumbs moistened in verjuice, and strain and bray again very well, then strain once more and put them all together and season with vinegar.

Nota that it is a good pickle, but let there be no bread.

Nota that for all spices, many only put in rosemary leaves.

A GREEN PICKLE (SOUCIÉ VERGAY) FOR PRESERVING SALT-WATER FISH. Take parsley, sage, herb bennet, vinegar and strain them; but beforehand have brayed basil, hyssop, sorrel, clary, marjoram, ginger, cinnamon flour, long pepper, clove, and grain and be they taken out of the mortar and poured over your fish when all are strained; and let it be green. And some add thereto gillyflower, root and all.

For freshwater fish let a chawdon [sauce] be made in the same manner, save that you put in no herbs, and instead of herbs put saffron and nutmegs and verjuice, and it should be a thin yellow broth, and poured hot over cold fish.

The sauce for a roast capon is to dismember it and put salt and verjuice and a third part of white or red wine on the joints; and press it hard as you do a chicken.

Item, in summer, the sauce for a roast chicken is half vinegar, half rose-water and press, etc. *Item*, orange juice is good thereto.

Boiled Sauces

Nota that in July the old verjuice is very weak and the new is too crude; wherefore in the vintage season, verjuice half old and half new mixed is the best. *Item*, in pottage you dilute it with vegetable water, but in January, February, etc., the new is the best.

YELLOW OR SHARP PEPPER. Take ginger and saffron, then take toasted bread moistened with sewe of meat (or still better with vegetable sewe) and boil and when it boils add the vinegar.

BLACK PEPPER. Take clove and a little pepper and ginger and bray them well; then bray burnt bread dipped in this sewe of meat or thin vegetable water, which is better, then let them be boiled in an iron pan and when it boils put in vinegar; then put it into a pot on the fire to keep hot. *Item*, some add cinnamon thereto.

GALENTINE FOR CARP. Bray saffron, ginger, clove, grain [of paradise], long pepper and nutmegs and moisten with the greasy sewe in which the carp has been cooked, and add thereto verjuice, wine and vinegar and let it be thickened with a little toasted bread, well brayed and colourless (nathless strained bread maketh the best sauce) and let it all be boiled and poured over the cooked fish, then put on to plates. It is good warmed up on a dish on the grill, better than quite cold. *Nota* that it is fair and good without saffron and *nota* that it sufficeth to set on each plate two slices of carp and four fried gudgeons.

SAUPIQUET FOR CONEY, RIVER FOWL OR WOOD PIGEONS. Fry onions in good fat, or mince them and set them to cook in the dripping pan with sewe of beef, and add not verjuice or vinegar until it boils, and then add half verjuice and half wine and a little vinegar, and let the spices be strongest. Then take half wine and half verjuice and a little vinegar, and set all in the frying-pan beneath the coney, pigeon or river fowl, and when they be cooked, boil the sauce and have some pieces of toast and put them in with the birds.

CALIMAFRÉE OR LAZY SAUCE (SAULCE PARESSEUSE). Take mustard and powdered ginger and a little vinegar and the greasy sewe of the carp and boil them together; and if you would make this sauce for a capon, instead of putting the greasy sewe of the carp, put verjuice, vinegar and the fat of the capon.

JANCE OF COWS' MILK. Bray ginger, yolks of eggs without the germ, and pass them through the strainer with cows' milk; or in case it should turn, let the yolks of cooked eggs be taken and then brayed and passed through the strainer; moisten with cows' milk and boil well.

GARLIC JANCE (JANCE A AULX). Bray ginger, garlic, almonds and moisten with good verjuice and then boil; and some put in a third part of white wine.

JANCE is made in this manner: take almonds, set them in hot water, peel them and bray them and likewise two heads of ginger; or put therewith spice powder, a little garlic and white bread, rather more than the almonds and let it not be burnt but moistened with white verjuice and the fourth part of white wine; strain it, boil it well and serve it forth in bowls. And you must serve more of this than of other sauces.

A POITEVINE SAUCE. Bray ginger, cloves, grain [of paradise] and some livers, then take them out of the mortar; then bray toasted bread, wine and verjuice and water in equal quantities, and boil them with the fat of the roast and then pour it over your roast or serve in bowls.

MUST FOR YOUNG CAPONS (MOUST POUR HÉTOUDEAUX). Take new and black grapes and crush them in a mortar and boil them once and then run them through a strainer; and then sprinkle spice powder over them, a little ginger and more cinnamon, or cinnamon alone, because that is better, and mix a little in a silver spoon and throw therein little crusts, or brayed bread, or eggs or chestnuts to bind it; brown sugar and serve forth.

Item, if you want to make this sauce after St John's Day and before that there be any grapes, you must make it of cherries, wild cherries, quinces, mulberry wine, with powder of cinnamon and no ginger or very little, boil as above and then sprinkle sugar thereon.

Item, after that no more grapes are to be had, *scilicet* in November, the must is made of wild sloes, with the stones taken out, then brayed or broken up in the mortar, boiled with the shells, strained, spice powder added and the rest as above.

QUICK SAUCE FOR A CAPON. Have some fair clean water and set it in the dripping pan below the capon while it roasteth, and sprinkle the capon with it continually, then bray a sprig of garlic and moisten it with this water and boil; then serve forth. It is good as *jance*, if you have none.

SAUCE TO BE PUT TO BOIL IN PASTIES OF HALEBRANS, DUCKLINGS, LITTLE RABBITS AND WILD CONEYS. Take plenty of good cinnamon, ginger, cloves, grain [of paradise], half a nutmeg and mace and galingale, and bray them very well, moisten them with equal quantities of verjuice and vinegar and let the sauce be clear. And when the pasty is about cooked, pour the sauce therein and set it in the oven again to boil once only.

(*Nota* that *halebrans* be little ducklings which cannot fly until they have had the August rains.)

And *nota* that in winter you put more ginger for the spice to be stronger, for all sauces ought to be stronger in winter than in summer.

A BOAR'S TAIL (UNE QUEUE DE SANGLIER). Take umbles of pigs, hares and river fowl and set them on the spit with a dripping pan below and real wine and vinegar. Then take grain [of paradise], ginger, clove, nutmegs, long pepper and cinnamon and bray them and take them out of the mortar; then bray toasted bread moistened with wine and run through the strainer; then pour all the liquid into the dripping pan and the spices and bread into an iron pan or pot, with sewe of meat, and put therein whatsoever roast you are cooking and stick it first all over with cloves.

Nota that nutmegs, mace and galingale make the head to ache.

SAUCE FOR A CAPON OR HEN. Set a very small quantity of bread-crumbs to soak in verjuice and saffron and bray them; then put them in the dripping pan, with four parts of verjuice and the fifth part of the fat of the hen or capon and not more, for more would be too much, and boil it in the dripping pan and serve it forth in bowls.

SAUCE FOR EGGS POACHED IN OIL. Have onions cooked and par-boiled for a long time like cabbage, then fry them; afterwards empty the pan wherein you have fried your eggs so that nothing remain therein, and in it put water and onions and a fourth part of vinegar, to wit, let the vinegar form a fourth part of the whole, and boil it and pour it over your eggs.

Beverages for the Sick

TIZANNE DOULCE. Take water and boil it, then for each sester [here no doubt the sester of 8 pints] of water put in a bowl heaped with barley, and it matters not if it be hulls and all, and two *parisis* [2½d.] worth of liquorice, *item*, figs, and let it be boiled till the barley bursts; then let it be strained through two or three pieces of linen, and in each goblet put great plenty of crystallised sugar. Then the barley is good to give to poultry to eat to fatten them.

Nota that the good liquorice is the newest and it is a fresh greenish colour, and the old is more faded and dead and is dry.

BOCHET. To make six sesters of *bochet* take six pints of very soft honey and set it in a cauldron on the fire, and boil it and stir it for as long as it goes on rising and as long as you see it throwing up liquid in little bubbles which burst and in bursting give off a little blackish steam; and then move it, and put in seven sesters of water and boil them until it is reduced to six sesters, always stirring. And then put it in a tub to cool until it be just warm, and then run it through a sieve, and afterwards put it in a cask and add half a pint of leaven of beer, for it is this which makes it piquant (and if you put in leaven of bread, it is as good for the taste, but the colour will be duller), and cover it warmly and well when you prepare it. And if you would make it very good, add thereto an ounce of ginger, long pepper, grain of paradise and cloves, as much of the one as of the other, save that there shall be less of the cloves, and put them in a linen bag and cast it therein. And when it hath been therein for two or three days, and the brochet tastes enough of the spices and is sufficiently piquant, take out the bag and squeeze it and put it in the other barrel that you are making. And thus this powder will serve you well two or three times over.

Pottages for the Sick

FLEMISH CAUDLE (CHAUDEAU FLAMENT). Set a pot of water to boil, then for each bowl beat up four yolks of eggs with white wine and let it run slowly into your water and stir it very well, and put in salt to the right amount; and when it has well boiled take it from off the fire.

Nota. If you are only making one bowl for a sick person you must put in five yolks.

MILK OF ALMONDS. Parboil and peel your almonds and set them in cold water, then bray them and moisten them with water in which onions have been cooked and run through a strainer; then fry the onions and put a little salt therein, and boil it on the fire, and then add sops. And if you are making milk of almonds for the sick, do not put in onions and instead of using water of onions to moisten the almonds as is aforesaid, moisten them with clean warm water and boil it and put in no salt, but plenty of sugar. And if you want to make it for drinking, run it through the strainer or through two pieces of linen, and add plenty of sugar to the drink.

CHICKEN MOULD (COULIS D'UN POULET). Cook the chicken until it is all soft, and bray it with all its bones in a mortar, then moisten it with its own gravy, strain it and add sugar.

Nota that the bones ought to be boiled first, then taken out of the mortar, strained and the mortar cleaned; then bray the meat and great plenty of sugar.

Nota that after the great heats of June, spiced pottages come into season, and after St Remy's Day (1 October) civey of veal, hare, oysters, etc.

Other Small Things that be Needful

THIS IS THE MANNER OF MAKING PRESERVES (COMPOST). *Nota* that it must be begun on St John's Day, which is the 24th day of June.

First, you shall take 500 new nuts towards St John's Day, and look that the shell and the kernel be not yet formed, nor the shell too hard or too soft as yet, and pierce them in three places right through or in a cross. Then set them to soak in Seine water or spring water and change it daily; and they must be soaked for ten or twelve days, until they become black and you can taste no bitterness when you bite them; then set them to boil for a while in sweet water, for the space of time wherein you can say a Miserere,[94] or as long as you shall see is needful, that they be neither too hard nor too soft. Afterwards empty away the water, and set them to drain upon a sieve, and then melt a sester of honey, or as much as shall suffice to steep them all therein and let it be liquid and well skimmed; and when it shall have cooled down until it is just warm, put your nuts therein and leave them for two or three days, and then set them to drain. Take as much of your honey as they may soak in, and set the honey on the fire, and bring it well up to the boil once only, and skim it, and take it off the fire; and in each of the holes in your nuts set a clove on the one side and a crumb of ginger on the other, and afterwards put them in the honey as long as it shall be warm. And you shall turn them twice or thrice a day, and at the end of three days take them out; and boil the honey again and if there be not enough add some more and boil and skim and boil it, then put your nuts into it; and so every week for a month. Then leave them in an earthen pot or in a little cask, and turn it once a week.

Towards All Saints' Day [1 November] take large turnips and peel them and cut them into four pieces and set them to cook in water; and when they have been cooking for a short while, take them out and put them in cold water to make them tender, and then set them to drain; and take honey and melt it as you did for the nuts, and be careful not to cook your turnips too long.

Item, at the season of All Saints', you shall take as many carrots as you will, and scrape them well and cut them into pieces, and cook them like the turnips. (Carrots be red roots which be sold in hand-fuls in the market, for a silver penny a handful.)

Item, take choke pears (*poires d'angoisse*) and cut them into four quarters, and cook them like the turnips and peel them not; and do them no more and no less than the turnips.

Item, when pumpkins be in season, take neither the hardest nor the softest among them, and peel them, and take out the centre, and cut them into quarters, and do as with the turnips.

Item, when peaches be in season, take the hardest and peel and cut them.

Item, towards St Andrew's Day [30 November] take roots of parsley and fennel, and scrape them over, and divide them into little pieces, and cut through the fennel and take out the hard centre, but do not take out that of the parsley, and do everything as for the things abovesaid no more and no less.

And when all your preserves are ready, you can do what is required, according to the recipe which follows:

First, for every 500 nuts take a pound of mustard seed and half a pound of anise, a quarter and a half of fennel, a quarter and a half of coriander, a quarter and a half of caraways, to wit a seed which is eaten in comfits, and powder them all up; and then bray them all in a mustard-mill and soak them well in very good vinegar and set them in an earthen pot. And then take half a pound of horse radish, to wit a root which is sold by herbalists, and scrape it well and cut it up as small as you can, and grind it in a mustard-mill, and soak in vinegar.

Item, take half a quarter of clove wood, called *stem of cloves*, half a quarter of cinnamon, half a quarter of pepper, half a quarter of ginger, half a quarter of nutmeg, half a quarter of grain of paradise, and reduce them all to powder.

Item, take half an ounce of saffron of Ort[95] dried and pounded, and an ounce of red cedar, to wit a wood which is sold by spicers and it is called 'cedar from which knife sheaths be made'. And then take twelve pounds of good honey, thick and white, and melt it on the fire and when it is well cooked and skimmed, let it settle, then strain it and cook it again, and if it scums, you must strain again or allow it to get cold; then steep your mustard in good red wine and vinegar in equal parts and put it in the honey. You shall moisten your powders with wine and vinegar and put them in honey, and boil your cedars awhile in hot wine, and afterwards put the saffron with the other things and a handful of coarse salt.

Item, and this done, take two pounds of the raisins which be called raisins of Digne, to wit small ones, with no pips or seeds of any sort therein, and let them be fresh, and bray them well in a mortar and soak them with good vinegar, then run them through a strainer and put them with the other things. *Item*, if you add thereto four or five pints of must or boiled wine, the sauce will be all the better.

TO MAKE COTIGNAC (QUINCE MARMALADE), take quinces and peel them, then cut them into quarters and take out the eye at the end and the pips, then boil them in good red wine and then let them be run through a strainer; then take honey and boil it for a long time and skim it and afterwards set your quinces therein and stir them well up and boil until the honey is reduced to half the amount; then cast therein powdered hippocras, and stir until it is quite cold, then cut it into pieces and keep it.

FINE [SPICE] POWDER. Take of white ginger an ounce and a dram, of selected cinnamon a quarter, of cloves and grain [of paradise] each half a quarter of an ounce, and of lump sugar a quarter and reduce them to powder.

NUT JAM. Take new nuts before St John's Day, and peel and pierce them, and set them to soak in fresh water for nine days and each day renew the water; then let them dry, and fill the holes with sticks of clove and ginger and set them to boil in honey, and leave them therein as a conserve.

TO PREPARE WATER FOR WASHING THE HANDS AT TABLE, set sage to boil, then pour out the water and let it cool until it is just warm. Or you may instead use camomile or marjoram, or you may put in rosemary; and boil them with orange peel. And bay-leaves too are good.

HIPPOCRAS. To make powdered hippocras, take a quarter of very fine cinnamon selected by tasting it, and half a quarter of fine flour of cinnamon, an ounce of selected string ginger (*gingembre de mesche*), fine and white, and an ounce of grain [of paradise], a sixth of nutmegs and galingale together, and bray them all together. And when you would make your hippocras, take a good half ounce of this powder and two quarters of sugar and mix them with a quart of wine, by Paris measure. And *nota* that the powder and the sugar mixed together is [hight] the Duke's Powder.

For a quart or a quarter of hippocras by the measure of Béziers, Carcassonne or Montpellier, take five drams of fine cinnamon, selected and peeled; white ginger selected and pared three drams; of cloves, cardamom, mace, galingale, nutmegs, nard, altogether a dram and a quarter, most of the first and less of each of the others in order. Let a powder be made thereof, and with it put a pound and half a quarter (by the heavy weight) of lump sugar, brayed and mingled with the aforesaid spices; and let wine and sugar be set and melted on a dish on the fire, and mixed therewith; then put it in the strainer, and strain it until it runs a clear red. *Nota* that the sugar and the cinnamon ought to predominate.

SAGE. To make a little cask of sage, take two pounds of sage and cut off the stems, then put the leaves into the cask. *Item*, have half an ounce of cloves in a linen bag and hang it within the cask by a cord; *item*, you may put in half an ounce of bay; *item*, half a quarter of string ginger, half a quarter of long pepper and half a quarter of bay. And he that would have sage on the table in winter, let him have an ewer of sage water and pour it upon his white wine in a hanap.

TO MAKE WHITE WINE RED AT TABLE, take in summer the red flowers that grow in the corn and be called *perceau* or *neelle* or *passerose*,[96] and let them dry until they can be made into powder, and cast it privily into the glass with the wine and the wine will become red.

IF YOU WOULD HAVE VERJUICE AT CHRISTMAS FROM YOUR VINE ARBOUR, when you see the grape opening before it is in flower, cut it off by the stem and the third time let it grow till Christmas. Master Jehan de Hautecourt says that one ought to cut the stock below the grape and the other shoot beneath will put out new grapes.

IF YOU WOULD HAVE CHOKE PEARS OF A RED COLOUR IN NOVEMBER AND DECEMBER, put hay to cook, and cover the pot so that no smoke cometh forth. *Nota* that it behoves you to put on the pears fennel seed boiled in new wine and then dried, or comfits.

TO MAKE WHITE SALT, take a pint of coarse salt and three pints of water, and set them on the fire until the salt is melted in the water, then strain it through a cloth, towel, or sifter, then set it on the fire and boil it well and skim it, and let it go on boiling until it is quite dry and the little grains that have been throwing up water be dry; then turn the salt out of the pan and spread it on a cloth to dry in the sun.

TO WRITE ON PAPER A LETTER WHICH NONE SHALL SEE IF THE PAPER

BE NOT HEATED, take sal ammoniac and moisten and melt it in water; then write therewith and let it dry. And this will last for about eight days.

TO MAKE GLUE, it behoves you peel holly when it is at the sap (which is commonly from the month of May up to August) and then boil the bark in water until the topmost layer separates; then peel it off, and when it is peeled, wrap up that which remains in elder leaves or other large leaves, and set it in some cool place, as in a cellar, or within the earth, or in a cold dung heap, for the space of nine days or more, until it be decayed. And then behoveth it to pound it like brayed cabbage and to make it up into cakes like woad, and then go wash the cakes one after another, and break them up like wax; and let them not be too much washed in the first water, nor in too hard a water. And after you may break it all up together and knead it in running water and put it in a pot and keep it well covered.

And he who would make glue for water, let him warm a little oil and therein melt his glue; and then lime his line.

Item, another sort of glue is made from corn.

IF YOU WOULD KEEP ROSES RED, take a dozen buds and put them together as in a ball, and then cover them round with linen and tie them up with thread into a ball and make as many balls as you would preserve roses; and then set them in a crock of Beauvais earthenware and of none other, and fill it with verjuice; and as the verjuice is sucked up fill it up again, but let the verjuice be very good. And when you would have the buds full blown, take them out of the bags and set them in warm water and let them soak for a little.

Item, to keep roses in another manner, take as many buds as you would, and put them into a bottle of Beauvais earthenware, as many as you can get in. Afterwards take some of the loosest sand that you can have, and put as much of it as you can into the bottle and then stop it up well, so that nothing can pass in or out, and set the bottle in running water; and the rose will keep fresh there for the whole year.

TO MAKE ROSE-WATER WITHOUT LEAD ALEMBIC, take a barber's basin, and cover it with a kerchief spread right over the mouth in the manner of a drum, and then lay your roses on the kerchief, and above your roses set the bottom of another basin filled with hot cinders and live charcoal.

TO MAKE ROSE-WATER WITHOUT EITHER LEAD ALEMBIC OR FIRE, take two glass basins and do as is said at the back of this page [i.e.

in previous paragraph] and instead of ashes and charcoal, set it in the
sun; and in the heat thereof the water will be made.

The roses of Provins be the best for putting in dresses, but they
must be dried and sifted through a sieve at mid-August so that the
worms fall through the holes of the sieve, and after that spread it
over the dresses.

TO MAKE RED ROSE-WATER, take a glass flask and fill it half full of
good rose-water and fill the other half with red roses, to wit with the
petals of young roses, from which you shall have cut off the end of
the petal, which is white, and leave it nine days in the sun and nine
nights likewise, and then pour it out.

TO MAKE BIRDS LAY AND SIT AND REAR YOUNG IN AN AVIARY. *Nota*
that in the Hesdin[97] aviary, which is the largest in this realm, and in
the king's aviary at Saint-Pol,[98] and in Messire Hugues Aubriot's[99]
aviary, they were never able to make birds sit and rear little ones;
and in Charlot's[100] aviary they do so, *scilicet* laying, sitting and feed-
ing. In the first case the fault lieth in that the little birds be fed upon
hempseed, which is hot and dry, and they have nought to drink.
And in the second case, they be given chickweed or groundsel, sow-
thistles set in water ever fresh and constantly renewed, changed
thrice a day and in clean leaden vessels, and therein with the chickweed and the groundsel all green, all field thistles with their stems
well moistened in water, and hempseed sorted and broken up, with
the shells removed, and moistened with water. *Item*, let carded wool
and feathers be put in the aviary to make their nests. And thus have
I seen turtle-doves, linnets and goldfinches lay and rear their young.
Item, you should also give them caterpillars, worms, flies, spiders,
grasshoppers, butterflies, fresh hemp in leaf, moistened and soaked.
Item, spiders, caterpillars and such like things which be soft to the
little bird's beak, which is tender.

(And with such things do the peacocks feed their chicks, for you
have often seen a hen sit upon a peahen's eggs with her own, and the
shells break at the same time, but the little peacocks cannot live long
for their beaks be too tender, and the hen doth not seek soft things
for them according to their nature; and the chickens live well on
corn or soft paste, which is not so meet a food for peacocks. Again,
you will see that though you give a hen the best corn and the best-
sifted in the world, she will scratch it to find worms or flies.)

Item, at the end of April it behoves to go to the woods to seek branches forked with three forks, and nail them to the wall and cover them with other greenery, and within the fork the birds make their nest.

TO CURE TOOTHACHE, take a covered earthenware pot, or a pot without a lid with a trencher over it, and fill it with water and set it to boil; then undress and go to bed and let your head be well covered, and then take the covered pot and let it be well covered all over, with a hole in the middle, or let it be covered with a trencher pierced in the middle. And hold your teeth against the hole, with your mouth wide open, in order to breathe the steam of the water passing through the hole, and let sage and other herbs be set therein and keep yourself well covered up.

TO MAKE SAND FOR HOURGLASSES. Take the grease which comes from the sawdust of marble when those great tombs of black marble be sawn, then boil it well in wine like a piece of meat and skim it, and then set it to dry in the sun; and boil, skim and dry nine times; and thus it will be good.

POISONS FOR SLAYING A STAG OR A BOAR. Take the root of the herb aconite, which hath a blue flower, and bray it in a mortar and put it in a bag or a piece of cloth, and wring it to get out the juice; and set this juice in a basin in the sun, and at nightfall set it under cover in a dry place that neither water nor any other dampness get to it, and go on putting it back into the warmth of the sun until it has become a thick jelly, like gummed wax, and put it in a well closed box. And when you would use it for shooting, smear it between the barbs and the iron socket, so that when the beast is wounded, it enters into the flesh, for if you do otherwise, to wit if you otherwise anoint the iron, when it enters into the beast's hide the ointment remains in the hide and the hit is of no avail.

MEDICINE TO CURE THE BITE OF A DOG OR ANOTHER MAD BEAST. Take a crust of bread and write what follows: †*Bestera* †*bestie* †*nay* †*brigonay* †*dictera* †*sagragan* †*es* †*domina* †*fiat* †*fiat* †*fiat*†.

TO SEPARATE WATER FROM WINE, put water and wine in a cup and have a thread of cotton and plunge one end thereof to the bottom of the cup and let the other end hang over the edge and below and outside the cup, and you will see that the water will run colourless along the thread. And when the water has all dripped away, you will see the wine begin to drip red. (*It would seem that the same could be done with a cask of wine.*)

WAFERS (GAUFFRES) be made in five ways. By one method you beat
up the eggs in a bowl, then add salt and wine and throw in flour, and
mix them, and then put them on two irons, little by little, each time
as much paste as the size of a leche or strip of cheese, and press them
between the two irons and cook on both sides; and if the iron doth
not separate easily from the paste, grease it beforehand with a little
cloth moistened in oil or fat.

The second method is like to the first, but you put in cheese, that
is to wit you spread out the paste as though to make a tart or pasty,
and then you add the cheese in leches in the middle and cover the
two ends; thus the cheese remaineth between the two pastes and is
thus set between two irons.

The third method is that of Strained Waffles (*Gauffres couléisses*)
and they be called strained for this reason only, that the paste is
clearer and is, as it were, boiled clear, after the aforesaid manner;
and on to it one scatters grated cheese; and all is mixed together.

The fourth method is flour made into a paste with water, salt and
wine without either eggs or cheese.

Item, the wafer-makers make another kind called big sticks (*gros
bastons*), which be made of flour made into a paste with eggs and
powdered ginger beaten together, and then made of like size and in
like manner to chitterlings, between two irons.

Other Small Matters which need no Chapter

TO KEEP ALL POTTAGES FRESH WITHOUT ADDING OR TAKING AWAY
ANYTHING, take a fair white cloth and set it upon your pot and turn
it often; and the pot must be kept away from the fire.

TO TAKE AWAY THE TASTE OF BURNING FROM A POTTAGE, take a
fresh pot and put your pottage therein, then take a little yeast and
tie it in a white cloth and put it into your pot and do not let it
remain there long.

TO MAKE A LIQUID FOR MARKING LINEN, take coom, that is the
black grease that is at the two ends of the axle of a cart, and add ink
and oil and vinegar and boil all together, and then warm your mark
and dip it therein and stamp it on to your linen.[101]

IF THOU WOULDST MAKE A GOOD KINDLING to light the fire with a
steel, take the old bark of a nut-tree and then put it in a pot full of
very strong lye, whole or in pieces the size of two fingers, whichever
thou dost prefer, and keep it boiling for the space of two days and a

night at the least. And if thou hast no lye, then take good ashes and put them with water and make a thick paste thereof, and then set your bark to boil therein for the aforesaid time, and keep on mixing it as it boils. If thou art boiling it in lye, mix it with lye, if thou art boiling it in ashes, mix it with water; and nathless whatever thou art boiling it in, if thou can procure animal urine to mix with it, it will be all the better. And when it has thus boiled, press out the moisture and then wash it in fair, clean water, ready to dry it again, and then set it to dry in the sun or in the chimney corner, away from the fire, so that it burn not, for it must be dried slowly and at leisure. And when it is dry and it is desired to use it, then it must be beaten with a hammer or a stock, until it becometh like unto a sponge. And when thou wouldst light a fire, then take a piece the size of a pea, and set it on thy flint and forthwith thou shalt have fire; and it needeth only to have lighted wicks and to light the candle. And it must be kept clean and dry.

TO MAKE CANDIED ORANGE PEEL, cut the peel of an orange into five pieces and scrape away the loose skin inside with a knife, then set them to soak in good, fresh water for nine days and change the water daily; then boil them, letting them come once to the boil only, in fresh water, and this done, spread them on a cloth and let them dry thoroughly, then put them in a pot of honey until they be quite covered therewith, and boil on a slow fire and skim. And when you think that the honey is cooked (to try if it be cooked, have some water in a spoon, and pour a drop of the honey into the water and if it spreads it is not done, and if the drop of honey remains in the water without spreading, then it is done), then you must take out your pieces of orange peel and set out a layer in order and sprinkle powdered ginger thereon, then another layer, and sprinkle etc., *usque in infinitum*; and leave them for a month or more and then eat them.

TO MAKE SAUSAGES, when you have killed your pig. Take the flesh of the ribs . . . and the best fat, as much of the one as of the other, in such quantity as you would make sausages; and cause it to be minced and hashed up very small by a pastrycook. Then bray fennel and a little fine salt, and afterwards take your brayed fennel and mix it very well with a quarter as much of fine [spice] powder; then mix thoroughly your meat, your spices and your fennel and afterwards fill the intestines, to wit the small ones. (And know that the intestines of an old pig be better for this, than those of a young one, because they be larger.) And afterwards put them in the smoke for four days or more and when you would eat them, put them in hot water and boil them once and then put them on the grill.

TO TAKE SALT OUT OF BUTTER, put it in a bowl on the fire to melt and the salt will precipitate at the bottom of the bowl, and salt thus precipitated is good for pottage; and the rest of the butter remaineth sweet. Otherwise put your salt butter in fresh sweet water and rub and knead it with your hands therein and the salt will remain in the water.

(*Item*, note that flies will never swarm on a horse that is greased with butter or with old salt grease.)

MAGPIES, CROWS, JACKDAWS. These be slain with the arrows of a crossbow, the which are blunt; and with weak crossbows you may shoot at those crows that be on the branches, but those that be in their nests must be shot at with stronger bolts to bring down nest and all. They should be skinned, then parboiled with bacon and then cut up into pieces and fried with eggs like shredded meat (charpies).

RIQUE-MENGER. Take two apples as big as two eggs or a little bigger and peel them and take out the pips, then cut them up into little slices and set them to boil in an iron pot, then pour away the water and set the rique-menger to dry. Then fry butter and while you are frying it break two eggs into it and stir them up; and when it is fried sift a fine [spice] powder on to it and colour it with saffron and eat it on bread in the month of September.

ROAST HARE. I have seen a hare roasted in the skin of a pig's fry, that is called the caul, and it costs three silver pence, wherefore the hare is not larded otherwise. *Item*, I have seen it larded.

FARCED CHICKENS, COLOURED OR GLAZED. They be first blown up and all the flesh within taken out, then filled up with other meat, then coloured or glazed as above; but there is too much to do, it is not a work for a citizen's cook, nor even for a simple knight's; and therefore I leave it.

Item, DES ESPAULES DE MOUTON, *quia nichil est nisi pena et labor.* [And the same concerning shoulders of mutton, for it is nought but pain and trouble.]

Item, HEDGEHOGS can be made out of mutton tripe and it is a great expense and a great labour and little honour and profit, wherefore *nichil hic.*

TO HULL BARLEY OR CORN TO MAKE FRUMENTY. You must have very hot water and put the corn or barley in it, and wash and knead it long and carefully; then pour and drain away all the water and let the corn or barley dry and then bray it with a wooden pestle, then winnow it in a washing basin.

Notes

[In the following notes those which are followed by the initials [J.P.] are translated and sometimes condensed from the notes of the French editor Jérôme Pichon. The rest are my own.]

I: NOTES TO THE INTRODUCTION

¹ Pichon fixes the date as follows: 'The *Ménagier de Paris* is evidently one of the results of the literary movement of Charles V's reign and the impulse, given by the king's encouragement, to everyone to write upon the subject which he liked most and knew best. The author had seen the whole reign of this great prince, since he was at Melun in 1358 [p. 103], at Niort in 1373 [p. 73] and had known Aubriot in his power [p. 199], but he did not write until several years after the accession of Charles VI. He speaks indeed of the duke of Orleans, who cannot be Philip of France, brother of king John, 1st, because that prince, who died in 1372, would not be referred to as alive in a book written after the capture of Niort; 2nd, because the author who names the dukes of Berry, Burgundy and Bourbon in the order of their kinship with the king [p. 145] would not, if he had been writing in the reign of Charles V, have placed the king's uncle before his brothers; 3rd, the duke of Anjou, younger brother of Charles V, who died in 1384, would undoubtedly have been mentioned in this enumeration, if it had been written before the year of his death; 4th, there is an allusion in the book to a sedition which I believe I have proved to be that of 1382 [pp. 97-8, 211]. If then we admit (and it seems impossible to deny it) that the duke of Orleans mentioned in the *Ménagier* is not Philip, king John's brother, he can only be Louis, the brother of Charles VI, and since this prince, who was at first duke of Touraine, only received the title of duke of Orleans on June 4th, 1392, it follows that the *Ménagier* cannot have been written before June, 1392. But neither can it be later than September, 1394, because the author speaks of Jews "now in this realm" [p. 67]; now the Jews were expelled by an ordinance dated the 17th of that month, which was promptly executed, but to which he would certainly have made some reference in this part of his book, if it had been even promulgated when he wrote. The *Ménagier de Paris* was thus written between June, 1392, and September, 1394.' [J.P.]

² He had read all the following books and possessed most of them: the Bible, the *Golden Legend*, St Jerome (*Life of the Fathers*), St Augustine, St Gregory, the *Histoire sur Bible* of Pierre le Mangeur, Livy, the *Roman de la Rose*, the historian Josephus, the *Catholicon*, Gratian's *Decretals*, Petrarch's *Tale of Griselda*, the *Seven Sages of Rome*, the *Dream of Scipio* (by Cicero, with the

commentary of Macrobius), the *Jeu des échecs moralisé* of J. de Cessoles, the *Chemin de povreté et de richesse* of J. Bruyant, *Melibeus and Prudence*. [J.P.]

3 He had been in Beauce and Picardy, at Niort, at Bar-sur-Aube, at Chaumont, in Gascony, at Béziers, in Flanders and probably at Tournai, which he mentions several times. [J.P.]

4 His references to the Duke of Berry are particularly interesting. He was with him at Niort, when he and his lords came to see the faithful dog on the grave of its master, who had been slain in battle with the English in 1373 [p. 73]. In his treatise on gardening he mentions that the Duke of Berry had told him that the cherries of Auvergne were bigger than those of France (the Ile-de-France), because they layered their cherry trees there [p. 134]; and in the course of his section on cookery he gives a detailed account of the consumption of food by the duke's household, gathered from his servants ('*les gens de monseigneur de Berry dient* . . .') [p. 145], and elsewhere remarks that at the court of lords like this duke they make rissoles out of beef marrow, every time that they slaughter an ox [p. 186].

5 See pp. 73, 103 and notes III 19, III 20.

6 *Le Livre du Chevalier de la Tour Landry*, ed. A. de Montaiglon, 1854. This book was translated into English in the reign of Henry VI and the translation has been edited as *The Book of the Knight of La Tour-Landry*, ed. Thomas Wright, Early English Text Society, 1868; revised edition, 1906. It was later translated and printed by Caxton. A translation into German was also made in the fifteenth century and first printed in 1493.

7 *How the Good Wife taughte hir Doughter* (c. 1430) in *The Babees Boke*, ed. F. J. Furnivall, EETS, 1868, p. 39.

8 From John Russell's *Boke of Nurture* in *Early English Meals and Manners*, ed. F. J. Furnivall, EETS, 1894 edit., p. 64.

9 Quoted from Laurens Andrewe, *The Noble Lyfe and Natures of man, Of bestes, serpentys, fowles and fisshes y^t be most knowen* (a very rare black letter book). Ibid., p. 108.

10 *Gespraechbuechlein, Romanisch und Flamisch*, printed in *Altniederländische Sprachwörter* hgg. von Hoffmann von Fallersleben, in *Horae Belgicae*, pt. ix, Hanover, 1854, pp. 63–95. The passage I have quoted will be found on pp. 90–3. I owe my introduction to this dialogue to a charming book by Mr Malcolm Letts, *Bruges and her Past*, Bruges and London, 2nd edit., 1926, pp. 158–60. See also F. Callaey, 'Illustrations of Social life in Belgium derived from French–Flemish conversation manuals of the fourteenth and sixteenth centuries', *Bulletin de l'institut histoire belge de Rome*, vol. V.

11 There is an article on the Ménagier's treatise on gardening in the *Gardener's Chronicle*, LXV, 1919, p. 105, but I have not been able to consult it.

12 For an admirable collection of illustrations of gardens, drawn from illuminated MSS, paintings and early printed books, with an introduction, see the

late Sir Frank Crisp's *Medieval Gardens*, 1924, 2 vols.

13 The treatises of John de Garlande and Walter de Biblesworth will be found in *A Volume of Vocabularies*, ed. Thomas Wright, 1857. Other vocabularies printed in this collection contain important lists of plants.

14 T. H. Turner, 'Observations on the State of Horticulture in England in Early Times, chiefly previous to the fifteenth century', *Archaeological Journal*, V, 1848, p. 302.

15 One roll has been translated in full by the Hon. A. Amherst (Mrs E. Cecil) in her *History of Gardening in England*, 3rd edit., 1910.

16 Thomas Wright, *The Homes of Other Days*, 1871, p. 313. See *Palladius on Husbandrie* (*c*.1420), ed. B. Lodge, EETS, 1872–9, 2 vols.

17 It has been edited by the Hon. A. Amherst (Mrs E. Cecil) under the title 'A Fifteenth Century Treatise on Gardening by Mayster Ion Gardener' in *Archaeologia*, vol. LIV, 2nd series IV, 1895, pp. 157–72.

18 *Knightes Tale*, ll. 190–97.

19 *Volume of Vocabularies*, ed. Wright, p. 136, and see *Homes of Other Days*, pp. 309–10.

20 *La Manière de langage qui enseigne a parler et a écrire le Français*, ed. Paul Meyer, 1873, p. 395. (Extract from the *Revue Critique*, 1870.) Compare the list of herbs and vegetables in a fourteenth-century book of dialogues in French and Flemish which was subsequently adapted by Caxton as a French–English manual. 'Under this trees Ben herbes suete smellyng. There ben roses reed, white, Mynte, confyte and grayne . . . Yet Ben in the gardynes Rede cool [cole] and white, Porreette, oynyons, Betes, cheruyll, persely, Sauge, ysope, tyme, Letews, porselane [purslain], kersses [cresses], geloffres [gillyflowers], Rapes, gharlyk, fenell, Spynache, borage.' William Caxton, *Dialogues in French and English*, ed. H. Bradley, EETS, 1900, p. 13.

21 The list is to be found in MS Sloane 1201 and was first printed by Wright, *Homes of Other Days*, p. 312, from whom I take it. It has been reprinted by the Hon. Mrs E. Cecil in her *History of Gardening in England*, and by Sir Frank Crisp in the preface to his *Medieval Gardens*.

22 Cecil, *Archaelogia*, vol. LIV, pp. 165–6.

23 Wright, *Homes of Other Days*, p. 313.

24 *Early English Miscellanies in Prose and Verse*, ed. J. O. Halliwell, Warton Club, 1855, pp. 67–8.

25 *Prologue*, ll. 333–54.

26 Those interested may consult the following books: *A Collection of Ordinances and Regulations for the Government of the Royal Household*, Society of Antiquaries, 1790; Warner, *Antiquitates Culinariae*, 1791 (contains *The Forme of Cury*); *A Noble Boke off Cookry*, ed. Mrs Alexander Napier, 1882; *Liber Cure Cocorum*, ed. R. Morris, Transactions of the Philological Society Supplement, 1862; *Two Fifteenth Century Cookery Books*, ed. T. Austin, EETS,

1888. Variants of the Ménagier's recipes will be found in all of these and I have found them of great help in translating this somewhat technical section.

[27] Russell's *Boke of Nurture* in *Early English Meals and Manners*, ed. Furnivall, pp. 33–4.

[28] Ibid., pp. 35–7.

[29] See *A Feste for a Bryde* (at the end of a little treatise *Ffor to serve a lord*), ibid., pp. 360–1.

[30] From *A dynere of flesche* in Russell's *Boke of Nurture*, op. cit., p. 50.

[31] *Prologue*, ll. 379ff.

II: NOTES TO THE PROLOGUE

[1] The Ménagier always addresses his wife as 'Sister', which was used in a general way as a term of affectionate respect. It will be remembered that the Wife of Bath's last husband addressed her as 'dere suster Alisoun' on a memorable occasion. *Wife of Bath's Prologue*, l. 804.

[2] There are only seventeen.

[3] I do not know what is intended by *puys* here; the *exemplum* referred to seems to be that on pp. 97–8.

[4] Several of the *exempla* named in this section have been omitted in the translation, viz. those of Sarah, Rebecca, Rachel, and Melibeus.

[5] The castle is mentioned in the poem *Le Chemin de povreté et de richesse*, by Jean Bruyant, which has been omitted in the translation.

[6] The second article relating to hawking (which is omitted in this translation) is the only one found in the three surviving MSS of the *Ménagier*.

III: NOTES TO THE FIRST SECTION

[1] *Le colet de vostre chemise, de vostre blanchet, ou de vostre coste ou surcot.* The *chemise* has the same significance as today; the *blanchet* was a short garment of white cloth or flannel worn over the chemise; the *coste* or *cotte* here signifies robe, and the *surcot* was an upper garment which went over it, usually not so warm and more elegant than a *houppelande*. [J.P.]

[2] Compare the Knight of La Tour-Landry's remarks on deportment. 'Affterwarde, in sayeing youre praiers atte masse or in other place, be not like the crane or the tortu [tortoise]; for thei are like the crane and the turtu that turnithe her hede and fases bacward, and lokithe ouer the shuldre; and, euer steringe with the hede like a vessell, hauithe youre loke and holdithe your hede ferme as a best that is called a lymer [bloodhound]; the whiche lokithe euer afore hym, ... euer forth right. And therfor bethe ferme and lokithe forthe

right afore you plainly, and yf ye luste to loke asyde, turnithe youre body and
uisage togedre, and so youre countenaunce shal be most ferme and sure; for thei
that lokithe bak and ar ofte stering with the hede, ar ofte scorned & mocked.'
The Book of the Knight of La Tour-Landry, ed. Wright, p. 15.

³ *De opere monachorum.*

⁴ The moral disease of *accidia* – part sloth, part ennui and part melancholia –
has been excellently described by Chaucer, *Persones Tale*, §§53–9, and Dante
has crystallised it in four lines:

> *Fitti nel limo dicon: Tristi fummo*
> *Nel' aer dolce che dal sol s'allegra,*
> *Portando dentro accidioso fummo:*
> *Or ci attristiam nella belletta negra.*

An interesting modern study of *accidia* is to be found in a book of sermons by
a late Bishop of Oxford, Dr Paget, *The Spirit of Discipline*, 1891, and see also
H. B. Workman, *The Evolution of the Monastic Ideal*, 1913, pp. 321–31, and
E. Power, *Medieval English Nunneries*, 1922, pp. 293–7.

⁵ By Jacques de Voragine, Archbishop of Genoa.

⁶ By St Jerome.

⁷ The Jews were expelled from France by an ordinance of 17 September
1394, which was punctually executed. This passage is proof positive that the
Ménagier was written before September 1394. [J.P.]

⁸ 'A Chaldean philosopher, who, according to Jacques de Cessoles, author of
the *Game of Chess Moralised*, invented the game of chess. The author of the
Ménagier is here citing Jacques de Cessoles' work, in which the tales of
Romilda, Lucrece and Papirius occur; he tells them, but develops them considerably.' [J.P.] On the *Solacium ludi schaccorum*, compiled by the Dominican
Jacques de Cessoles in N. Italy before 1325, see J.-Th. Welter, *L'Exemplum
dans la littérature religieuse et didactique du moyen age*, Paris, 1927, pp. 351–4.

⁹ 'The duchess is Romilda, widow of Gisulf, duke of Friuli, killed in 611 in
a battle against the Avars. After the death of her husband, by whom she had
four sons and four daughters, she was besieged by the Khan of the Avars in
Forojulium, today *Civita di Friuli*. Attracted by the appearance of the Khan,
she offered him (not one of his lords) her position and hand; her offer was
accepted but when the Khan was master of the palace he had Romilda impaled
and carried away her children and the chief citizens into captivity. The four
princes escaped on the way. The two elder, Taso and Cacco, were dukes of
Friuli from 621 to 635. The third, Rodoald, was duke of Benevento from
642 to 647, and the youngest, Grimoald, was duke of Benevento after his
brother and king of the Lombards in 662, dying in 671. The story is taken
from Paul Deacon.' [J.P.]

[10] 'Les autres jouans au *bric*, les autres à *qui féry?*, les autres à *pince-merille*.'
It is not very easy to identify these games and doubtless they are among those
which the Ménagier would have described in his last section, if he had finished
it. *Bric* was played with a little stick; *qui féry?* was evidently hot cockles; *pince-
mérille* is mentioned among the games played by Gargantua [Rabelais, bk I,
ch. xxii]; the player seems to have had to pinch another player's arm, saying
'Mérille', but what the point of it was is unknown.

[11] Chaucer, *Legend of Good Women*, ll. 1869–70.

[12] Some biblical *exempla* follow in the original.

[13] 'The dukes of Berry, Burgundy and Bourbon and the constable Du
Guesclin conquered almost the whole of Poitou from the English in 1372; they
returned to Paris on December 11th and on the following day the duke of
Berry did homage to the king his brother for the county of Poitou. But Niort
and a few other places remained in the hands of the English. Du Guesclin,
having defeated at Chisay the English garrisons, which had united under the
leadership of messire Jehan d'Esbreux, according to Cuveliér, clad his soldiers
in English armour and so took Niort by surprise. According to Froissart, the
Battle of Chisay took place on March 21st, 1372 (1373 new style), and Niort
was taken by April 28th at least. It seems likely that the incident of the dog,
which our author tells as an eyewitness, took place at Niort during the sojourn
of the duke of Berry in that town in July, 1373.' [J.P.]

[14] The story of Griselda was first written in Italian by Boccaccio and then
paraphrased and put into Latin by Petrarch. It was several times translated into
French and is familiar to all readers as the *Clerk's Tale* in Chaucer's *Canterbury
Tales*. Chaucer also was paraphrasing Petrarch's version in English verse; and
there is no better way of appreciating his surpassing genius than to compare his
tale with that of the Ménagier. Both followed their original closely, but
Chaucer's additions and comments raise his version head and shoulders above
all the others; compare for example his treatment of the scenes in which
Griselda's children are taken from her; there is hardly any addition but the
pathos is infinitely more touching.

[15] Nothing shows the Ménagier's good sense better than his comment on the
tale of Griselda, which may be compared with the comments which Chaucer
lets fall after each of the successive trials in his version. Chaucer's Envoy will be
remembered for a gay cynicism which the Ménagier lacks:

> *Grisilde is deed and eek her pacience,*
> *And bothe atones buried in Itaille;*
> *For which I crye in open audience*
> *No wedded man so hardy be t'assaille*
> *His wyves pacience, in hope to finde*
> *Grisildes, for in certein he shall faille!*

O noble wyves, ful of heigh prudence,
Lat noon humilitee your tonge naille,
Ne lat no clerk have cause or diligence
To wryte of yow a story of swich mervaille
As of Grisildis pacient and kinde;
Lest Chichevache yow swelwe in hir entraille! . . .

¹⁶ The *Historia Scholastica* of Pierre le Mangeur (Petrus Comestor), chancellor of the university of Paris, who died in 1179. 'The historical and legendary stories of the Bible had at all times a great attraction for the faithful and consequently enjoyed a legitimate vogue among them. From the second half of the twelfth century Pierre le Mangeur of Troyes, while adding profane legends and rabbinical fables to them, co-ordinated them chronologically in his famous *Historia Scholastica*, the influence of which was to be enormous, not only upon preachers, but also upon letters and art during the centuries which followed.' J.-Th. Welter, op. cit., pp. 84–5, and see article by L. Delisle on '*Bibles historiées et allégorisées*' in *Histoire Littéraire*, t. XXX, pp. 218–46. A copy of the *Histoire sur Bible* translated from Pierre le Mangeur's work by Guiart des Moulins (1291–4) was made about 1400 for the Duke of Berry and is now one of the treasures of the British Museum (Harl. MS, 4381, 4382).

¹⁷ Pichon considers that this episode probably took place in Paris during the aftermath of the rebellion of the *maillotins*, which broke out in Paris on 1 March, 1382. After Charles V (who was at the time a child, under the influence of his uncles) had been victorious at the battle of Rosebecque (27 November, 1382), he entered Paris on 11 January, 1383, and during the days which followed three hundred wealthy burgesses were arrested and a hundred were executed, the rest being condemned to pay huge fines.

¹⁸ Pichon thinks that the *bailli de Tournay* here spoken of was probably messire Tristan de Bos, a fairly important person and first *bailli* of Tournai, who had previously been *bailli* of Lille and of Vermandois, and was made *bailli* of Tournai in 1383. These stories of wagers to try the obedience of wives were very common in the Middle Ages. The Ménagier gives two others, one the tale of the abbots and the husbands and the other drawn from his own experience. There is an amusing one in ch. xix of *The Book of the Knight of La Tour-Landry*, ed. Wright, pp. 26–8. The famous proof of Katharina by Petruchio in *The Taming of the Shrew*, Act V, sc. ii, is familiar to all.

¹⁹ 'The castle of Melun, and consequently that part of the town which lay on the Gâtinois side, was surrendered to the Navarre troops and the English by Queen Blanche on August 4th, 1358, four days after the death of Etienne Marcel and the re-entry of the Regent into Paris; but the part of the town which lay in Brie remained French and messire Jean d'Andresel was from that month captain of Melun and Brie for the Regent. Peace was signed between the

Regent and the king of Navarre on August 21st, 1359, but the Navarre troops were still in occupation of Melun in September. The curious adventure narrated by the author of the *Ménagier* must have taken place between August, 1358, and October, 1359.' [J.P.]

²⁰ 'Jean sire d'Andresel, knight, was sprung from an ancient and illustrious family and was the eldest son of Jean d'Andresel, the much-loved chamberlain of king Philippe de Valois. He was chamberlain to the dauphin, then to king Jean and then to Charles V. At least as early as 1346 he married Jeanne d'Arrablay, daughter of one of the king's masters of the household and niece of a chancellor of France. In August, 1358, he was captain of Melun and Brie, and in August, 1359, captain-general of the latter province. After the treaty of Bretigny he, together with several princes of the blood and some of the most illustrious lords of the period, was among the hostages of king Jean, taken by the king of England from Calais on October 31st, 1360. He was back in France as early as the beginning of 1366, at least, because in the April of that year a second marriage contract was signed between him and Jeanne de Maligny, widow of Jean lord of Rochefort and Puiset. He died early in 1368. The incident recounted in the *Ménagier's* narrative clearly refers to his first wife, Jeanne d'Arrablay.' [J.P.]

²¹ This famous collection of tales was of Indian origin. It was composed in Latin verse under the title *Historia Septem Sapientum Romae* towards the end of the twelfth century, probably from still older versions, by the Cistercian monk Jean de Haute-Seille, and shortly afterwards translated into French by the French poet Herbert, under the name of *Dolopathos*. See Ward, *Catalogue of Romances*, II, pp. 199–234.

²² Compare the ballad of the death of Robin Hood, who was bled to death by his cousin, the Prioress of Kirklees:

> '*Set a chafing-dish to the fire*', *she said,*
> '*And strip thou up thy sleeve.*'
> *I hold him but an unwise man*
> *That will no warning 'leeve!*

> *She laid the blood-irons to Robin's vein,*
> *Alack, the more pitye!*
> *And pierc'd the vein and let out the blood*
> *That full red was to see.*

> *And first it bled the thick, thick blood,*
> *And afterwards the thin,*
> *And well then wist good Robin Hood*
> *Treason there was within.*

²³ This was a favourite saying. Compare Chaucer's use of it: 'Men seyn that thre thynges dryven a man out of his hous, – that is to seyn, smoke, droppyng of reyn and wikked wyves.' *Tale of Melibeus*, §15; and

> *Thou seyst that droppyng houses and eek smoke*
> *And chidyng wyves, maken men to flee*
> *Out of his owene hous.*
> *Wife of Bath's Prologue*, ll. 278–80.

²⁴ *Palettes*, little flat shovels, like the whisks sold for killing flies with today.

²⁵ This tale was a favourite one in the Middle Ages and is found in several variants. The usual version is that a squire told his wife that he had laid an egg and she spread the tale. This version is to be found in *The Book of the Knight of La Tour-Landry*, ed. Wright, pp. 96–7, in the *Proptuarium Exemplorum* (see *Selection of Latin Stories*, ed. T. Wright, Percy Society, 1842, p. 104), and in the *Gesta Romanorum*, ch. cxxv, in which the knight is made to void a black crow instead of laying an egg. It was told in French verse by La Fontaine, *Fables*, liv. VIII, fable vi.

²⁶ In the original there follows a very long *exemplum*, which is here omitted, the tale of *Melibeus and Prudence*, first written in Latin in 1246 by Albertanus of Brescia and several times translated into French. Although intolerably dull to modern taste, it enjoyed considerable success in the Middle Ages. Chaucer translated it into English prose as his own contribution to the *Canterbury Tales*.

²⁷ 'The story of Jehanne la Quentine was reproduced in the sixteenth century by queen Margaret of Navarre in her *Nouvelles*, but she attributes it to a *bourgeoise* of Tours (38th Tale, or 8th of the 4th day). But as the author of the *Ménagier* gives the names and says that he had it from his father, it is impossible [?] to doubt that it took place in Paris. The Queen of Navarre may have heard the story told by someone who read it in the *Ménagier*, and may have placed the scene in Tours. She gives similarly in her 37th Tale, attributing it to a lady de Laval-Loué, and with a few variations, a similar example of conjugal indulgence, reported by the chevalier de La Tour as having actually happened to his aunt, then lady de Languillier.' [J.P.] The chevalier de La Tour tells (chapter xvii) how she had 'tolde me diuerse tymes of that she had suffered. She was a ladi of Fraunce, that might spende more thanne fyue hundred pounde bi yeere, and helde a noble estate, and she had a knight to her husbond that was merueilously lecherous, the whiche had eueri day in his hous one or two women besides the lady his wiff. And ofte tyme he rose from her to go lyge with his leude women, and all wey, whanne he come agein from hem to bedde, he fonde euer the candell light, and water to wasshe his hondes, and he saide he come from the priue. And thanne saide the ladi, "somoche haue ye the more nede to wasshe you"; and she saide neuer no thing ellys to hym, but yef if were atte sum

tyme whanne thei were meri and allone, she wolde saie, "Syr, y know all youre
doinge by suche women and suche, but sethe it ys youre lust, and that y may
sette no remedie thereon, y will make you nor them neuer the worse chere; For
y were a fole to slee my selff for youre sportes. But y praie you, sethe it is well,
that ye make me neuer the worse chere, and that y lese not youre loue, nor that
ye make me not the worse semblaunt, and of the remenaunt y reporte me to
you, y woll suffre it." And so with her goodly wordes he repented hym, and was
conuerted in goodnesse atte the laste, and he dede nomore euell; and thus with
fairenesse she ouercome hym.' *The Book of the Knight of La Tour-Landry*, ed.
Wright, pp. 23–4.

IV: NOTES TO THE SECOND SECTION

[1] In the original this is followed by a very long moral and allegorical poem
(here omitted) entitled *Le Chemin de povreté et de richesse*, by Jean Bruyant,
king's notary at the Châtelet in Paris, and written in 1342. The Ménagier sets
it forth at length 'to show the diligence and perseverance that the newly wed
ought to display' and it forms the whole of the first article of his second section.

[2] *Porrée* is used in the Middle Ages of beets, spinach or green vegetables in
general, or of the soup made therefrom; the word *porray* or *poret* (as well as the
usual *worts*) is found in English, e.g. in a fifteenth century *Nominale* under the
heading *De Speciebus liguminis* we find '*Nec porreta, porray*'. *A Volume of
Vocabularies*, ed. Wright, p. 241. Compare Langland: 'With grene poret and
peson to poysoun hunger thei thought.'

[3] *Marquets chevelus*. The words *chevelue* and *marquet* or *marcotte* or *margoute*
both mean a layer, viz. 'a shoot or twig of a plant fastened down and partly
covered with earth in order that it may strike root while still attached to the
parent stock and so propagate the plant' (*Oxford English Dictionary*). The
word usually applies to vines.

[4] The Armenian violet is possibly, Pichon thinks, what we know as the
Parma violet.

[5] 'This is the famous Bureau de la Rivière, Charles V's favourite, who died
August 16th, 1400, and was buried in the abbey of Saint-Denis. The Avignon
lettuce would seem to be the same as our Roman lettuce, the only lettuce with
white seed, which was already known in the sixteenth century.' [J.P.]

[6] i.e., so that the water might fall drop by drop on to the roots of the plant.

[7] It is rather difficult to translate the Ménagier's different cabbages. Further
on, in speaking of pottages, he distinguishes five sorts of cabbage: (1) *choulx blancs*
(white cabbages), which he here says are identical with *choulx cabus* (headed
cabbage or cabbage heads), (2) *pommes de chou* or *choulxpommés* (cabbage hearts),
(3) *choulx Romains* (Roman cabbages), (4) *minces* (sprouts), and (5) *choulx
pasquerés* (Easter cabbages, i.e. to be eaten at the Easter season).

⁸ Compare the instructions in an English treatise of about the same date. 'To make cheris to growe withowte stonys. Cleve a yonge schote of a yonge cherytre that is a spanne longe or ij. fro the toppe evene downe to the rote, but let hym stond stylle on the stalke, and thanne drawe owte the pyth one every syd with some maner of iryne, and anone joyne every perty togedyre, and bynd hem welle, and donge hem welle with clay one every syd fro the toppe to the rotte, and when a yere is past there hys wond is, sowde a graffe in the same stoke a syone that never bare frute, and thereon schalle growe cherys withoute ony stonys. Also a grape to growe withowte pepyns, whenne the pythe of the vyne is take owte. Also of alle othyre y-like.' *Early English Miscellanies in Prose and Verse*, ed. J. O. Halliwell, Warton Club, 1855, p. 71.

⁹ i.e., Steward. The office is that from which the Despensers and Spencers took their name.

¹⁰ The Béguines were a sort of religious order or lay sisterhood, living in the world under certain vows and somewhat analagous to the Franciscan Tertiaries or Third Order.

¹¹ This witness to the antiquity of the term 'bloody' as an expletive (*de males sanglantes fièvres, de male sanglante sepmaine, de male sanglante journée*) is interesting and disproves finally the popular belief that it is derived from the phrase 'By our Lady' much as the inn sign 'The Goat and Compasses' is said to be derived from 'God encompasses us'. Mr Coulton has discovered an example two centuries earlier, when the *viguier* of Béziers in the days of Louis XI addressed some villagers who refused to pay a royal levy, 'You bloody peasants! whether you will or whether you won't, you shall pay all the same!' (*O rustici sanguinolenti, vos dabitis velitis vel non*). See G. G. Coulton, *The Medieval Village*, 1925, p. 342.

¹² The Ménagier uses the term *blanc*, which I have roughly translated throughout as 'silver penny'. It was worth 10d.

¹³ The sun parlour upstairs.

¹⁴ Here follows a short treatise on the points of a horse and its care in health and sickness, which I have omitted. It contains some odd remedies, including two charms of the nature of the charm to cure the bite of a mad dog, given on p. 200. It also contains the eighteen points of a good horse, which were often printed in the sixteenth century. 'Three of the points of a fox, to wit, short upright ears; good coat and strong and stiff; bushy tail. Four of a hare, to wit narrow head, wide awake, light in movement, fleet and swift in going. Four of an ox, to wit haunches large, wide and open, large cod, large eyes jutting forth from the head, and low jointed. Of an ass three: good feet, strong backbone, debonnair manners. Four of a maid, to wit, fine mane, fine chest, fine thighs and large buttocks.' Which shows that standards of feminine, if not of equine, beauty change.

¹⁵ These statistics of the consumption of meat in Paris (amounting annually

when he wrote to 30,316 beefs, 188,552 muttons, 30,794 pigs and 19,604 veals, counting the consumption of the royal household and the households of the dukes of Orleans and Berry) would be interesting if we could rely upon their accuracy; but Pichon gives reason to doubt this (*Le Ménagier de Paris*, I, Introd., pp. xliii–xliv).

[16] i.e., as 20 is to 25, or one-fifth less than the king.

[17] 'A *Pike*, first a Hurling pick, then a Pickerel, then a *Pike*, then a *Luce*, or *Lucie*'; thus Randolph Holme, quoted by Furnivall in his edition of *Early English Meals and Manners*, p. 99. The Ménagier's French terms are '*des brochets, l'en dit lancerel, brochet, quarrel, lux et luceau*'.

[18] *Franche*. This may be a misreading for *fraîche*, or it may denote a special kind of eel.

[19] A sweet Greek wine. '*De l'isle de Candie il leur venoit très bonnes malvoises et grenaches*' (Froissart).

[20] A pimpernel was a little fish.

[21] Cyvey or civey is the form which contemporary English cookery books give to the French *sivé* or *civé*. For the recipe see p. 174.

[22] So called because it was divided into four parts by two lines crossing, as in heraldry. The Ménagier describes a *potage parti* in a recipe not given here, and concludes, 'serve it in bowls and cast thereon cinnamon powder and sugar, to wit cast it on one half of the bowl and not on the other; and it is called Party Pottage.' In Quartered Pottage the spice would no doubt be spread so that two plain alternated with two spiced losenges. Further on a 'party blankmanger' is mentioned.

[23] Dodine was a sort of sauce made of almond, garlic and eggs, sometimes with the white meat of capons too.

[24] I use the Anglicised version of the name *bourrée*; the dish was composed of meat cut up into little gobbets, boiled and seasoned.

[25] Again I use the contemporary English version of the French word *flaonnés*; they were open tarts, modern French *flaon*; modern English cooks still call them 'flans'. For a recipe see pp. 182–3.

[26] A spiced wine which took its name from the particular sort of bag, termed Hippocrates' sleeve, through which it was strained. (Furnivall, op. cit., p. 88.) For a recipe see p. 196. There is a rhymed recipe for it in Russell's *Boke of Nurture* (Furnivall, op. cit., pp. 9–12).

[27] *Taillis* or *tayles* (as the English cookery books have it) is thus defined by Cotgrave, 'A Hachee; or made dish of Creuises, the flesh of Capons, Chickens, or Veale, bread, wine, salt, verjuyce, and spices; also a kind of gellie.' See recipe for meatless *taillis*, p. 181.

[28] *Doreures*: the English also used the word to 'dore' or 'endore', meaning to glaze or wash over a piece of meat etc. with yolks of eggs or some other liquid, to give it a shiny appearance like gilt, when cooked.

²⁹ Cotgrave, '*Soupe*: A sop, or peece of bread in broth; also pottage, or broth (wherein there is store of sops or sippets).' Contemporary cookery books have many recipes for different kinds of sops, as 'Soppes Chamberlayne', 'Soppes Dorre', etc. It will be remembered that Chaucer's Franklin liked a 'sop in wyn' in the morning.

³⁰ *Soupe*; here and in the menu the word seems to be used in the modern sense and gravy is the nearest equivalent.

³¹ Cotgrave, '*Crepez* ou *Crepets*: Fritters; also Wafers'; modern French *Crêpe*. They were favourites in England under the name of crisps. For recipe see pp. 186-7.

³² I have preferred to use the old English word brewet for *brouet*, rather than the modern broth; the brewets were served in bowls, the solid gobbets of meat from which the broth had been made at the bottom, then the broth, and a powdering of spices or sugar over the surface. The *Brouet d'Alemaigne* (German brewet) here mentioned was a very favourite dish and is found under that name in most of the English cookery books. For the recipe see pp. 173-4.

³³ I use the word used in the *Forme of Cury*, for this herb dish, which the Ménagier calls an *Arboulastre*. See Ducange, *Herbolasta*, a cake stuffed with herbs. For the recipe, see p. 180.

³⁴ Cotgrave, '*Cretons*: The crispie peeces, or mammockes, remaining of lard, that hath been first shred, then boiled and then strained through a cloth.' For a vegetable *cretonnée* see pp. 170-1.

³⁵ I can find no definition of *raniolles*, but it may be a misreading for *rauiolles* (*raviolles*), found in old English cookery books as *raffrolys*, and in modern Italy as *raviuoli*. T. Wright gives a recipe from an English cookery book in *Homes of Other Days*, p. 362. Pichon, however, notes that in the *Grand Cuisinier* the word is written *ramolle*.

³⁶ A *rosée* was so called from being made of roses, but the Ménagier's *rosée* on p. 170 has no roses in it, nor has the rosee in Warner, *Antiquitates Culinariae*, p. 43 (No. 47); but the rosee in the same tract (No. 41) befits its name: 'Tak the flowris of rosys and wasch hem wel in water and after bray hem wel in a morter; and than tak almondys and temper hem, and seth hem; and after tak flesch of capons, or of hennys and hac yt smale, and than bray hem wel in a morter, and than do yt in the rose, so that the flesch accorde wyth the mylk, and so that the mete be charchaunt; and after do yt to the fyre to boyle, and do there to sugur and safron, that yt be wel ycoloured, and rosy, of levys and of the forseyde flowrys, and serve it forth.'

³⁷ This is the dish in which Chaucer's cook excelled – 'Of blankmanger, that made he with the best' (*Prologue*). It was so called from its white colour, but had nothing to do with our blancmange of today, being usually made with capons. For recipe see p. 173.

³⁸ *Leschefrites* i.e. fritters; I use the term used in the English cookery books.

Cotgrave, '*Lesche*: a long slice or shive of bread,' or of meat or other edibles.

[39] Cotgrave, '*Darioles*: Small pasties filled with flesh, hearbes and spices, mingled and mixed together.' The Ménagier gives no recipe, but they are common in English cookery books. See e.g. Warner, op. cit., pp. 32, 66; *Two Fifteenth Century Cookery Books*, ed. T. Austin, EETS, 1888, pp. 47, 53, 55, 56.

[40] *à la soupe courte*. Perhaps like the *soupe despourvue* on p. 168, or the *saulce brieve pour chapon* (Quick sauce for a capon) on p. 191.

[41] A recipe for the famous cameline sauce (of which we read much in English cookery books too) is on p. 188.

[42] 'O.F. *Nombles*; cf. Late Lat. *Nombrilus*, for Lat. *Lumbrilus*' (Austin, op. cit., p. 137). See p. 176 and recipes in English cookery books under this name.

[43] '*Hastelet*, dimin. de *haste*, viande rôtie' (Godefroy). They were little fillets or pieces of meat roasted on the spit and the name was sometimes applied to vegetable rissoles of like shape.

[44] Cotgrave, '*Talmouse*: a cheese-cake; a Tart, or cake made of egges and cheese.'

[45] Perhaps glazed and silvered over.

[46] *Losenges* or *orillettes* were little pasties doubtless so called from their shape. There are two recipes for 'Loscyns' in *The Forme of Cury* (Warner, op. cit., pp. 12, 24). An *oreillette* was an earring, or the flap covering the ear in a head-dress or helmet; little cakes under that name, fried in olive oil, are still eaten in the Montpellier district in carnival time; see the recipe in a book greatly to be recommended to modern gourmets, A. de Croze, *Les Plats régionaux de France*, Paris, 1928, p. 256 (*Oreillettes montpéliéraines*).

[47] Puffs or pummels. See p. 184.

[48] *Chastelliers*, so called because they were shaped like castles. A recipe under the title 'Chastletes' is given by Richard II's Master Cooks in *The Forme of Cury*: 'Take and make a soyle (*crust*) of gode past, with a roller, of a foot brode, and lynger by cumpas (i.e. *long in proportion*). Make four coffyns (*crusts*) of the self past, upon the rolleres, the gretnesse of the smale of thyn arme, of six ynche deepnesse. Make the gretust in the myddel. Fasten the soile in the mouth upwarde, and fasten thee other foure in every side. Kerve out keyntlich (*quaintly, cunningly*) kyrnels (*battlements*) above in the manner of bataiwyng (*embattling*), and drye them harde in an ovene, other (*or*) in the sune. In the myddle coffyn do a fars (*stuffing*) of pork, with gode pork and ayren (*eggs*) rawe with salt and color it with safron, and do in another creme of almandes; and helde (*cast*) it in another creme of cowe mykle with ayren; color it with sandres (*sandalwood*). Another manner. Fars fyges of raysons, of apples, of peeres, and hold it bron (*make it brown*). Another manner. Do fars as to frytors blanched and color it with grene. Put this to the ovene and bake hit wel, and serve it forth with ew ardant (*hot water*).' (Warner, op. cit., p. 33.)

49 i.e. stuffed pigs; to stuff was called to 'farce', from the French *farcir*, whence our 'forcemeat'. See pp. 175-6.

50 Cotgrave, '*Oublie*: a wafer cake; such a one especially as is sweetened onely with honie' (the word is still in use). '*Estrié*: a kind of bread, or paste, of fine flower kneaded with water, white wine, the yolkes of egges, salt and sugar.'

51 Clarry was a claret or mixed wine, mixed with honey and seasoned with spices. For a long and elaborate recipe for making it entitled 'An excellent approved medecine both for the stomach and head of an elderly person', see Warner, op. cit., p. 90. A short recipe from Arnold's *Chronicle* is also quoted there: 'The craft to make clarre. For eighteen gallons of good wyne, take half a pounde of ginger, a quarter of a pound of long peper, un [one] ounce of safron, a quarter of an ounce of coliaundyr, two ounces of calomole dromatycus and the third part as much honey that is claryfyed, as of youwre wyne; streyne thym through a cloth and do it into a clene vessell.'

52 A sort of ragout; the term *salmis* is still in use. See p. 155.

53 I have found no recipe for *chapons pelerins*.

54 Doubtless some sort of fish, but I have been unable to identify them.

55 A *bécuit* was a fish dish; possibly it consisted of fish on a flat open pastry tart.

56 I cannot discover what method of serving peas this was.

57 Either twice boiled, or with some sort of boiled sauce.

58 Here and in one or two places hereafter the author uses the word *beschet* or *bequet*, which was a popular name for the salmon. He also uses the word *saumon* elsewhere and I do not know whether a special kind of salmon is here intended.

59 *Nieulles*, 'light pastry, perhaps a sort of oublie'. [J.P.]

60 *Graspois*. Further on (in a passage here omitted) the Ménagier explains: '*Craspois*. It is salted whale and should be in strips all raw and cooked in water like bacon; and serve it with your peas.' (*Le Ménagier de Paris*, II, pp. 200-1). Pichon has an interesting note on the subject. 'There is mention of *graspois* or *craspois* in many medieval works, but to my knowledge only the Ménagier explains what it is. From a trial which lasted for several years in the Parlement de Paris and which concerned the seven stalls, five for cuttle fish and two for *craspois* owned by the king in the *halles* of Paris, we know that *craspois* only came to Paris at Lent; it was the Lenten bacon, the fish of the poor; forty thousand persons lived on craspois, cuttle fish and herrings during Lent. These fish were sold by something like a thousand poor market women, who were only forbidden to stand beneath the covered part of the *halles*, where the big stalls were.' [J.P.]

61 'There was in 1379 an abbot of Lagny who was present in the Parlement, either because he was a member or because he was one of the King's Council ... and it is very likely that this account refers to him. I notice him mentioned as

present in the Parlement for the first time on March 1st, 1378–9 (*Plaid. civiles*); and it may be that the dinner of which our author gives the menu was an inaugural dinner which took place at that time. Easter fell on April 10th, 1379, so that it was still Lent, and the dinner is in fact *maigre*. If I am right on this conjecture and if the dinner actually did take place in 1379, M. de Paris is Aymery de Maignac, bishop of Paris ... The President (doubtless the first president) is Arnault de Corbie, afterwards chancellor of France, one of the most illustrious and most honourable statesmen of the fourteenth century, who died in 1413 at a ripe old age. The Procureur du Roi is Guillaume de Saint Germain, first avocat *solennel* at the Châtelet, then Procureur Général in the Parlement, or Procureur du Roi (it was the same thing), from 1365 until his death in February, 1383–4 ... Of the two Avocats du Roi, one may be Jean Pastourel, who exercised the office in 1364 and 1373, but the other was certainly the famous Jean Des Mares or Des Marès, who died so unhappily in 1382.' [J.P.]

⁶² I translate the word *escuelle* or bowl by cover here. The custom seems to have been for each guest to have his own trencher for solid food, but to share a bowl or soup plate with his next-door neighbour for liquid foods, each dipping his spoon into it. Thus a meal served for a certain number of *écuelles* would signify a meal for double that number of persons. Pichon points out that the use of separate soup plates for liquids for each guest was still new and not very general under the minority of Louis XIV.

⁶³ Cups.

⁶⁴ Flat slices of bread, several or more days old, used as plates.

⁶⁵ I do not know if by this is to be understood the servants or perhaps also persons of less elevated rank who dined after the first guests. [J.P.] The phrase also occurs on p. 157.

⁶⁶ *Pommes de rouvel*. Cotgrave: '*Rouveau. Pomme de rou*. The Ruddocke, Redding, Summer Goulding'.

⁶⁷ *Becquets* again.

⁶⁸ A preserve of fruits, or jam. See pp. 194–6.

⁶⁹ I am not sure whether 'soup' or 'sops' is here intended; Pichon thinks the former.

⁷⁰ *Oubloier*, or maker of the wafers called *oublies*. I have not attempted to find English equivalents for the names of the different sorts of wafers, *supplications, estriers, gros bastons, portes, galettes* and the rest. Some of them are more fully explained on pp. 161 and 201.

⁷¹ Cotgrave: '*Blandureau*: the white apple, called (in some parts of England) a Blaundrell.'

⁷² Compare Russell's *Boke of Nurture*:

For good gynger colombyne is best to drynke and ete;
Gynger valadyne & maydelyn ar not so holsom in mete.

Furnivall, op. cit., p. 10.

73 Sugar cooked in rose-water.

74 In which were placed portions of the food in front of the guests, to be subsequently given to the poor.

75 'The hotel of the bishop of Beauvais, either that which seems to have been the personal possession of the famous Miles de Dormans, bishop of Beauvais (d. 1387) in the rue de la Verrerie, or more probably the hotel of the bishops of Beauvais, *rue des Billettes*, which belonged to the bishopric and which Charles, cardinal de Bourbon, sold for 30,000 livres in 1572 . . . We read in the relation of the embassy of Jerome Lippomano to France in 1577 that the concierges of Paris houses let them by the day or month during the absence of their masters (*Amb. vénitiens*, 1838, II, 609); this was already customary in the fourteenth century, for later on it is remarked that Jean Duchesne paid the four francs here mentioned to the "concièrge of the hotel de Beauvais", who also hired him the tables, trestles, etc.' [J.P.]

76 'In 1385 there was a Jehan Duchesne attached to the Châtelet, possibly as usher, who to all appearances is the same whose wedding is described for us by the Ménagier.' [J.P.]

77 *Asséeur*. I use the old English word for the man who arranged the dishes on the table. See 'Office of a sewer' in Russell's *Boke of Nurture* (Furnivall, op. cit., pp. 46–7).

78 Pichon quotes the following ceremony for the blessing of the nuptial bed. '*Benedictio thalami ad nuptias et als* [*sic*]. Benedic, Domine, thalamum hunc et omnes habitantes in eo, ut in tua voluntate permaneant, requiescant et multiplicentur in longitudinem dierum. Per Christum, etc. *Tunc thurificet thalamum in matrimonio postea sponsum et sponsam sedentes vel jacantes in lecto suo. Benedicentur dicendo*: Benedic, Domine, adolescentulos istos; sicut benedixisti Thobiam et Sarram filiam Raguelis, ita benedicere eos digneris, Domine, ut in nomine tui vivant et senescant, et multiplicentur in longitudinem dierum. Per Christum, etc. Benedictio Dei omnipotentis, Patris et Filii et Spiritus sancti descendat super vos et maneat semper vobiscum. In nomine Patris, etc.' *Le Ménagier de Paris*, I, Introd., p. lxxxvi.

79 'We shall further on [p. 197] find this Hautecourt called *Maistre Jehan de Hautecourt*. It seems fairly certain that it was the same man who on June 3rd, 1385, made an accord with the Abbess of Hyères in the matter of a case which she had brought against him . . . Sire Jean de Fleury, last provost of the merchants in 1382, the famous treasurer Bernard de Montlhéry cited by Christine de Pisan, and Jehan de Longueil councillor in Parlement, were friends of his; there is thus reason to believe that he was in a sufficiently elevated position to

be able to give as expensive a bridal feast as that of which we have the menu here.' [J.P.]

⁸⁰ This was another of the dishes at which Chaucer's cook excelled. See p. 181.

⁸¹ 'Ducange cites, at the word *Manus*, an account of 1334, in which there appear two marchpanes, the one of *manuchristi*, the other of *confiegs*. These words would seem to refer to a fruit or almond, but which I know not.' [J.P.]

⁸² The *Viandier* which follows is very long and has been abbreviated here by the omission of a number of recipes, including some general directions as to preparing meat, etc., at the beginning.

⁸³ I use this old English word for the pot-water in which meats or vegetables have been cooking.

⁸⁴ i.e., boil slowly.

⁸⁵ Here again what seems to be intended is a series of soups in which to serve sops, for they are served up in bowls.

⁸⁶ Probably charcoal is meant by *charbon* all through; but mineral coal was in use at this period too.

⁸⁷ Argus, full of eyes (i.e., holes); Helen, white; Magdalen, moist; Lazarus (leper), seems to represent scaly. Pichon explains Martinus as standing for hard, obstinate or resisting, in allusion to Martin Grosia, professor of law at Bologna in the twelfth century, whose hardness and obstinacy became proverbial, according to Baronius, quoted by Ducange under the word *Martinus*. He thinks that *respondens pontifici* ought then to be translated by heavy, possibly in allusion to the pontifical gravity. The men of the Middle Ages were fond of these lists of the qualities of things – compare the qualities of a horse given on p. 215, and Alexander Neckam's list of the virtues of good wine '*quid quidem lacrimarum penitenciam agentis claritati conformetur. Cujus color bubali cornu virorem representat. Sumptum descendat impetuose ad modum fulminis, sapidum ut nux Philidis, repens ad modum esperioli, gesticulans ad modum caprioli, forte sicut edificii grisorum monachorum, emicans ad modum scintille; subtilitati Parvipontane veritatis equiparetur; delicatum ut bissus; frigitatem cristalli excedat.*' The editor also quotes a much longer description in old French. *A Volume of Vocabularies*, ed. Wright, pp. 102–3.

⁸⁸ The remarks in brackets and italics are the Ménagier's own comments on the recipes which he is copying.

⁸⁹ *Planta genista*, whence our Plantagenet.

⁹⁰ The Ménagier divides this into two sections, round and flat fish, and has a large number of recipes and directions for cooking different sorts of fish, all interesting.

⁹¹ 'The *Maison Rustique* (1570 edit., p. 105) says that when the liquid in the woad has been pressed out in the press, the grounds are made up into little pastilles, which are dried in the sun, and that these pastilles are thrown into the

vats where the wool is put to be dyed. It is these pastilles or *pasteaux*, the size of which was doubtless fixed by custom and well known, that our author uses here as a basis of comparison.' [J.P.]

92 'At the end of the *Calendrier des Bergiers*, Paris, 1493, f. N vj, there is a very curious poem on the snail, in the course of which it is remarked:

> *Oncques Lombard ne te mangeat*
> *A telle saulce que (nous) ferons,*
> *Si te mettrons en ung grant plat,*
> *Au poyvre noir et aux ongnons.'*

[J.P.] 'Never Lombard ate thee with such a sauce as we will do; we will put thee on a big dish with black pepper and onions.' For black-pepper sauce see p. 190.

93 Cotgrave, '*Pignolat*: The preserved kernell of a Pine-apple; or conserve of Pine-kernells'.

94 In a more pious and clockless age these directions for judging the time would doubtless be adequate.

95 Name of a place. In the *Dit des pays* (printed in the sixteenth century) we read 'En Orte est le bon saffran'. [J.P.]

96 *Agrostemma githago* (according to Littré). It is rather difficult to identify the flower. The modern meaning of *passerose* is hollyhock and of *neelle* fennel-flower or sweet saviour.

97 'The aviary of the castle of Hesdin in the town of Artois, where the dukes of Burgundy of the last line often used to reside. The town of Hesdin, razed to the ground by Charles V in 1553, is now a *bourg* called Vieil-Hesdin, about a league from the present Hesdin, which is the old village of Mesnil, enlarged and fortified in 1554 by the duke of Savoy.' [J.P.]

98 The hotel Saint-Paul, rue Saint-Antoine, in Paris. [J.P.]

99 The famous provost of Paris. [J.P.]

100 Doubtless a citizen of Paris, but nothing is known of him. [J.P.]

101 i.e., linen was then marked by means of a stamp or seal. [J.P.]

Index

Of related interest

Brief Lives
John Aubrey
Edited by Richard Barber

Full edition, in modern spelling, of Aubrey's racy portraits of great figures of
16–17c England, from Sir Walter Raleigh to John Milton.
336pp, 1 84383 112 0

The Buccaneer Explorer
William Dampier's Voyages
Edited by Gerald Norris

An edited account of Dampier's voyages which gives an admirable picture of
this fascinating and unorthodox figure – buccaneer, explorer, naturalist,
adventurer – in his own words.
296 pp, 1 84383 141 4

The Diary of John Evelyn
Edited by Guy de la Bédoyère

The diaries of a man at the centre of English social and political life in the
17th century, a friend of Charles II and a member of Royal Society.
384pp, 1 84383 109 0

The Loss of the Wager
John Bulkeley and John Byron

Two contrasting versions of the struggle for survival following shipwreck on
the ferociously inhospitable Patagonian coastline. This story formed the
basis of Patrick O'Brian's historical work, The Golden Ocean.
272pp, 1 84383 096 5

Particular Friends
The Correspondence of Samuel Pepys and John Evelyn
Edited by Guy de la Bédoyère

'Intriguing insight into the minds of two exceptional men whose contribution
to our understanding of 17th-century England is incalculable.' – *Spectator*
352 pp, 1 84383 134 1

The Pastons
A Family in the Wars of the Roses
Edited by Richard Barber

Vivid first-hand accounts of life in England at the time of the Wars of the
Roses, presented in their historical context.
208pp, 1 84383 111 2

The Siege of Malta 1565
Francisco Balbi di Correggio
Translated by Ernle Bradford

The story of one of the greatest-ever battles, a few men under the Knights
of St John against a huge Turkish armada, written as witnessed
by a participating soldier.
192pp, 1 84383 140 6

The Service of Ladies
Ulrich von Liechtenstein
Translated by J. W. Thomas

Extraordinary medieval autobiography, full of the adventures of a
knight-errant, and one of the most vivid records of chivalric life.
Helped to inspire the motion picture, A Knight's Tale.
189pp, 1 84383 095 7

The Unconquered Knight
Gutierre Diaz de Gamez

A chronicle of the deeds of the fifteenth-century knight Don Pere Niño,
Count of Buelna, written by his senior lieutenant.
248pp, 1 84383 101 5

For more information, see our web site at www.boydellandbrewer.com